THE REAL DEAL

*JOURNEY
OF A
BILLION DOLLAR
REAL ESTATE
BROKER*

ISBN 978-0-9890855-5-7
[First softcover edition]

Pascal Editions
New York   POB 90889 14609
www.pascaleditions.com

DEDICATION

To my loving parents Sikander and Hajra Susiwala.

Thank you for all you have done for me, the life you gave me and for instilling the confidence to allow me to take the path less travelled. You have set my moral compass and I cherish you for recalibrating me throughout my life. Your sacrifices are unparalleled, your strength is extraordinary, and your love has been the greatest gift I could ever have received. Thank you.

And to my wife Natalie, my son Yusuf and my daughter Anisa.

I further dedicate this book to all those people – there have been many, and you know not only who you are, but also why – who deserve my sincerest and most heartfelt thank you.

City teen sold on real estate business

TABLE OF CONTENTS

INTRODUCTION

On February 25, 2020, I was backstage at the MGM Grand Hotel in Las Vegas, the largest single hotel in the United States. I was wondering if this would turn out to be the day I'd been waiting for the past thirty-two years.

As I stood there, the announcer's voice went out to the thousands upon thousands of people in the audience from all around the globe. "... And now! The top agent in all of Canada for the most homes sold—Faisal Susiwala!"

I was shocked. I tried to find the strength in my legs to move forward. I felt the same way I'd felt on the day my name was called decades earlier at Avenue Road Public School in Cambridge, Ontario. I was ten, and I'd sold the most chocolate bars door-to-door for the school fundraiser. "Faisal Susiwala—most chocolate bars sold!" The award I received was an all-expenses paid trip to McDonald's. Back then it just didn't get much better than that.

I didn't really like selling chocolate bars door-to-door. Building a successful real estate career, on the other hand—that's something I've loved from the very beginning. So when the announcer called my name, and I stepped out as thousands stood up and cheered, recognized by my peers in RE/MAX as Canada's Number One salesperson, I was on top of the world.

Me—Canada's top-selling Realtor. I'd sold almost three billion dollars worth of property by then to reach that distinction.

Now I'm here to show you how I did it.

My name is Faisal Susiwala, and I'm a real estate agent and investor. I take so much pride in that short simple description of who I am and what I do that it's hard for me to adequately explain it to you. In the pages to come, I 've done my best to share my journey. Not only my journey, but what I learned along the way. The experiences I've had, the wins and the failures, the ups and downs—and we all have them—led me to reflect on what brought me at last to that stage at the MGM Grand at the very top of my game. Those reflections led me to develop what I call the Susiwala System—my roadmap to success in real estate and in life.

I've had the good fortune to work with, and be mentored by, some incredible people. They're an important part of the story I'm going to share with you, and I'll always be indebted to them. This book chronicles some of the key lessons I learned from those people. Their foundational insights, plus my own experiences, have allowed me to materially help others while truly living the life of my dreams. I hope my story and my System will inspire you, awaken you, and show you ways you too can excel in your career and create a beautiful and satisfying life.

As you follow my journey, you'll begin to understand the unique approaches and strategies I've applied to achieve success beyond my wildest dreams. Guess what? They're really not that complicated. As you'll see, I often go against conventional wisdom. But my system certainly worked for me, and I'm convinced it can work for you too. So let's get started!

Faisal receiving his awards at the global RE/MAX Awards in Las Vegas in 2020.

My journey began in England, where I was born. But it truly began as a young boy when I came to Canada as a three-year-old immigrant. I began working almost as far back as I can remember, delivering papers, working as a stock boy, and picking strawberries for two dollars an hour.

Today I have a beautiful family, great friends, homes I could never have imagined, a collection of cars I once only dreamt of, rental properties, homes, plazas, land. Everything I ever wanted.

The Real Deal.

I've been named the #1 top-selling real estate agent in Canada by the #1 top-selling agency in Canada—RE/MAX. I've earned tens of millions in commissions alone, and I've sold nearly three billion dollars in property. I travel the world, donate to schools, hospitals and charities, am connected with a wide variety of people, including individuals of wealth, stature and influence, and I've partnered with some brilliant and amazing people.

But this is not only the story of how I made it. It's the step-by-step account of how you can make it too.

Now I don't mean to brag. Far from it. There were some hard times when I was growing up. My family and I lost our home when I was a child. As a young man I went bankrupt. Then I came within an inch of being blown up in the Twin Towers on 9/11 along with nearly 3,000 others. I was lucky. I survived, and I've been grateful to God ever since.

But my real estate success hasn't been a matter of luck. It hasn't even been a matter of hard work and hustle, though there were years when I worked hard, very hard, and hustled even harder. Working hard isn't working smart, though. I've known agents and investors who worked even harder and got nowhere. I am where I am today because I developed a system. I'm going to share this system with you by showing you the steps to take so that you too will have the tools to do what I did. These tools are tried and true—processes I've applied and tested over the course of thirty years. They work.

I'm going to show you the actions I took that led me to the top of my profession, and the experiences that sharpened my understanding so that I could see what it was that I was doing and pass it on. Learning these steps didn't just fall into my lap. I had to figure them out, sometimes the hard way, gaining knowledge from experience. Bitter experience. Though more often than not, I learned the easy way, too, by watching others and learning from their experience.

No matter who you are, real estate is a wonderful profession if you do it right. How you look, where you come from, and a host of other factors are all secondary. What counts is your intelligence, your personal integrity, and your understanding of the ideas and actions that make it all work. Sadly, a lot of people in the business—even some of the most successful ones—know how to do a great job without being able to explain it very clearly in detail. They're doers, not thinkers. There's nothing wrong with that, but the problem is, when asked about the secret of their success, they pass along the same old clichés everyone keeps repeating.

Well, a lot of the things people tell you work great in real estate don't work at all. In fact, what works best is often the exact opposite of what most people are telling you. You're much better off copying what they do than listening to what they say. (Of course, if those people are making tens of millions in commissions, you may want to listen to what they say too and keep listening to them. But if they haven't, and you haven't yet either, you might want to keep reading.)

Faisal Susiwala.

I wrote this book for two reasons.

The first is that I'm often asked to give talks at real estate conferences, and to young people. I've found that if you just give people abstract rules and principles, they don't always get it, and they don't always follow through. Why should they? No one's there to show them how to apply these guidelines in real life. It's like I said: sometimes we learn from experience, and sometimes we learn from others' experiences.

This book is a chance for you to learn from my experiences; that's why I'm sharing them here, and explaining how they led me to develop my system, so you'll be able to understand and apply it more easily. Now, maybe you won't draw the same lessons from my experiences that I did. For people who want their principles spelled out directly and clearly, I spell them out too. I've arranged this book so that the chapters that tell my personal story, the story of how I arrived at the principles of my system, also summarize it in a few brief pages at the end of each chapter.

In fact, if you're one of those people who wants to skip personal material entirely and go straight to the heart of my system, that's fine too. You can. It's all there in the chapter near the end called, "The Susiwala System."

That chapter points you to another systematic approach I've developed that you may want to review called the LEXIT Strategy. (There's also an earlier chapter on "Getting the Listing," the key element in building your own professional success).

If you want to make money in real estate and retire comfortably, I believe you'll find everything you need to know in those core sections.

The Susiwala family. Family has been an important part of Faisal's motivation and success, and one of two underlying reasons why he wrote this book.

But I recommend following the story, and not just because there's useful extra material in there for you. There's more to a journey than just the map. Following the journey of someone who's travelled the road you're about to take can make your own journey much more profitable and pleasant. I'd like to hear about your own journey, too, and I've included contact information at the front and back of this book. Let me know how this book has helped you. Read the book. Put the principles in practice. If you have any questions, or think there's a way to make my system even better, or just want to share your own real estate stories, get in touch. I look forward to hearing about your journey, too.

The second reason I wrote this book is for my children.

When I was a young boy, my family and I went through some very hard times. We weren't destitute, but we were close enough to poverty to be threatened by it, and afraid of it. I can't begin to express the love and gratitude I feel for my parents for all they did to hold us together during those times and keep us above the storm. And yet, looking back, I find that it's exactly the storm, the wolf at the door, the challenges, that gave me the motivation, the drive and the will to work hard enough to get where I am now.

It comes down to a sense of responsibility. All along the way I knew the people I loved were depending on me. I couldn't let them down. I couldn't afford to take it easy. Even today that sense of responsibility has driven me to write this book.

Trappings of success: Nearly 20, fresh out of high school and already two years into his real estate career, Faisal Susiwala bought his first car, a Mercedes. It was suitable for use when conducting business and showing houses. At 30 he treated himself to a Porsche; at 40, a Ferrari (right); at 50, a Lamborghini (left). At the same time, his ingrained sense of responsibility has extended to community philanthropy, and he has been a generous donor to various organizations such as his local hospital.

My children don't have those experiences or that fear to motivate them. I'm glad they don't. There's nothing more enjoyable about money than being able to make sure your family is well-off and comfortable, free from want and from the threat of poverty.

But—just in case things ever change and times get tough—I want my children to have something to support them. A manual. A book of counsel from Dad so that if things ever do change and they find themselves having to struggle, they'll have a clear guidebook showing them what to do and how to get back on top.

This book is my legacy to them. More, even, than the money I've made, I believe this book can ensure a prosperous and honourable future for my children—and for you.

If you follow the steps laid out in this book, if you think hard about them and really understand the lessons, if you then go out and apply them in practice, will you become the #1 Realtor in your nation? I can't promise that.

But I honestly believe that the principles in this book will help you become much, much more successful, and not just in the world of real estate.

Maybe even as a person.

Chapter 1

I WAS A TEENAGE REAL ESTATE AGENT

When I was seventeen, I was sitting in my living room late one night watching an infomercial.

It was a Vietnamese gentleman named Tom Vu. He didn't look like a movie star, but he was sitting on a yacht surrounded by beautiful women in bikinis.

He had sports cars. He had a Rolls Royce. He lived in a mansion and was showing pictures of all the homes he was buying, renovating, renting, flipping and selling.

I was astonished, even mesmerized.

How did this guy manage to do that?

I wanted to do it too! I wanted to be that guy!

In hindsight, he wasn't the role model I was seeking, but he was the spark. I was seventeen, still in high school and living with my parents. I couldn't do what Tom Vu was doing even if I had the money to go out and start buying houses that very minute, which I didn't. I was a minor and there were laws. I couldn't buy property or rent it or flip it—whatever that meant.

I couldn't do what he was doing.

But I could learn. I could take some courses and learn about real estate.

So I did. It was the summer of 1988. Students were enjoying their summer vacations. I was working in a factory to help the family make ends meet. I was also picking strawberries, stocking shelves at BiWay, and working at the drug store. Somehow, though, I still managed to have a few minutes to spare, and Tom Vu had set me on fire. I wanted to learn about real estate, and I wanted to learn badly! Of course, I didn't have the money to go to Tom's seminars and buy his books and tapes. (Good thing – it turned out later that Tom got himself into some trouble. Still, I'll always be grateful).

I asked around and talked to some real estate people. I didn't get very far. Most told me to get lost; moreover, they didn't

14

seem to know Tom Vu from a hole in the ground. That didn't get me very far.

Then I found out our local college offered a real estate course and you didn't have to be a student at the college to enrol.

So that's what I did.

The courses consisted of three phases, two weeks at a time. I was so clueless I didn't even know it was a licensing course till I was halfway through. What, you needed a licence to do real estate? I thought licences were only for fishing.

Anyway, there I sat, this 18-year-old sitting next to forty- and fifty-year-olds, trying to figure out the difference between duplexes and bungalows. I scratched my head. I raised my hand and asked questions. I took notes. And by the end of eight weeks I think I was the youngest licensed real estate agent in the country.

That didn't matter to me. I was on fire. I wanted the lifestyle I saw in that infomercial. More importantly, I wanted to be able to help my father, my mother, and my family. I wanted to be the #1 real estate agent in Canada. I wanted to buy and sell!

Then someone explained the fine print. Having a licence was one thing, but buying and selling houses as an agent was something else. To be an agent, I had to be part of a brokerage. Real estate agents needed to be registered by real estate brokers. What broker was going to hire an eighteen-year-old? My resumé was impressive, all right. Senior year student at Galt Collegiate Institute high school in Cambridge. One of these days (if I passed my exams) I might even graduate.

Still, opportunities are everywhere, and when you really know what you want, you start to see them. I'd made a friend at school, Jeremy Potvin, and when I told him about my real estate ambitions, Jeremy told me his father ran a nearby Century 21. Yes!

I sat right up. Would Jeremy mind setting up an introductory meeting? After all, I'd finished my courses. Real estate agencies were always looking for new young faces. My face was young. Heck, it was probably younger than any face that had ever applied. Still, however young I was, I'd passed. I was qualified.

Jeremy set up the meeting.

I can't tell you how excited I was that day I walked down the Water Street hill from my high school to Dickson Street where the Century 21 office sat. If all went well, they'd soon be tossing me the keys to my own yacht.

That feeling didn't last long. My friend's father, Tom Watson, and his partner, Len Peace, took one look at me and said, very politely, "No way."

As soon as they saw me, I knew they weren't going to sign me on. I was just too young. Sure, they encouraged me. They discussed the opportunities in real estate for an ambitious young man. They couldn't have been more kind or polite about it. But in the end they advised me to finish my education first and consider getting into the business later.

Much later. "Come back in four or five years!"

I was crushed.

The Century 21 office was just a block away from the local bus terminal. I went there and sat and waited for the bus so I could have something to throw myself under.

But as I sat there waiting, I remembered something. Mr. Menary! He was an old friend of our family. We hadn't seen him for years, but I remembered that he was in real estate, too. He had an office downtown on Main Street—in fact, right across from the bus terminal.

When my father first came to Cambridge, Mr. Menary found him his first apartment. As a child, I would see Mr. Menary now and again as he stopped by to see how we were getting along. My father worked in a factory in Cambridge, and in 1975 there was an industrial accident in which my father lost his right arm at the elbow in a press. I was five at the time, my brother Zeb was six and my sister Sameera was three months old. Our family was devastated. Mr. Menary was the first person to come along and to tell us we were going to be OK. I never forgot that visit.

Before the accident we had just arranged to buy a townhouse. We were immigrants, new to Canada, and Mr. Menary was doing all he could to help us find our first home. We were right in the middle of that purchase when our whole world turned upside down.

How are you going to close on a home when you've got no job, no money, and you're in the hospital? When you're not even fluent enough in English to read and understand all the words in the property contract? We had no car—my mother had to walk several kilometres each day to get to work. My brother and I were children, too young to contribute. Things could not have looked worse.

But we did have friends and relatives. The community helped. Somehow we managed to survive. It took time, and help from Mr. Menary, but eventually we even ended up in a home of our own, though keeping it was a struggle.

Then, after a few years passed, in 1979, interest rates spiked. Home interest rates reached an almost unprecedented twenty-one per cent. Twenty-one per cent! The monthly payment became impossible to meet. It was just too much. We had to file for bankruptcy.

Again, Mr. Menary was there, trying to ease us through it the best way he could, and finding us a decent apartment where we could live until things turned around.

I thought the world of him. He treated my dad, my mother, and even nine-year-old me, with the utmost good manners and respect.

Though years had passed since those days, I looked up at the buildings across the street from the bus terminal. There it was, above some retail stores—'Reid C. Menary Real Estate.' It looked like he was still in business.

His company wasn't Century 21, but he'd been in the business since the early 1960s, and his agency was still there operating. That counted for something.

I thought about it for a second. The bus wouldn't be along for another 20 minutes. I was already in the vicinity. Why not visit Mr. Menary and tell him I was now qualified to be an agent? Maybe he was short-handed. Maybe he'd be willing to take a chance on me. What did I have to lose?

I made my decision and got up. I didn't know it at the time, but it was possibly the most important moment of my life. I walked across the street and went up the stairs. There was his company name on the door: Reid C. Menary Real Estate.

I knocked.

Mr. Menary himself opened it, and there, greeting me, was the same friendly face I remembered as a twelve-year-old boy.

"Hello sir, I'm Faisal Susiwala. Sikander's son. Do you remember us?"

"Faisal!" he said. He broke into a big smile. "Of course. How are you? How is your father?"

He remembered my father very well and had nothing but good things to say about him as he invited me in.

By now Mr. Menary was more than seventy years old. He went and sat in his big black chair behind his large oak desk.

"How was your family, Faisal? Is everyone doing well? How are you doing?"

"Well, I'm doing well, Mr. Menary, I'm doing well," I said, "but I have a problem—you see, I've taken a course in real estate. I'm really interested in it, and I really want to make a real estate career. I've taken a college-level course, and now I'm certified and qualified and everything. Only I can't get a licence unless someone hires me. I'm only eighteen, and no one seems to care if I'm qualified or not. They see how young I am and they tell me to come back in a couple of years.

"Sir—would you be interested in hiring me?"

He rubbed his chin and looked at me thoughtfully.

"Well, actually I'm retiring," he said.

I was crushed. Twice. In one day.

"But," he added, "I'm not retiring right away. There's no reason you couldn't work for me till then." He smiled at me. "Sure, Faisal, I'd be happy to get you started. Why don't you come see me tomorrow and fill out the Real Estate Council paperwork, and we'll get you registered?"

I felt like I had just won the national lottery.

That was the beginning of my journey.

In the next few months I would sell 2.2 million dollars in property for the independent brokerage of Reid C. Menary Real Estate. I'd be featured in a newspaper story that would make me locally famous in the Cambridge community. I was on my way. On my way, and as grateful to Mr. Reid Menary as an eighteen-year-old starting out on his chosen career could be.

I would have been even more grateful if I'd known how much more Mr. Menary would go on to teach me. Not just about real estate, but about the ethics of real estate—about honesty and integrity, about decency and patience. He was the kindest soul a man could be, and from that moment on, he not only patiently held my hand through every procedure and every aspect of each transaction, but, more importantly, he taught me to think not just about the money but about what the money was all about: people wanting a home, families needing a safe investment for their future, folks looking for a place for themselves and their families and businesses, a place to live and grow and thrive.

"Just do a good job. Be fair, be honest," he said, "and the money will come." Words I still live by.

That's how, on November 18th, 1988, just days before Mr. Menary would turn 73, when I was still in my final year of high school, I became an officially licensed and registered real estate agent in the Province of Ontario.

I can't tell you how proud I was. I told everybody I could about who I was now and what I did. I was a businessman now. An entrepreneur. I had a pager!

I was Faisal Susiwala—real estate agent.

And I was blessed to have the best mentor in the business.

Lessons

Later on in life, a friend told me about one of the leaders of the French Revolution, a man named Georges-Jacques Danton. Enemies were surrounding Paris, the Revolution was in danger, and Danton gave a speech. What could they do to save themselves? Danton roared, "Dare, dare again, always dare!"

That's my whole lesson for this chapter.

Dare.

Start.

Take action.

Make a decision and throw all you've got into it.

How much preparation did I have before I launched my career? Are you kidding? I saw one infomercial and took a six-week college course. I was living with my parents. I didn't have a car. I had no experience in the business whatsoever. I couldn't afford to pay a nickel on marketing and advertising. I was an immigrant, a visible minority, a religious minority, a teenager. I wasn't even out of high school. The first time I so much as asked for a job I was told to go away and not come back for years! To say I started out at the bottom would be an understatement.

Today? I'm the number-one agent for the number-one real estate brand in the entire country.

Don't listen to the naysayers. Don't listen to the "conventional wisdom." Don't listen to those who seem to have all the answers and advice. Don't even listen to the doubts you tell yourself. Above all, don't sit around and daydream.

Starting Out: As a young real estate agent fresh out of high school, Faisal Susiwala bought his first car, a Mercedes.

If you've found something that inspires you and excites you and fills you with ambition, go for it.

Start today.

Start now.

Take action.

Get going!

Dare.

Chapter 2

WORKING WITH MR. MENARY

I generated over five million dollars' worth of sales in the first year Mr. Menary and I worked together. Most of it happened the very first few months. I did it at the same time I was still going to classes and successfully completing my final year of high school.

Did Mr. Menary pass on some magic formula to me?

He did.

Eight wonderful words: "Do a good job. Do the right thing."

The effects were magical.

Needless to say, I didn't make those sales the first day. Not much happened at first, at all. My parents could see how happy I was about the job. They were a little surprised about this strange development with their son, but they were tolerant. I had a lot of little side jobs. As long as I kept my grades up in high school, they were good with my after-school activities. I suppose they thought that after a while my real estate fever would cool down, and I'd go on to college like everyone else.

My mentor and friend, the late Mr. Reid C. Menary.

I think Mr. Menary realized that my fever was going to turn into a lifelong romance. But, just in case it didn't, he too wanted me to have my high school diploma, so I'd be able to open that door to a university degree if need be. I only had a few months to go till graduation, and he was flexible. He agreed to let his teenage real estate associate start work a little late—after all, high school came first.

So, I began my career in real estate by going to high school all day; and as soon as classes were over, I'd walk down to Mr. Menary's (I still didn't have a car) and get to work.

Since then I've seen agencies where people are hired and are pretty much left alone to sink or swim. The new hires either figure out how to meet their goals, or they don't. If they don't, they're out. That wasn't how Mr. Menary did things. He always found time to talk to me. He would take a moment to sit down and go over each document in detail, or explain what some item on a listing meant, or why I needed to bring along this form here, or get a signature on that one there. He was a natural teacher, and he'd hired someone hungry to learn. We'd sit and talk for hours about neighbourhoods and historical data and construction and mortgages and how to go about evaluating properties and all sorts of tiny and technical things. The more I learned, the more I wanted to know.

But the biggest thing he taught me was how to deal with people. That was, by far, the most important lesson I learned from Mr. Menary.

Faisal Susiwala's first business card, as an agent with Reid C. Menary Real Estate agency.

And it was easy. Really easy. I recall him saying to me one time, "Look, you're a young man. Never think about the money. Never count the dollars. Just do a good job and the money will come."

Just do a good job and the money will come. It sounds so simple; and yet it contains absolutely everything. That's really the whole key. Just do a good job.

And how do you do a good job? It was more than just a matter of getting the paperwork right or doing due diligence properly. Of course, those things mattered too. They mattered a lot.

But the main thing was to put the good of your clients first, and the money second. Everything he did, everything about the way he handled his own prospects and accounts, demonstrated that.

Mr. Menary would talk people out of purchasing a property, and do it all the time! I thought this was just amazing. There are so many people in real estate driven to *sell, sell, sell*, to push people into buying, to twist their arms into instantly pulling that trigger and closing the deal.

Yet here was someone honestly saying to a customer, "No, I don't think this is right for you," or "I know you love the house, but it's got serious problems," or "There's another house that's just as good in every way, and it'll cost you a lot less." A lot less meant less commission. Why was he doing this? I'd never seen a salesperson act in that manner.

I know now—because I've had time to see how things work and think about it—that this is the best possible business move you can make. What Mr. Menary did was to think in the long term. He understood that a person who got honest treatment and good advice from him would come back, sometimes for an entire lifetime. They'd recommend him to family and friends. Nowadays he would be getting five-star reviews on Facebook and Google.

He was acting as a good steward for his clients, and today we would say he was branding himself and developing customer evangelists. The label didn't matter; he had the common sense and personal decency to know that doing the right thing might mean taking a slight reduction in commission today, but multiple commissions would be coming down the pipeline tomorrow as a result. Mind you, he wasn't acting cynically, or out of greed. He really wanted his clients to have the best house he could get them. But he also understood that what was best for them was ultimately also best for his business.

Typically, a salesperson will tell you that everything they show you is the best thing ever, just perfect in every way. Not Mr. Menary. He always tried to get the best deal for people, not a deal that might benefit him at their expense. He made money, but he made it honestly and honourably. He was a modest man, lived simply, and didn't even hold onto the money that he worked hard for: he'd give it to his children, or donate land he acquired to the Salvation Army.

I was young and seeing him handle himself this way really had an impact on me. He was a very generous person, and I don't just mean in terms of the time and advice he gave me. He gave to the community. He reminded me of my father. My father might have nothing, but he never turned anyone away. If a friend in need came to the door and asked, he would write a cheque on the spot. Sometimes he would have to post-date it two weeks, and work like hell for those two weeks to make sure those people had what they needed. But he never turned them down. Mr. Menary was like that.

I expected to learn about real estate from Mr. Menary, and I sure did. I didn't expect to learn about charity. Or about honour and decency. But I did.

Yet even then, part of my real estate brain was operating, watching, weighing and trying to separate what worked from what didn't. You could always count on Mr. Menary to do the right thing. But it wasn't just that it was right. It also worked! Thanks to Mr. Menary I began to see that making a sale wasn't purely about making a quick profit. You were making an investment at the same time—an investment in your reputation and in your future.

Mr. Menary didn't sell people. He helped people; so when the time came for them to move up into a new place, Mr. Menary would get the call. When people asked where to find a good Realtor, they'd say: "Reid Menary." He dealt with people fairly and honestly and they told others. Their recommendations brought other people to the office and gave us new and steady business. He gave—and they gave back.

Seeing it led me to a principle I've come to call 'I.O.U.' It's a core idea that I'll be coming back to, and Mr. Menary was the man who first helped me to see it—to see that doing the right thing for others in the long run means doing the right thing for yourself, too. And understanding this key principle is even more important now than it was back then, because of social media and the Internet. Today the way you act, the way you treat people, follows you around your whole life. A bad online review sits there forever. A good review does the same; they don't just reach a few friends, but hundreds of people, even thousands!

However, there's a secret to being a decent human being. You can't fake it. You can't pretend to care about people, just so they'll give you business. It has to be genuine; you have to really care. Mr. Menary really cared. He wasn't in it solely for a quick buck.

24

I was lucky—I had parents who cared about me and my siblings and each other. I knew what it was to care about others long before Mr. Menary reinforced that lesson by example. But that was in everyday life. Mr. Menary taught me that you didn't have to stop being a good guy to be successful in business. He showed me, through personal example, that in business, good guys finish first, not last.

You didn't expect me to start this book by talking about ethics, did you? Hang on, don't worry. We'll get into sales in a moment. It's just that you need to know that ethics underpin everything. You've got that, right? Good. So now you'll want to know how I sold my first million in my first few months as a real estate agent.

OK: it was like this. About a week after I got licensed, my parents and I were invited to a dinner party, a big family gathering in Toronto. Among the guests were some people who were distant relatives of my parents who were visiting from South Africa, the place where they settled some years earlier. They weren't really that well known to us, but they were related, and also related to a friend of ours named Dr.. Paruk, from Jamestown, New York.

Family is family, so when we gathered, we all got to talking. I listened respectfully but stayed in the background. They were the elders. I was a kid. Eventually one of the visitors from South Africa decided to be polite and turned a little attention my way.

"So, young Faisal! Are you still in school?"

"Yes," I said, noting I was almost finished "but.. I'm a real estate agent too."

He blinked.

"Really?"

Suddenly I was more than just an object of attention. I was the centre of attention. They had all sorts of questions about Cambridge and the land and the community and its real estate. I was hardly the best-informed real estate agent in Canada after being licensed for just one week, but I had studied hard enough to be able to talk intelligently about it. To my surprise, they were hanging on my every word!

They were concerned with how things were playing out in South Africa. They'd started several successful businesses there, and were very well-to-do there, but things in their country were turning upside down. Apartheid was coming to an end, the political structure of the whole country was changing. The African National Congress (ANC—a Communist party, after all) was coming into power, and there was talk of nationalizing everything. They wanted to take their money out of a volatile situation and put it somewhere safe and stable. But where? They'd already moved a good deal of their money into the UK, but they wanted to diversify further. So they were looking into Canada.

Was Canadian real estate a good investment, they asked me?

Well, I didn't need a college course to know how to answer that one. I gave them all the information about the Canadian market I could, handed out my card, and told them to give me a call.

The following Monday I got a call. It was Dr.. Paruk and the South African group of investors. They wanted to come to Cambridge and see what was available. I skipped school that day. I took them downtown to show them a commercial building.

The first floor was a street level storefront. The second floor had offices. The third-floor, apartments. The cash flow looked good, and the price was $850,000. It all looked OK on paper, so they said, "Great, let's see it." While they were looking, they asked if we had anything else to show them.

Now Mr. Menary had a friend developing homes in Ingersoll, so he suggested I show them those. I did. They loved it. They bought four homes. The builder in Ingersoll was so impressed that I'd sold four of his townhome units that he gave me twelve more units to sell, and I started selling those as well.

As for the building, they decided to offer $750,000. We put the offer in and went back to handling our other clients.

Then we got word. The offer was accepted.

When Mr. Menary handed me the commission cheque and I saw the numbers, I nearly fainted. It was more money than I had seen in my entire life.

Now you would imagine that my parents would be proud and happy at my success. You'd be half right; my parents were proud and happy at my success—and very worried about it. I was out of high school now, and working. I was making decent money too. *Very* decent money.

But what about my career? Not 'real estate,' but my real future, serious, respectable, college education and career? Time was passing. I wasn't sending my applications out. Shouldn't I start putting more effort into it? I didn't want to be late for my freshman year.

I put it off as long as I could. Finally, we sat down and I told them my decision. I explained to them that I had found my calling. I wasn't going to go to university. At all. Ever.

I can't begin to describe the scene that followed. Were they happy? Proud? They were horrified. The disappointment on their faces was awful. They wanted me to get an education so badly that they pulled out all the stops. My Mom pointed to my Dad's arm and said, "Your father lost this so you could have a better life. I get up at four in the morning and walk to work in a factory and get home at seven at night, so you'll never have to. And now you tell us *this?*"

The worst thing about it was that I understood their feelings. Their entire lives, the whole reason they'd stayed in this country, was to provide a proper education for their three children. They sacrificed so much to give us that chance. And now I was throwing it away? I could be a doctor, a lawyer, a professor. And instead I had decided to be a—a mere salesman?

I pointed out that my salesmanship had paid off half the family home mortgage in six months. It meant nothing, and I knew why it meant nothing: because my future meant so much more to them than the mortgage or the money. The love I could feel behind their distress was what really twisted the knife. I was breaking their hearts, and it was breaking mine. I was in tears.

In the Indian culture, those lacking education are frowned upon. If you don't have an education, you are simply not a respectable person. You bring shame upon yourself and your family. "You will be an embarrassment to your brother and sister," they argued. "No girl will ever, ever want to marry you!" On and on it went. Night after night I crawled off to my room feeling like a worm.

My older brother Zeb was my saviour. He and I shared a room and I was so fortunate that he was there for me. He said he'd support me in any decision I made, and he did. To this day, he's got my back. Thank you, Zeb.

Support or not, my decision had been made. I had no doubt about my path. When I pictured Tom Vu, when I remembered what Mr. Menary and his kindness had done for us when I was a boy, when I looked at tracts of bare land and could see the developments that could be built on them, it all just spoke to me. This was what I wanted to do. What I was *meant* to do.

But however promising this path seemed to me, and however successful I might become, I was the only one who wanted me to stay with it. My parents immediately went out to consult everyone—family, friends, and trusted members of the entire community, and in unison they all agreed: Faisal, how can you be so ungrateful? Go to university. Now. Period. End of story.

There, too, I understood. Their hearts were in the right place. They wanted the best for me and believed an education would be a wise and safe decision; a degree would confer status. And they were right! Who would throw all that aside to become a real estate agent? As a relative put it to my parents, to be a real estate salesperson, in the Indian and Pakistani communities, is to become a mere *peddler*. "If Faisal does this, he'll be an embarrassment to the entire family. He'd be a peddler." For my parents, that was it! The end of the world. I felt like the character in the Charles Dickens novel, where the father of the house throws his disgraced offspring into the snow and points his disgusted finger down the dark, lamplit street, crawling with tramps and beggars. "Go!"

Faisal Susiwala—banished from decent society forever.

I guess you could say emotions were running pretty high.

But just when it seemed like things couldn't get any worse, there emerged one small sliver of sunlight. I reached out to my one hope: Uncle Rasheed.

Uncle Rasheed (his original name was Richard) was British —in fact, his name was Bond, like the legendary spy. William Richard Bond, to whom I owe so much. He passed away not long ago, may he rest in peace. Before I was born, he fell in love with, and married, my Pakistani grandmother's youngest sister, Auntie Rabia. She had gone to England to study, and there met William at school in the early Sixties. Through her, he developed an interest in, and sympathy with, Islam, and converted. When he did, he took the name Rasheed—Rasheed Bond.

Uncle Rasheed was held in the highest possible esteem by our family. As a full professor of education at Brock University in St. Catharines, he was as polished and eminently British and respectable as it was possible to be. His judgment carried weight. Moreover, he and my family had always been close, and he'd taken a certain delight in my young entrepreneurial ways.

Once, when I was four and we'd all gone to Pakistan for a visit, he'd bought me some Popeye candy cigarettes; he soon saw me going seat to seat on the airplane selling them to passengers for five cents apiece. He enjoyed passing that story along. "That young lad has a bright future in sales," he would say.

So I called him up. I told him my story. He could see that I was very upset. He realized how distressed my parents probably were as well. I pleaded with him to advise us. He said he'd come down and talk to us all and see if we could work something out.

When he came, we all sat around the kitchen table; and after my parents had made their case, he sat back very judiciously and said, "Hajra, Sikander—I agree with you completely. Faisal should go to university and get an education."

My last hope was gone. I had hit rock bottom.

Despite sharing my parents' sentiments, he was sympathetic. He understood my entrepreneurial side, and spoke to it. "The fact is, Faisal, real estate is an unstable profession. The market fluctuates. Many agents don't make enough of a salary to survive. Many drop out. Whereas people in the academic world can eventually make as much as sixty or seventy thousand dollars a year—more, if they go into administration, or write books and get royalties, or consult with businesses. Your parents are asking you to make a safe and reasonable decision. We don't know how well you'll do in real estate. We don't know if you'd make a cent."

"But Uncle Rasheed," I said, "I've already made $60,000 in commissions this year."

He blinked at me.

"—What?"

"And I've got another $30,000 in commissions coming."

He turned his head and looked at my parents.

"Is this true?"

"Yes," said my father—with pride. "And he gave us $35,000 of that to pay off our mortgage."

He looked at each of them, one after the other, straight in the eyes.

"Let this kid do what he wants," he said. "He's making more money than I am!"

And in fact, he called me two weeks later, to invest! "Faisal, I have a little bit of money. Put it into some property for me—on the condition that you're my partner."

I thought about it—for a nanosecond.

"OK!"

I soon began to appreciate that the best thing about finally having money wasn't so much the money itself. The best thing was being able to use it to pay off my parents' house. No sheriff would put a lock on that door ever again. It was all ours, all paid, free and clear.

But even though I was happy to be able to pay it off, I didn't relax. I kept all my other side jobs or businesses going—my jobs at Shoppers Drug Mart and at Canada Trust, where I was a bank teller. I kept selling my custom T-shirts. After all, Uncle Rasheed had a point. Who knew if real estate would work out in the long run? I didn't believe giving up on an income source so long as the income kept flowing. Even then I could see the value in diversification. If it brings in income, let it! (At least until you find a more lucrative substitute). If you absolutely must set it aside, don't just abandon it, sell it! I eventually sold my T-shirt business to someone for $5,000.

Soon my income started getting bigger and bigger. It wasn't because of my two other jobs, either. It was because of real estate. I was still in my teens, but now that I was a real estate agent, my income was approaching six figures. And this was in 1989!

But there were bigger changes coming for me—and for all of us—than just the one filling up my bank account.

Mr. Menary was not a young man. He was nearly seventy-three years old at the time I joined his agency. With that age came a good deal of insight into people, and into life. A good deal of kindness and wisdom. Most of what he made he spent on his children, helping set them up in businesses. I have no doubt that he was a great father, and in a lot of ways he was more like a parent to me than a boss. He treated me the way a father would treat a son.

But though he was old, and even Old School, he was open to new ideas. And so, a funny kind of dynamic began to build up between us. I began pointing out some of the ways that the new technology could help the company.

Mr. Menary was the senior man at his firm, and he'd been in the business for so long that a lot of the old ways of doing things were taken for granted. We had an office phone, and a manual typewriter, but that was it. Nowadays people are so used to their smartphones and their laptops that they don't always realize how different things used to be. They used to be slow and clunky. At Mr. Menary's there wasn't even a fax machine. When we had an important document to send or receive, I crossed the street to another office that let us use theirs!

But though Mr. Menary often did things the old-fashioned way, he wasn't stuck in the past. He was willing to experiment— to give new ideas and new innovations a shot. All you had to do was make a good case for them. That was another priceless lesson he taught me.

Remember, this was 1988. These days smartphones are an essential part of life. Back then, there weren't any. There wasn't even an Internet to connect to. Cell phones were only just coming out and they were expensive cutting-edge high-tech stuff. Well, we needed these things. I'd just gotten a pager and purchased a plan, and Mr. Menary could see that it was a useful tool. So why not take the next logical step?

It wasn't until later the next year that I finally decided to approach him. I had to. It was the up-and-coming thing.

"Mr. Menary," I said, "the pager helps, a lot, but I really think if I had a car phone, I could provide better service, and do a lot more business. I could get back to people quickly from wherever I might be; I wouldn't have to waste time looking for a pay phone; I could…"

"Well, maybe," he said, "but car phones are expensive. That's a pretty tall order."

True enough, it was. A car phone cost a little over $3,000 at the time, and you paid a dollar fifty per minute for each minute you used the phone. No free Wi-Fi back then! On top of the price of a phone, Mr. Menary would also be getting a bill for $500-$600 each month. Ouch.

"They're not cheap, that's true," I admitted. "I can't afford to get one on my own." I tapped into my entrepreneurial spirit. "But I'll tell you what. Why don't we work something out together? If you could buy me a cell phone for my car, and pay my monthly cell bill, I'd be willing to pay back the money from whatever deals I'm doing over time. I honestly think a phone will help me get so much more business that we can both come out ahead. Why not try it and see? OK?"

He leaned back. He thought about it. Then he said —"OK."

And that's how Faisal Susiwala and the Reid C. Menary agency got wired.

The phone was a GE phone, and it was huge—the size of a military Walkie-Talkie. The company selling it installed it in my car, and I was right. It did get us a lot more business. I was fortunate enough to bring that business in quickly and demonstrate to Mr. Menary that the technology paid off. Callers and clients were astonished at how quickly I responded. Back then, people were not plugged in like we are today, and they expected that someone would get back to them by the end of that day or the next. I got back to them in minutes. So I made deals faster and closed deals faster. It was a big win for the company —thanks to Mr. Menary's open-mindedness.

That was another thing about him that impressed me, something I hope I've learned to copy. He wasn't completely sold at first, but he was free from prejudiced conclusions and open to experiment—receptive to trying new things out, even if it might not work. After hearing a reasonable argument, his attitude was, "OK, let's hop on this technology bandwagon and see where it takes us." Maybe it would work, maybe not. But you'd never know till you try. He was old in body but not in spirit. He was like that French guy, Danton: ready to push the envelope.

It snowballed. Our initiative took us out of the nineteenth century and into the twenty-first. In no time, there was a fax machine in the office, and we were downloading the everyday listing we called the 'Hot Sheet.' There was a tiny digital screen and data would come in; a dot-matrix printer with reams of perforated sheets churned it out. Incredible! We got information right away! No longer did we have to wait for the regular Multiple Listing Service book to come around once a week, which was the norm.

Did that help us? It sure did. We needed the help; we needed every edge we could get if we wanted to compete with the big firms. Me, Mr. Menary, and another older gentleman named Ron Crosby were the whole agency. The big firms had resources we couldn't match. Yes, they were ramping up their technology too, and sooner or later they'd be leaving us behind. Fortunately you don't have to be the biggest to get there first, or to be one of the first few. For the moment we were holding our own.

That didn't mean that plain old nineteenth-century networking didn't work too. That was another principle I took from Mr. Menary: don't knock Old School approaches if they still work. Shmoozing worked! One day I was having a casual conversation with a friend of the family named Mr. Khan, and talking about real estate (which I was now doing with just about everyone I met), and Mr. Khan was good enough to let me know that houses were very nice, and commercial buildings were also nice, but just plain land could be even nicer! He was an investor who worked with several Italian partners and they were quietly buying parcels of land throughout Ontario. Development was happening, and more development was sure to follow. When it did, those parcels of land would skyrocket in value.

"You don't say?" I replied.

"I do say," he said.

I began looking for land.

Sure enough: there was a parcel of 25 acres on the city limits that was maybe 20 to 25 years out for development, and it was going for a song—a mere $500,000.

$500,000 was a little out of my range. (After all, I still needed to find a way to pay for my high school lunch and gym shoes. By now I was almost out the high school door, but not quite. Some of the teachers weren't too sorry to see me go, either. My pager would keep going off in the middle of a lesson. "Sorry," I'd say. "Closing on a real estate deal. Go on without me.")

But thanks to Mr. Menary, I had gotten in the habit of thinking about others and what might be in their best interest. Mr. Khan was not just one of my Dad's dearest friends, and almost an uncle to me. (I even called him 'Uncle Shabbir.') He was also an up-and-coming land developer, I now knew. As I went through the hot sheets and saw this parcel of land available for future development, I thought at once that it might be something that Uncle Shabbir might want to know about.

I called him.

"Uncle Shabbir, you should look at this. It's 25 acres, it's listed for $500,000, and it's a beautiful spot for development."

He was involved with the outlet's developments on the Canadian side of Niagara Falls at the time, but he was intrigued.

City teen sold on real estate business

By ELIZABETH LeREVEREND
Staff Writer

Faisal Susiwala doesn't dare shave off his moustache.

"Being 18 in this business can be a disadvantage, and appearance is everything," he says.

"There's no way I can shave off my moustache."

The business is real estate, and Mr. Susiwala — who got his Grade 12 diploma last year from Galt Collegiate Institute — is doing well despite his youth.

In his first four months as a real estate agent for Reid Menary, Mr. Susiwala has closed about $2 million in sales.

Sales already top $2 million

"My best commission was almost $8,000," he said noncha-lantly.

Mr. Susiwala has been selling real estate full time for just over a month.

For three months before that, he sold real estate part time, went to school full time, and had a part-time job as a bank teller.

"I was worried I'd go broke" in real estate, he said. "I guess I'm over-ambitious."

His first sale was to an acquaintance, who mentioned before Mr. Susiwala got his licence that he was interested in Cambridge property.

Within a week of earning his licence from Conestoga College, Mr. Susiwala had sold a 23-acre parcel of land to the man.

"That really gave me a boost. The first sale is important to build up your confidence."

Since that all-important first, he has sold subdivision properties, and a high school friend's parents' home, among others.

Mr. Susiwala said he has to try just a little harder than his older colleagues to be taken seriously.

"I have to make my voice

deeper on the phone and try not to get too excited. I read the Financial Post, and the Globe and Mail, and other publications, to stay on top of things. You have to know where the action is and be part of it."

His friends are fascinated with the real estate business now, he said.

"At first, they said, 'Why are you doing this?' but they're really interested. I'm just one of the guys. I like to have fun, but I'm not the type of person to just

sit around and wait for things to happen."

He's been compared to Family Ties character Alex Keaton more than once.

With his navy blue suit, leather shoes and red tie, Mr. Susiwala could be mistaken for a smart-alecky young capitalist.

He's not.

He still lives at home, and said he couldn't be a real estate agent without support from his family.

"This isn't as easy as it may seem," he said.

"It's a lot of work. A lot of nights I've been up til 1 a.m. on the phone trying to make a sale. The rewards are good, but it's a lot of running around and a lot of paperwork. I'm not just out to make lots of money."

The real estate business is going so well Mr. Susiwala has put off plans for a university business degree.

"This is what I want to do. Even after five years in school and a BA, I'd want to do this."

At first, other agents were skeptical of the young newcomer, but now he's getting job offers, Mr. Susiwala said. He's turned them down.

"It's to my advantage to be in

Reporter photo by Elizabeth LeReverend

Faisal Susiwala keeps up with the Financial Times. The 18-year-old Cambridge man is a real estate agent.

a small office, and Mr. Menary is my mentor, I guess. For 25 years, he's been in this field. There aren't many people who would hire an 18-year-old for a responsible position, but he did."

Now, he's working on selling subdivision investment properties in Ingersoll, trying to convince his employer to spring for a car phone, and hoping the Cambridge housing boom lasts a while longer.

"If it doesn't work out, there's always university," he said.

At 18 Faisal Susiwala was already starting to gain attention in local newspapers. Sporting a moustache, and initially lacking a car (perhaps a first among real estate agents in Canada), he needed to garner all the credibility he could muster.

He said he'd drive down and see the area. That's what he did. I was no land development expert, but Mr. Menary was there to have my back if and when it came to details like zoning. (Thank goodness. Just two or three months earlier I had no idea what zoning even meant.)

Uncle Shabbir checked it out, asked me a few questions, and looked over at Mr. Menary.

"This is great. I want to buy it."

He signed the offer on the trunk of my new (used) car.

And that was it. $475,000. Cash!

The year was almost over. From November 1988 to December 1988, I'd written up over two million dollars in real estate. My commission: $60,000.

When I walked into the McDonald's after school the next day, where all my friends were working, I had no trouble covering the Big Mac and (my favourite) Filet-o-Fish. It reminded me of my celebration at the same McDonald's after selling the most chocolate bars only a few years earlier.

Soon after that I got a lesson in real estate marketing that put my $60,000 in the shade. The New Year came and went and the newspapers were looking for fresh stories. They'd heard that some kid had sold $2 million worth of real estate. They wanted to write a story about me.

"Go ahead," said Mr. Menary. "You may get a few more calls."

A few? As soon as my face hit the papers, boom! Everyone in my little community started treating me like a rock star. Nearly everyone started noticing me. I got more calls than I could believe.

Before that news story, no one in the business—and I mean not the banks, not the other agents, not anyone other than Mr. Menary, really, I mean no one—regarded me as an actual licensed, qualified real estate agent, which is what I was. Normally brokers are all over you, because they hope to get business out of you, but as far as the local real estate community was concerned, I was the Invisible Man. More like the Invisible Kid!

There was one exception: a real estate attorney by the name of Calvin Johnson. He invited me over one day for a cup of coffee. He was a well-known, well-respected, well-placed figure in the real estate community. He couldn't have been nicer. He said if I needed help, advice, anything, to reach out and give him a call. He asked me how I was doing. I mentioned the South African investors and the Ingersoll properties and the townhouses, and he was impressed.

"I'd be interested in buying a couple of those myself," he said.

And he did! Four more units sold!

His reaching out to me all those years ago only reinforced a longstanding principle that I live by, the one I call 'IOU.' It's very simple: Give to Get. Reach out and do good to others, and it will come back to you. Cal Johnson treated me like an adult and a human being when others wouldn't give me the time of day. In turn, I sent him every piece of business I could for the next thirty years, until the day he retired. All because of that one cup of coffee and his kindness.

Cal was literally the only person in the business, aside from Mr. Menary, who noticed I was alive. Once the news story hit, though, it was like the ice had been broken. Suddenly I stopped being a non-person. It wasn't just that I became universally known and celebrated in the immigrant community, which I did ("One of our guys did good!"). It wasn't even that heads started turning when I walked down the street, which they did). I began to feel that 'rock star' buzz that successful real estate people feel. Suddenly I started being accepted by my peers and colleagues. I was no longer on the outside looking in. I was on the inside now—looking up.

Sometimes in Mr. Menary's office I would daydream about those big firms on the other side of the street. I remember looking out from our second-floor office window above the Royal Trust at a company on the other side of the street—Homeway Real Estate—and I would think, "Wow…" I could see computer screens. They had big bulky monitors and modems and keyboards on rows of desks. They had individual desks. Talk about cutting-edge. They didn't need to share a desk like us. What would it be like to actually work at a place like that?

Eventually I got to meet some of the Homeway Realtors. After all, we were sort of next-door neighbours. We'd go out at the same time and have lunch. One day I introduced myself as a fellow real estate agent. They were surprised at my age, but one of them had read about me in the papers. That was all it took. He pulled out a chair for me. The other agents raised their eyebrows.

"Hey, relax. Let the kid sit in," said the man from Homeway. "He's the real deal." (Thank you Walter).

We became friendly in no time and started talking and exchanging ideas. I didn't know it at the time, but I was becoming a part of the professional community.

In those days that community was very small and very local. Every Wednesday morning the Real Estate Board would meet at a place called The Matador. It was a large nightclub, but no one went there on Wednesday mornings to hear crooners or dance. Everyone who was anyone in local real estate went there to hear the latest real estate news. Agents from different firms would sit around the tables till their turn came, then get up with their MLS books and make announcements. This new property just came on the market. That property had just been sold. These listings here had gotten price reductions. Those were scheduled to have open houses.

It was an entirely different way of doing real estate, because the technology that's everywhere today just did not exist at all back then. If you wanted to communicate or share information with your peers you got together in a big hall, and then, table by table, one person after another would stand up and talk about their listings and the features of the listings. That was it. That was how it was done.

Looking back now, I'm sure it sounds like the Dark Ages. I mean, forget zooming in on a roof with Google Earth, we didn't even have the luxury of decent photographs. We were lucky to see a burnt-looking grainy black-and-white postage-stamp fax image next to the description. Unbelievable! It was pretty much a men's club in those days, too, though an avalanche of spectacular lady agents was about to completely change the make-up of the whole industry and inject a tidal wave of new talent. The guys chain-smoking around the table didn't have a clue what was on the horizon.

But that's part of the beauty of real estate, though, this evolution. Seeing and living through this amazing transition has been one of the most exciting parts of my career. It's like being there watching the first steam-driven motor car roll off the assembly line and then still being there to see it develop in front of your eyes into sports cars and self-driving trucks and superhighways.

Mr. Menary had taught me everything there was to know about the basics, and the best things there were to know about the traditional ways of doing business. He showed me, and modeled, what every person needs to know about ethics, responsibility, and being open to change.

But what he was willing to try, I wanted to embrace. Compared to Mr. Menary, I was like a surfer aching to catch a monumental racing wave. When I looked at the technological changes, I could sense what was coming, and it was new and amazing and world-changing, creating fresh opportunities at every turn. I loved it and wanted to jump in. I longed to become part of it.

But the Reid C. Menary Agency had no such plans. That first day I walked in to see Mr. Menary, he'd said that after a few months he planned to retire and close shop. Those months came and went and the shop stayed open, and I like to think that Mr. Menary's unusually young novice agent, and the energy and new developments I argued for and got, were among the factors that kept the firm open far longer than Mr. Menary had anticipated. A year and a half had gone by now, and not only was the company still open, it was flourishing. Mr. Menary still talked about downsizing and stepping down. But it never quite seemed to happen.

To tell the truth, I think it was because of me. He liked me, and he liked mentoring me as much as I loved being mentored. He had so much life experience, practical business experience, and professional skill. He'd seen so much, learned so much. There was a part of him that wanted to pass it along. There was part of me that wanted to learn everything he had to teach.

Like I said: I was blessed, and not just with a mentor. With a friend. We got together regularly for lunch once a week and, sure, we'd go over real estate, but we also talked about our families, about Canada, about the way the world was changing and the way it used to be. I've worked with lots of people in the real estate world, including the very best. But Mr. Menary was special. We remained friends until the day he passed away. Honestly, in my heart, he's never passed away.

We became a team, and during those last years the firm did well, all right. Even so, we all knew that retirement was coming. And no one had earned a peaceful retirement more than Mr. Menary. The fact remained, the time was coming when I'd have to leave the nest. I was already getting attention from other people in the business just by showing up at The Matador and announcing all the sales I was making. At first the agents looked at each other and asked, "Who is this kid?" But I wasn't a kid, not anymore. I was now a registered, experienced, successful real estate agent. I was out of high school, soon to be in my twenties and closing deals that any one of them would like to have had. If I knocked on the door of a Cambridge agency now —any agency—it would open. And I wanted to open those doors. There was so much still to learn. So many resources and opportunities waiting.

But which door?

And how to break it to Mr. Menary?

Around that time there was a new real estate company coming in from Vancouver that was getting a lot of attention.

They were making it clear that they wanted new people—young people in particular. Most Realtors at the time were in their 30's to 50's, and company recruiters tended to focus on that demographic. I had experience, but I was only 19. Recruiters weren't exactly knocking my door down to sign me. OK, maybe I could get an interview now. But it didn't mean I was guaranteed a desk.

This new company was different. They had it all: Dial up Internet, up-and-coming technology, independent offices, a great storefront, colourful signs, public exposure. It was 1990 and they called themselves Realty World; they were doing everything right, checking off every item on the business-leader checklist. There was something electric and vibrant about the firm. I wanted to be part of it.

Two partners owned the local firm—Mike Tremblett and Gerry Stocks—and Mike, in particular, was always looking for new potential. Whether by chance, or fate, my family had recently bought a new home that happened to be right across the street from where Mike Tremblett lived. He and I would often run into each other, and Mike didn't believe in beating around the bush.

"Hey, Faisal, why don't you come over and work for us? Come on. You've gotta come over. Stop playing hard to get. Realty World is where you need to be."

He kept at it. Kept at it? He hounded me! And he was right. Mr. Menary was still planning to retire. He'd put it off, but we both knew it was coming. No one could have had a better mentor, but I couldn't have him put off his retirement forever on my account. Besides, we could have lunch together wherever I worked. The job might come to an end, but our friendship— never.

Mike was dogged. He simply would not let up. So finally I said to Mike, "All right, I know Mr. Menary is retiring. Let me give it a shot. Let me talk to him."

So Mr. Menary and I set up a time to talk. It was absolutely one of the hardest conversations I've ever had in my life. I sat across the desk from him, and I thanked him so much for all that he'd done, I told him how much I appreciated everything he taught me, how much working with him had meant to me. But… there was a new company that I really wanted to work for… and —.

Well, I couldn't finish what I was trying to say. I was completely overcome. I sat there crying. Tears were running down my face. He'd become like a grandfather to me. I felt like I was abandoning him. He looked at me and there was a sadness in his eyes that broke my heart. It was more than just me leaving. If I left, the last thing keeping him from retiring would be gone. His lifelong career and the business he'd built would be going away too. He knew that day was coming; he'd even looked forward to it and gotten everything all arranged and in place.

But it doesn't matter how well prepared you are. When things that mean a lot to you come to an end, it hurts. That's just how it is, and there's nothing you can do about it.

Of course, he took it like the perfect gentleman he was. He said he understood, and that he was retiring anyway, and told me how much he'd enjoyed working with me and having me around. He said the new company was very lucky, and that he was sure I'd have a great future, and that whatever happened, we'd always remain the best of friends.

All of it was true, especially that last part. We did remain the best of friends. Mr. Menary closed his business soon after, but we continued to have our weekly lunches and review deals and scenarios. I would go over to his house and he would come over to mine. He continued to give me wise advice, and I continued to take it. He might not have been busy leading an active real estate agency any longer, but he still liked to keep a hand in the game.

Through me he did; through me he saw his profession evolve even further in new and amazing ways. And me? I continued to have a guide, and a model of humanity and decency that kept me on the right path, and still does.

Every ending is really only a new beginning. I was no longer an employee of Reid C. Menary Real Estate, but I could carry on the lessons of the man who began it.

He's gone now, but I'm grateful to have the honour and the happiness of sharing his memory and some of those lessons with you. If what I'm passing along here helps you to be even a bit like the man who taught them to me, you'll be a success in a good deal more than real estate.

Lessons

There are so many things I learned while working with Mr. Menary that it's impossible to reduce them into one principle, or to ever pay him back. The story I've just told doesn't begin to cover it.

But if I could boil it down to its essence, it comes down to two things he would say to me:

Do A Good Job. Do the Right Thing.

It's just that simple. Be competent. Be energetic and active. Be truthful. Care. Do that, and everything else will fall into place —the money, the listings, the calls, the referrals. Don't be sloppy or lazy or cut corners or complain. Do the best you can. Be the best you can.

Yes, success takes time. Success takes work. You need to hit the books. You'll need to meet people, get your business cards printed, get marketing tools, show houses, review listings, schmooze. No, competence and honesty won't automatically make you a multimillionaire, or guarantee that you won't have tough days and make bad mistakes or poor decisions. Bad things happen to good people. That's part of life.

In the end, though, you'll be able to support yourself and your family, help people find a home they can afford and build a future they can enjoy, and go to bed with a clear conscience. And —who knows? —you may even become a millionaire along the way. I did.

Mr. Menary's two core principles are words I return to again and again. Whatever the situation, whatever may be happening to me professionally, or even personally as a husband and parent, I think of them and they centre me. I think you'll find they'll do the same for you.

Think About What You're Doing

"So, what you're telling me, Faisal, is that I should find a good mentor and do exactly as they say. Right?"

No. I'm saying you'd be smart to find a good mentor and to listen to good advice —but more than anything else, you need to think for yourself. Be observant. Look around you. What works? What doesn't?

Mr. Menary taught me to double-and triple-check the paperwork and do my proper due diligence. I still do that. But I got him to innovate and get a car phone. Doing what works is good. Figuring out what works better is even better.

I've succeeded because I've always been willing to go against the grain. If you do what everyone else does, you'll get the same results everyone gets. If you want to get extraordinary results, you must do things in an extraordinary way—an extraordinarily different way.

Writing this book has forced me to look back on my career and reflect on what I did to get where I am. I'm surprised to say this introspection has led to what I think is an entirely unique way of doing real estate—a system, the Susiwala System. I sure wish I'd known about it when I was starting out—I'd have been successful a lot sooner. But I didn't. I had to stumble into it after many years of trial, error and experiment, causing me to think about what I was doing. In the end, that isn't such a bad thing. Someone once said that making mistakes and experiencing failure aren't bad things if you learn from them. Thomas Edison said it best: "I have not failed. I've just found 10,000 ways that won't work."

As I occasionally stumbled along, always thinking about what worked and what didn't, I looked not just at what I was doing. I watched what others were doing, and what did I see? Some things worked, other things didn't. A lot of what didn't work was conventional wisdom; things like "knock on doors," or "make cold calls," and "always be closing."

'Wisdom'?' These things are poison! There are entirely different ways of going about it that are much more effective and better adapted to the high-tech world of doing real estate that we live in today. Yet people keep doing the same old things over and over again anyway.

I did things differently, and—obviously—they've paid off. But at the time I wasn't thinking about them in terms of principles and writing these tenets down. I was too busy applying them to sell more houses! I only started thinking about them systematically when I found myself looking back years later.

At each stage of my career new and more effective practices and guidelines gradually became clear, and I've summarized them all in the Susiwala System chapter. I want to present them in these early chapters more or less in the order they started to become clear to me at the time. Mind you, I didn't think of them as principles or even as part of a system at the time. I just did them and they worked.

But you can do things a whole lot better if you know what you're doing. So, let me spell out a few of those guidelines right now.

Scale Down

That one's simple, though perhaps not obvious. Don't think big. Think small. Concentrate. Use what's near to hand.

When I wanted to break into real estate, I went straight to a Big Name — Century 21. I got shot down. Then I went to a small, local independent real estate broker I personally knew and greatly respected. I got the job.

When I was looking for business, I didn't go to Toronto to buy and sell houses. Sure, the market was bigger there, but I didn't know that market. I knew the market I was raised in and lived in all my life — Cambridge. I knew the streets and its people. I delivered newspapers to each house! I focused on what I knew.

Turning what some saw as a disadvantage — being a visible minority — to an advantage, Susiwala was a proud Canadian who never forgot his heritage (as this article shows), and this gave him an early boost to his career.

Things that some people regard as disadvantages can become advantages on the small scale: for instance, my background is

South Asian. I came to Canada as a child immigrant. I'm a visible minority, a Muslim.

Don't get the wrong idea from that. My ancestors may have been born in Pakistan and India, but I'm as Canadian as hockey and poutine. I read the Globe & Mail, cheer when Team Canada fires a puck into the net, pour real maple syrup by the gallon over everything, and say "eh?" every chance I get. I wasn't born in Pakistan or India; I was born in England, and came to Canada at age three. I was raised here, became a Canadian citizen here. and I've been surrounded by Canadians all my life. I love my home, my country, and my fellow countrymen and countrywomen. I belong to this wonderful culture about as much as a person can.

Loving your home doesn't mean forgetting your ancestry or heritage. A lot of Canadians have parents or grandparents who came from other countries. They love their country too, but they also cherish their heritage. Why shouldn't they? It produced the parents and people they love.

A heritage makes a difference. When you have a heritage, you have a ready-made community in which people know and support one another. When a new immigrant from the old country arrives, they naturally offer help to find a home and a job, to help the newcomers get a footing and stand on their feet.

If you're in real estate, this is one of your greatest opportunities.

To scale down means to know your community, to know your circle, and to let them know what you do. When people in the South Asian community in Cambridge needed a home, who did they call? Faisal Susiwala. If an immigrant steps off the plane and can only speak Urdu, who can they talk to? Faisal Susiwala.

In the beginning my community was the foundation of my business—and why not? I was part of that community. I knew the challenges immigrants faced, I spoke their language, I socialized with them, I worshipped beside them.

How does this apply to you, you say? Easy.

Whoever you are, you belong to a community too—a circle of people with whom you have something in common, and who, because of that connection, are predisposed to work with you instead of another Realtor. That connection doesn't have to be ethnic, and it isn't simply networking. Networking for professionals doesn't have that informal personal connection I mean. Ask yourself what groups you belong to. Are you a college student? Your circle is your fellow students, your teachers, your professors. They need a place to stay too. Let them know that you can help. One of my first sales was to a professor—my uncle. Families and extended families are a circle too. Do you have relatives? Relatives relocate! Relatives need homes!

Find those groups in your life to which you belong and where you're welcomed and accepted. Let people there know that you're in real estate. Trust me, business will come to you without you having to lift a finger.

But two words of warning:

First: it's one thing to court and attract people from a certain demographic segment. It's another thing to favour them—to give them service that you would not give to others. It's even worse to restrict them to that segment—to send someone into a particular ethnic area because a lot of the people belong to that ethnic heritage and you think that's where they belong. And if you refuse service to people because they belong to an ethnic group or faith or circle you don't wish to cater to? That will kill your career on the spot.

If you're uniquely qualified to serve a particular group because you happen to know their language, say, it's all right to let them know you have that unique qualification. But you are obligated ethically and by law to treat all people of all backgrounds equally, and to the best of your ability.

Discrimination in real estate is not an option: it's a crime, and if you're not meticulously careful about giving fair and equal treatment to everyone, you will not last in this business.

Second: circles are a great place to start. They're a terrible place to remain. Don't restrict yourself to your circle or circles. If you're a good agent, anyone can use your services. Reach out. But—to use a phrase you'll be hearing again—maintain your core. Your circle, your community, the people who know and like you, are your core. They'll sustain you and support you—so long as you do the same for them.

Chapter 3

I WAS A (bankrupt) TEENAGE REAL ESTATE AGENT

Well, not quite teenage at that point. I was twenty. Twenty, and feeling pretty cocky. After all, there I was, fresh out of high school with my picture in the papers. As an eighteen-year-old, boom: I'd sold 2.2 million dollars' worth of property in my first few months. Move over, Donald Trump! I had arrived. I was news.

Yes, OK, maybe I didn't have all the knowledge and experience in the world. But I did have a mentor in his seventies with experience and wisdom to spare. I had a market almost all my own—the immigrant community in Cambridge. In those days it was small, but it was large enough to need housing, and proud enough of its own to celebrate the success of young Faisal Susiwala. Everyone knew me, and everyone referred me to others in the community.

"Need a house? Go see Faisal. He'll do right by you."

They were right. I bent over backwards to do right by them. After all, Mr. Menary was watching, and I wanted him to be proud of me more than anything.

All he asked of me were two simple things. Do a good job. Do the right thing.

Those two things didn't guarantee success, but without that as a foundation, no success was sustainable. Yes, I'd had a great start. I'd found a target market that I could depend on for business. I'd begun to get well known—building my brand, though I didn't know what that word meant at the time—and I'd even generated enough funds of my own to start investing. I even had an experienced real estate investment analyst on hand, Mr. Menary, to vet those investments and ensure they were sound.

But global and national markets fluctuate unpredictably. I didn't have the tools to predict those fluctuations with any precision. No one does, even today. I also didn't have the resources to weather the storm. Nowadays, I hedge my bets. I believe in backup: in having enough resources to ride out the storms, and maybe even pick up some bargains when the market is down. Back then I didn't. I didn't even think about hedging my bets. I paid the price.

What brought me down was the property I'd secured for the investors from South Africa. We had hit it off. The gentlemen wanted a building that generated a particular level of returns on certain specific terms. There was a commercial building in Cambridge that fit the bill exactly. It seemed like the perfect deal.

There was a catch: the principal owner would have to be a Canadian resident, and he or she had to put their own money into the deal. Suddenly I actually had money. I stepped up and put it into the deal. Eventually I committed to 5 per cent. Since the property went for $750,000, that meant $37,500 out of my own pocket. Not a huge amount, but after paying off my parent's mortgage, it didn't leave me a lot.

I was happy about making the commitment, though. Me, barely out of high school, becoming part-owner of a major commercial building! Wow. I was happy to put in as much as I could.

Under most any other circumstances it would have been a perfectly smart and safe investment. But the circumstances weren't safe, and my decision wasn't smart. Without warning, the market sank into a severe downturn. It was a good, though expensive, lesson: never, never, never put in more than you can afford to lose.

The world of real estate is like the ocean: there are big waves that go way up, and then those same waves go way down. Smart, experienced investors look at the trends and diversify, putting hedges and insurance in place to ensure that, when the inevitable downward adjustments come, and they will, the investor doesn't go down with them.

I wasn't that experienced.

I had paid off my parents' mortgage. We'd even bought a second house. I was invested in multiple properties. Then came 1991, and the market collapsed. We entered recession. Property values fell. Did I say 'fell'? They crashed by forty percent.

Suddenly, instead of making $60,000 a year, I was making $26,000. A year.

We survived. My parents continued working. I still had my T-shirt business. Hello again, Shoppers Drug Mart! No, I didn't give up on the real estate business. But real estate alone wasn't enough to keep me above water.

The investors from South Africa were under the water. They were drowning. They had put their money into a property whose monthly payments were now skyrocketing. They were having to pump increasingly huge amounts of money into their investment all the time, just to keep things afloat. All for a building whose value had dropped over 40 per cent. How long could they keep losing money? Some recessions lasted for years. It just didn't make economic sense for them to keep throwing good money after bad.

Faisal Susiwala as a young agent sporting a Realty World jacket.

I spoke to them and told them honestly that it was in their best interests to stop the bleeding. They understood, just as they understood that the recession had been entirely out of our hands, and that I was losing my share in the investment too. All of it.

I went to the bank. The bank said, "Well, we're going to have to come entirely after you, then, Faisal, because you're the Canadian resident—the owner."

I nodded.

"I'm sorry," I said. "I'm afraid I just don't have the money to make the payments."

"You'll have to file for personal bankruptcy then."

"I know," I said. "Do what you have to do."

The investors didn't hold the loss against me. The banks knew the failure of the deal had been out of my hands, and that I'd dealt with them honestly and honourably. They even let me know they looked forward to working with me again in the future, once all this had been resolved. I took it well. It wasn't the end of the world. I still had my licence and my skills. Yes, this was a serious hit, but my career wasn't over.

So I filed for bankruptcy, cleared the slate, regained my focus, and took what little I still had and started a flyer campaign to get some business.

I didn't have a lot. I began by sending my flyer to 2,000 homes. It worked. It got me some business. Then I took part of the profits and sent flyers to 4,000 homes. I got more business. Then 5,000 homes. I got even more business. Hmm. I was beginning to notice something, something that would eventually make me millions. Eventually, over the years, 25,000 homes would get a piece of literature from me every three weeks in their mailbox.

Soon I didn't need the newspapers—everyone knew my face because it looked up at them each time they opened their mailbox. I became the guy in the mail. They saw my face a thousand times, and every time they saw me, my face was associated with buying and selling homes. And when the time came to buy and sell their home, a good many of those people picked up the phone and gave the man in the mailbox a call.

I learned a lesson from those flyers, and it stuck. The more marketing I put out, the more calls came back in. Yes, putting them out cost a lot of money. But the money I made came to a whole lot more. It was a no-brainer: once I'd slowly built my funds back up, I took a quarter of the money I was making and put it back into advertising; on benches, billboards, buses and arenas. The more stuff I put out, the more calls I got.

I didn't reinvent the wheel. Everyone was doing what I was doing. They just weren't doing it across the board, or consistently. I made the decision to do all of it, all the time, 24/7, 365 days a year. After three or so years I surpassed all my competition.

What made the difference? Consistency and self-discipline. Others wanted to spend the fruits of their labours right away. I reinvested. If I made $100,000 a year, I put as much of that $100,000 a year as I could right back into the marketing. And so, the next year I made $250,000, and so on and so on. I just kept ramping it up and ramping it up. Like I say, it was a no-brainer.

You're probably thinking, "Well, OK, Faisal, you did a lot of advertising and got a lot of calls. Good for you, but calls with buyers and sellers are a lot of work. How did you manage to handle all the business you were getting?"

We're going to have to save that for a future chapter. I only mention it now to let you know that I crashed and burned, and to show you how I got back onto my feet. Fast.

But that's not the point I want to make. Yes, I'm a very successful real estate agent and investor. No, I'm not superhuman or any sort of genius. Nor am I incredibly lucky. I did have the good luck to start off high. Or maybe it wasn't good luck, because I soon crashed low. I did well at first because of certain reasons that I'm sharing with you—I had a circle, a tight target market that I was uniquely suited to serve. I stood out and got attention because I was young and different in attention-getting ways. Also I was willing to commit not just time but money. I committed my funds, first to investments, and later, in a major way, to marketing. I got caught short because of a completely unexpected market downturn. But I learned from that too. I had no backup, and I had invested more than I could afford to lose. My mistake. Never again.

Is it really bad luck when you learn from it? No, not at all. You're paying for your education, and your education will pay you back. In a later chapter I talk about the 2008 crash. That's when the housing market crashed across North America forcing millions of homes into foreclosure. The entire global economy hit the rocks in its wake. Did I lose everything then? Nope. It barely affected me at all. In fact, that collapse presented me with a whole range of bargains and opportunities. (It presented me with a few surprises too, ones that caused me some suspenseful moments.)

But I didn't crash this time around. I flourished.

You'll get the details later. Right now, I want you to get the principle:

Lesson: Hedge Your Bets

I got burned because I was violating a basic principle of investing that I had not yet worked out: I hadn't hedged my bets.

You must have Plan B, a backup, some way to salvage the deal if things unexpectedly turn sour, and if you don't, you *must* have enough resources to survive and come back if it doesn't. Otherwise the climb back up is long and steep.

I didn't know that. I was a high schooler who zoomed from picking strawberries and stacking shelves to six figures in less than a year. A newspaper story built up my ego and I felt like the star of the show. But I was performing without a net.

I couldn't have asked for a better teacher than my friend Mr. Menary, but everyone has another teacher whose lessons are unforgettable: *reality*. And the reality in real estate is that the market fluctuates, and you can't do much about it. There are highs. There are lows. No one knows when they'll hit or how long they'll last. If you prepare, and hedge your bets, you'll survive. I hadn't prepared.

How do you prepare? It's not rocket science. Put some funds aside for a rainy day. Don't invest every penny you have. Diversify. Insure yourself. Partner with others instead of bearing the whole burden of risk personally. Develop multiple sources of income—side businesses, teaching, royalties. Maintain your skills and your brand: whether the housing market is high or low, people will always need a place to stay and a Realtor to help them. Be there for them.

What would you do today if your income dropped in half? Draw up a plan. What do you do *'When Bad Things Happen to Good People'*? Good grief, there are entire books written on the subject. There are even books on getting through bad times in the real estate world specifically. Use your library card and go through a few, before the tornado hits. There are good suggestions everywhere on how to weather a storm.

But remember too that the most important thing about a challenge is your response. I took a hit, but I learned from it. And what I learned—about marketing, but also about dealing honestly with others, and about myself—in retrospect made it well worth the price.

When a deal goes badly, there's often an attempt to look around for someone to blame. Find a scapegoat and point the finger at others. It would have been easy for my partners to point the finger at me. I was young and inexperienced. I arranged the deal, and it went sour. But they didn't blame me, and my relationship with them and with the other investors didn't sour. My relationship with the banks didn't go sour either.

Why not? Transparency, integrity and having skin in the game.

If I had not been forthcoming with my fellow investors about the worsening financial developments, if I'd tried to cover it up in hopes that interest rates might change, at best I would be acting unethically, and at worst I'd be engaging in fraud.

Instead I made sure they were informed about every development, every concern. A downturn in the overall market was not something anyone could control. No one could be held accountable for that. The numbers that were compelling enough to get us all to invest were clear and open, and the risks were not concealed. We'd gambled and lost. But it was a reasonable gamble, and we'd all gone into it together with our eyes wide open. If we lost, it wasn't because of incompetence or unethical practice.

Plus, we all lost. I hadn't pointed the investors to a poor investment and put my own money elsewhere. I'd taken the same risks and got the same results. They were unfortunate results, but the circumstances were exceptional. No one was personally to blame. And so, although the venture had fallen apart, we parted with mutual respect, as friends.

That same transparency kept my reputation with the banks high. True, banks don't like investments to fail. They look forward to a long stream of regular payments, and they don't like to find themselves in possession of property they don't want and don't know what to do with. But they, too, had looked at the deal and found it sound. They, too, knew that no one could have anticipated a recession. I had lost, but I had only lost a battle. There would be more deals to come, and losing gracefully, responsibly, doesn't make you a loser. It only makes you someone who's lost one exchange on the chess board. If you've played well and honestly regardless, if you've shown the other players courtesy and respect, people will be more than ready to invite you to another game.

What should you do if you face this kind of problem? Don't 'fake it till you make it.' All that will get you is a charge of fraud. 'Face it and embrace it'. Don't wallow in anger or self-pity. Deal with it honestly and head on. Give it your best effort, your most honest and your most thoughtful effort.

Use your head. Ask yourself what your best possible move is, given the circumstances, and then make that move. It's that simple.

Chapter 4

REALTY WORLD

I couldn't have asked for a better introduction to real estate than working with Mr. Menary. But the truth is, it wasn't really an introduction to the whole vast world of real estate. I was learning the basics in a small office that was on the point of closing. Working with Mr. Menary was an honour and a privilege. A pleasure! But it was like working with a parent, a mentor, a friend. It wasn't being part of the scene. It wasn't making a breakthrough into the professional community, into the rapidly evolving world of realty.

That's—literally! —what happened next: I plunged headfirst into Realty World, a new and up-and-coming real estate firm taking Cambridge by storm.

I didn't have to knock on their door. They knocked on mine. Their door was literally next to mine. I've already mentioned our new neighbour, Mike Tremblett, who ran Realty World. He wanted me on their team so badly I thought he would tackle me on the sidewalk and drag me there by force. Talk about active recruitment!

Mike ran the firm with his partner, Gerry Stocks, and the full name of the firm was Realty World New Town. I think that was because they were looking at Cambridge as a 'new town' for their business, and so the people they were hiring were 'new people.' I'd just turned twenty, and you couldn't get much newer than that and still be licensed.

I resisted at first. I just hadn't yet reached the point where I could leave Mr. Menary. He'd come to mean too much to me. But I must admit that Mike's repeated invitations made me feel good about myself. I'd been turned down at Century 21 after barely so much as a single look. Now firms—dynamic, flashy, attention-getting firms—were looking to recruit me. What Mike told me about Realty World wanting to bring in young people was true. Most agencies back then were staffed mostly by older people in their 40's, and beyond. Realty World had a whole different perspective: they wanted fresh faces, more dynamic ideas—energy. They believed young people were the future, and younger Realtors would eventually grow into leadership roles in days to come. They wanted to get in on that ground floor.

With an attitude like that, I knew Realty World would be a good fit. Plus, they were all about networking, and that appealed to me too. It would be good to be part of a network of young people, of like-minded ambitious fellow professionals. I was already becoming a little concerned about stereotyping. I loved the immigrant community, and I served them as best as I possibly could. I still do, happily. But I didn't want to become known as the 'the immigrant agent' and be slotted into a niche. Your circle is the best possible place to start, true. But I'd gotten my start, and now I wanted to spread my wings and open up to all of Cambridge.

At Realty World there were important lessons to be learned. Here Faisal is shown left, at a President's Reception. At Realty World he embraced teamwork and the company's recognition program.

That's exactly what happened. I started meeting a ton of people; some of the key people in my story and my career, and in my ongoing understanding of real estate.

One big and lasting influence was a young man by the name Tony Puim, who introduced me to the whole world of learning from books and tapes and motivational speakers. I'd always been something of a Tony Robbins fan, but on and off. I'd listen to a CD but then drift away. Tony Puim not only got me listening with focus, he got me into workshops, fire-walking over coals, and shaking the hand of Tony Robbins himself. Not till I met

Tony Puim did I realize the value of complete immersion and total focus. Tony was passionate.

"You've got to embrace this scene, Faisal!" he said. "Buy all the CDs. Get all the audiotapes. Go see the speakers. Read the books. Embrace that network. Connect with these people!"

I did! We both did. His enthusiasm was infectious! We started attending workshops, seminars, presentations, and popped audiocassettes (remember those) into our cars' tape players every time we pulled out on the road. It wasn't all just about generating enthusiasm, either. We learned a ton of practical real estate tips and sound advice that I still use to this day. (Thank you, Tony Puim. Thank you to both Tonys!).

But that wasn't the big thing I took away from all the talks and seminars. The big thing was that it got me *thinking*. All the inspirational talks and the evangelical fervour coming from the speakers got my business mind going. I became more aware not just about buying and selling houses, but about the mental side of real estate, about the need to develop your attitude, your vision, to open yourself up to tremendously larger horizons.

Did I think when I walked into Century 21 that in a few more years I'd be the number one top-selling Realtor in all Canada? No way. I thought that one distant day maybe I'd own a yacht like Tom Vu and invite hot babes over to party. (Assuming I kept it real quiet and the news didn't reach my mom).

But Tony Robbins, Robert Kiyosaki, Robert Allen, Carleton Sheets, all helped me realize that I could build not just a career but expand as a person; that through my career I could continually become a better version of myself.

My ancestors came from India, and India has always had a long tradition of meditation and mental discipline. You pick it up in the culture—there's a feeling that you can and should lift up your heart, make your thoughts clean and noble, detach yourself from stress, fear and greed, cultivate wisdom and charity and compassion and service, aim for the highest state of mind you can attain. It's not enough to aim at accumulating more external material things. You also have to build yourself up on the inside —to develop qualities of the spirit.

Tony's enthusiasms and the speakers and ideas he introduced me to helped me see that real estate wasn't just a job I had to plug away at to pay the bills and help the family. In a way, he put into words what Mr. Menary showed by example: doing real

estate well, doing it competently and honourably, required and
helped to further develop personal qualities that every decent
human being needed to cultivate.

Success took intelligence, study, self-discipline, good
judgment, reflection, creativity and honour. Work wasn't a
burden: it was a noble path that led you to becoming a better
person. At least, if you followed it with discipline and integrity.

Gerry Stocks, Mike's partner and co-owner of Realty World,
had both. But discipline? He had *that* quality by the trainload.
He was the Compliance Officer at Realty World, and he went
straight by the book. No grey areas for Gerry! "This is what you
do, and this is exactly what you do, to the letter," was his
mantra. "It's black or white, period. There is no in-between."
He'd sit there behind his big desk and lay down one iron rule
after the other, while he chain-smoked one cigarette after
another.

I coughed, but I got the message. Gerry's talks about strict
compliance kept me very much grounded in ethics, but he went
beyond the goodness of heart that Mr. Menary always showed.
He was all detail every time. From Gerry I'd learn things about
contract law and how to stay out of the court system. He was
emphatic. "Do *this*. Don't do *that*. Sign this, and make sure you
witness that signature, and never, never say you did if you
didn't."

Basic due diligence? Yes, and everyone in the business takes
it for granted. But one single slip can kill deals and even destroy
your career if you fail to do them properly. A person might come
in, be asked to sign a piece of paper, and later they would leave
it behind with their signature, and you might not actually see
them sign it. Then, to get things moving, or finish the paperwork
early, someone would ask you to say that you witnessed the
signature. Many people would say, "Why not? So what? There's
the signature. There's the paper."

Then it turns out it was the husband or wife who was with
the person who signed. Or there's proof that you weren't present
to witness the signature. Then the whole deal becomes invalid,
you may end up in court, your career is toast, and the firm as a
whole could be liable.

To this day, I'll have lawyers or agents call and say, "Hey,
you failed to sign as witness," and the ghost of Gerry Stocks,
may he rest in peace, will appear at my shoulder blowing smoke

in my ear. I'll say, "That's right, because I didn't see them sign it."

Mr. Menary schooled me to be honest from the heart, but Gerry taught me to be *meticulously* correct, to line up all the details perfectly right. Clouds of smoke aside, it was almost spellbinding to hear him speak sometimes, explaining in rigorous detail how to do everything exactly right. You'd walk out of the office feeling you knew precisely what to do and would never go wrong following the straight and narrow.

Then I would walk down the hall into Mike Tremblett's office. Mike was Gerry's partner and the office manager, and every bit as important and knowledgeable as Gerry, and—he'll kill me for saying this—he would go, "Nah, forget everything you've just heard from Gerry... This is how things are done."

Now don't get the wrong idea. Mike never told me to do anything unethical or dishonest. Not once. It's just that Gerry went by the rule book 100 per cent of the time, all the time. Mike? He was kind of a jazzman—he had a creative, personal approach to doing business. He would improvise, and go with intuitions and gut feels, and look at things in unexpected ways. Every time after going to Gerry's office I'd always somehow end up in Mike's, and he'd go, "No, no, no. Throw all that out the window. Here's how it's really done." It wasn't that Mike was telling me to get the paperwork wrong. He was making the larger point that getting the paperwork right was not what mattered most about the whole process.

What did matter most? Here was another major takeaway I got from working at Realty World. Mike would emphasize again and again that real estate was about people. He would show me techniques which would help get people to like you, to allow you to be influential in a social way and not just in a cold, logical, show-them-the-numbers business way. Mike understood there was a human element to the process that every Realtor needs to remember. You won't get recommendations or referrals or lifelong loyalty from clients purely by getting their paperwork right. Of course you *should* get it right, and get it right every single time. That goes without saying. In fact, that's one of the ways in which you do earn their loyalty.

But there was more to it than that. Call it schmoozing, call it interacting with the client, call it charm, call it being a good listener, having a sense of humour—whatever. You had to connect with the client by bringing the client personally into the process and making them feel comfortable.

True, you weren't socializing just to be sociable, and it wasn't about getting them to like you just so you could get a higher commission. Connecting with them personally helped you do a better job for them. The more you knew, the more of a feel you got for the person, the better you could understand their needs and their likes and their dislikes. Get to know a person and you learn to tell what kinds of properties or prices or deals they would or wouldn't go for.

It also helped you do a better job because you enjoyed your job more. After all, who doesn't enjoy having a positive and pleasant conversation with people? Time and again I see people in real estate sales who think they can argue or badger or push people into buying a property. Not only doesn't it work, having unpleasant exchanges with people day after day kills your desire to keep going, and quashes any desire on their part to ever work with you again. It's like cold calling, which I also hate, and which I never do. Why make dealing with people unpleasant for everyone?

Mike did way more than just sit there and tell me, "Be nice." What I learned from Mike is that there are techniques that can build good, pleasant interactions. He was a true salesman, a character right out of Glengarry Glen Ross. Every day he'd have the wall chart up, like the coach going through plays for the Big Game, and he would go through the list point-by-point for agents like me about to take to the field. It was exhilarating.

We really were a team, too. We were like a major Canadian sports team. We had *attitude*. We were taking on the big-name agencies, and we were the up-and-coming champs! The Realty World contenders would walk into our usual restaurant like soccer players about to scramble; we'd get some appetizers, we'd down a couple hundred cups of coffee, and we would go for it. We connected: we applied Mike's focus on likability not just on customers but on each other. The truth is, real estate agents compete not only with agents from other companies but often against each other. If I get the listing, you don't, so some agents play their cards very close to the vest. Not at Realty World. The team at Realty World really enjoyed each other's company. We'd eat together. We'd party together. We'd go to conferences together from Toronto to Vancouver. (I think I was the first Indian in Calgary to attend the stampede wearing a white cowboy hat and boots).

It was a job, sure, but it felt good to be there. It was fun!

Still, I wasn't there just to have fun. I was there to get good at what I did. And day by day I got better and better—much better. At the back of my mind I had the ethics part from Mr. Menary, and the reciprocity—the 'IOU.' I added strict and meticulous compliance from Gerry Stocks. Now Mike Tremblett gave me the social skills. Those skills not only helped me in real estate, they helped me in my personal life. My circle of associates was expanding, and so was my circle of friends.

Individually, all these things mattered, but the combination lifted my professional skills and status to the next level. Thanks to Mike opening the social side, the fun side, of the real estate profession for me, I made some good friendships with other agents, friendships that have lasted. That mattered too. When you have friends, and your friends rise in their industry and in the world, so do you. Some of those people I would horse around with became very, very

Putting Cambridge on the world map!

Early success brought additional publicity, which Susiwala learned was an important aspect of gaining recognition in his community.

successful. They ended up working with the top firms, sometimes running them and having hundreds of agents working for them. I refer business to them, and they refer business to me. We do a lot more business now than then.

But back then we were just friends, and because we were friends, and hung out, and because we were all ambitious, they started inviting me to work with them on small development projects—not just the 'Realtor's office' part of real estate, but flipping houses, buying rental properties. Investment, but on a safe, modest scale. I was 'Scaling Down,' and because I was scaling down, I was expanding outward, growing a portfolio. We'd get other people involved too, people who had nothing to do with real estate. I had friends who were still in college and university who needed a place to stay, and didn't have a lot of money to spare. Sometimes I didn't either. So what?

"Hey, guys, let's get a group together and buy a big house that needs work, and renovate it. You can stay in one of the units and we'll rent out the rest."

Realty World became our hub. Everyone would show up there after school or after work and we'd be there till midnight or later, cooperatively planning and brainstorming different ways of making money and buying properties. How were we going to make that first million? Who was going to be the first billionaire real estate mogul? Who would control the Monopoly board?

It was at Realty World that I began to think of real estate not just as a game, but as a platform to build an empire.

I also began to see how many of the things that made working there enjoyable were also techniques that made the place productive, and how both worked because there was a carefully crafted playful quality to it all.

For example, ranking. At Realty World I learned what getting an award meant, what 'top salesperson' means, what 'salesman of the month' means, what it means to be part—wow!—of The Million Dollar Club. The rankings and rewards turned working in real estate from plain old dull work into ongoing competitive tests of skill: a game—and we love games. I sure did.

Once I realized what these accolades meant—that you were good, that you were the *best*—I wanted to play too, and play to win. I wanted to be on that winners list! I wanted to get that award! I dreamed of seeing my name on the next Hot Sheet going out across Canada: Faisal Susiwala, the guy with the most listings and the most sales. Mr. Real Estate Rock Star! There aren't many professions that foster that kind of industry stardom, but real estate does.

Does it make you work harder, do more, reach higher? You bet it does.

And how does it feel when you arrive, and all your peers, colleagues and friends are standing there applauding?

It feels good. Very good.

The competitive aspect—the *game* aspect—wasn't the only thing that made an impression on me. The power of marketing and advertising did too. I already knew what public attention could do from that newspaper article about me when I was eighteen. But I only got the attention in that case because of my age, and after the spike in attention, things went back to normal. I had no idea how powerful consistently getting your name and face in front of people could be.

But I was starting to. The papers gave me attention because I stuck out—I was a young kid in a traditionally older profession. Now I was getting attention because of my expertise. Back then they used to have these sales rallies—big rah-rah events where people would speak. By 1992 I was doing so well and getting so well-known through networking that I was asked to appear on one of the panels in Toronto and talk about what it was like being a young person in the business. That was my first experience of being on stage. It wouldn't be my last.

I also learned important marketing lessons about repetition and roll-out. At that time my entire campaign had just started. I put out flyers that I sent out into a farm area. (What's a 'farm area,' you say? Cows and barns? Nope. A 'farm area' is what we called a geographic area of, say, a thousand homes; we 'farm' it by distributing our literature to that population.)

That's what I did. It worked. The business I got from the flyers more than paid for the cost of making and distributing them.

And then, almost without thinking, I did something that has become a characteristic of my career, and is one of the reasons I've been so successful. I pushed the envelope. I said to myself, "If this works for a thousand homes, why not two thousand? And if it works for two thousand, why not three?"

From there I went to 5,000, 8,000, 15,000, all the way to 25,000 homes. I just kept growing and growing that farm area. And the responses and commission revenues just kept growing and growing, too.

Let me tell you: when that crop comes in, it is overflowing.

You could experiment in those days; there was an incredible creativity back then. Things were looser. Despite Gerry's heated insistence, registrations and compliances were 'loosey-goosey,' let's call it. Remember, this was the late 80s to early 90s and it was kind of a wild time. Things that are unacceptable now were acceptable then. There were ways of handling finances and abatements and such that you just can't do today. Back then you could buy a home for $500,000, but the offer would read $550,000. The $550,000 would be because they'd be giving you $50,000 back for renovations. It was true, they were giving you $50,000 back, but you were only actually paying $500,000. From the bank's perspective, though, the bank would be financing you for the $550,000, based on the ten percent down, which is the actual abatement you received.

Well, none of this is legal now. In those days, it was a grey area. So, it was common practice. The mortgage brokers called it "creative financing." The attorneys could and would work it out with everyone involved. It wasn't morally wrong, or even illegal (then). It just wasn't as crystal-clear as people with a Gerry Stocks mindset would prefer. Sometimes, in some cases, that worked out pretty well for everyone involved.

This was a part of my education as a Realtor too. I learned there are lines you never cross, ever, but there were creative methods used to everyone's benefit, including the client. There is a lot less of it now but learning about that flexibility was worthwhile. It inspired you to think outside the box. Instead of just running everything by the book

Susiwala's second business card as a Real Estate agent with Realty World

—the way Gerry insisted you should do—you would ask yourself how you could follow the letter of the law exactly, but still find ways to make use of it to get your client, the agency and yourself the best result. It was the Mike approach: clever, creative, intelligent real estate, real estate that engaged your brain. Lawyers probe for loopholes all the time in hopes of finding something that can help a client. At Realty World I learned that a real estate agent can do that too.

Yes, working at Realty World was fun, educational, profitable, creative, exciting and inspiring—just an excellent experience in every way.

So, I quit.

What? Didn't I say that I really enjoyed working at Realty World? I sure did. Gerry and Mike, Tony, the teamwork, the awards, the camaraderie, the dynamism, the sheer fun—it was great!

So why did I just walk out one day?

It wasn't an easy decision. But it was a matter of principle. Principles matter. At least they do to me.

You see, most every real estate office splits commissions. The agent gets a part, the agent's sponsoring broker gets a part, and the proportions change over the course of a year. Normally, they reset the split on agent commissions on December 31. On that day you go back to zero. When the real estate year begins, everyone starts off even, at a 60/40 commission split. What that means is that when a property is sold, and there's a commission paid, the salesperson gets 60 per cent of it, and the company gets 40 per cent.

As you sell more, your commission split gets higher too. The more you sell, the more of a percentage you get. So, when you reach $20,000 in commissions, for instance, you get 70/30 instead of 60/40. Then, at $50,000, your commissions are 80/20. And at $75,000 or whatever, you'd be at 90/10. At that point, 90 per cent of the commission on a sale is yours.

Need I say that this is one heck of a strong incentive for real estate agents to do as much business as they can and reach those goals? Agents hustle, because they make almost 30 per cent more per sale.

But it all ends on the last day of December. Come January 1, it resets, and you're back to 60/40.

Now in 1990 and 1991 things were tough. Those were very challenging years. It was the middle of the recession. Things were bad, and they stayed bad all the way through to 1994.

In December of 1993, I had a deal closing on the very last Friday of the month. (I still remember the street address. It was a house in Cambridge, and it closed for $130,000).

Although it was the last Friday of the month, it was still a workday, and the commission came in on that very day. I was in the high-level commission 90/10 bracket, so as a result, I'd be making a decent sum.

And because times were tough, I needed it. The salespeople at Realty World, myself included, were not making a lot of money. It was the holiday season on top of the recession and on top of the slow sales. Everyone was hurting. Struggling. Realty World itself was struggling. We were hungry. Every penny counted.

The deal was concluded, the commission was a done deal and the actual physical cheque arrived at our office well before the end of the year. But the commission check couldn't be processed. After all, it was the holiday season—Christmas and New Year's— and the banks were closed.

Given the circumstances, I understood why Realty World couldn't pay me out immediately. You can't cash a check at the bank if the bank is closed. That was fine. I could wait till after the New Year to pick up my commission. So, on January 2, I walked into the office to pick up my commission check. There it was, waiting on my desk. And when I opened it—the amount was based on 60/40.

Yet the deal had closed before the end of the year. The commission check arrived at the office before the end of the year. I didn't finish out the year at 60/40. I finished the year at 90/10.

What was going on?   I asked that it be corrected. Management refused.

So, I quit.

I understood why, of course. Before, when commissions closed in December, Realty World was doing well. Now, Realty World was hurting. They needed money too.

But fair is fair. And this wasn't fair. This was about more than the money. Commissions had closed in December before. I'd never heard of anyone getting treated like this before.

Talk about turning points. Leaving was a major move, especially in hard times. I was still only twenty-three, after all. I was still 'the kid,' and Mike and Gerry were still the bosses, expert professionals I looked up to. I liked them. I still do. Mike and I remain good friends. (Gerry passed away, may he rest in peace). I liked the company, and I enjoyed working there. Plus I had bills to pay and family to help support, and times were bad. Very bad. The last thing I wanted to do was start the New Year banging on doors in the depths of a recession to look for another job. On top of all that, the money wasn't even that much—a few hundred dollars.

But this was not about the money.

Letting yourself be mistreated, like mistreating others, can become a habit. A bad habit. What I learned from Mr. Menary was that integrity comes first. Always, always, do the right thing. But doing the right thing isn't just a matter of treating others fairly. You have to treat yourself fairly too. Respect for others begins with self-respect. Only if you treat everyone fairly, yourself included, will things turn out for the best.

And they did turn out for the best. In the long run.

In the short run, Realty World handed me a check for 60/40 when it should have been 90/10, and said "Take it or leave it."

I took the cheque—and left Realty World.

I don't think they ever really believed I would leave. We had such good rapport, we worked well together professionally, they taught me a lot, and in turn I gave them a ton of business. Letting me go over a few hundred dollars was as much a bad decision on their part as it was a brave one on mine.

But that's another takeaway lesson of this chapter: principles matter. You can learn techniques, you can comply with regulations, you can win awards, and pal around, and reach the top sales brackets. You can't do something you believe is genuinely wrong; or put up with something wrong when someone does it to you. If you do, you lose a lot more than money. You lose your self-respect. Yes, what I did took courage, but it wasn't about courage. It was about self-preservation.

So, at nine in the evening I called over a few friends who were in the office.

"Guys, I'm done here. Can you help me clean out my desk?"

They were my buddies. They looked at me funny, they asked questions, they got all upset, they told me I should reconsider and stay. It was only a couple of hundred bucks.

But I had made my decision.

And that was the last time I walked through the doors of Realty World.

At the time, driving home on that winter night as the snow fell silently, I felt.., I don't know what I felt. Serious. Principled. Brave. On the verge of new horizons. A new year had begun. Where would it take me?

Then I woke up the next morning, and the first thing I thought was, "Shit! Oh man—I don't have a job!"

I didn't have any place to go, either. I couldn't go back to Mr. Menary. He was retired, his agency was gone. Meanwhile the recession was still on, and the bills were piling up higher.

Bankruptcy was bad, but at least back then I'd still had a job and some money coming in. What little I had now was tied up in property. Once that last cheque from Realty World was gone, I had nothing.

So there I was—twenty-three, out of work, and on my own.

On my way to becoming the number-one best-selling Realtor in Canada.

Lessons

I learned a good many things at Realty World. So many that that there isn't space to list them all. But the big things weren't things you learn with your head. They're things you learn because you're part of a community. At Realty World I came out of my shell, and that was important. I stopped being a child prodigy and became a young professional, and that amped up my professional skills—big time. The awards I started winning even began to make me a name. I wasn't a superstar yet, but I started attracting notice—for my achievements, not my age.

At the same time, all that didn't really push me in the direction of building my own system and doing things my own way. I wanted to beat my colleagues at their game, by doing the things they were doing just a little better. I hadn't been analyzing the game itself.

But I was starting to. My time at Realty World planted the seeds. I began partnering with people and investing in properties. They weren't big properties or major developments, but it was a beginning. Thanks to Gerry, I learned to be meticulous when it came to contracts and details. Thanks to Mike, I learned to develop my social skills. An even bigger legacy of Mike's was realizing that you could do real estate creatively. So, without knowing exactly what I was doing, I began to build my own unique approach, and think about it and systematize it.

For instance? Everyone had an opinion at Realty World on how to get business. Knock on doors! Cold call! Send out flyers! How effective was that? I looked around and saw people knocking and calling and sending the whole day. They absolutely hated it. They hated it so much that some even dropped out of the business entirely. Even the ones that did manage to get some business calling and knocking sure didn't seem to get much. Did it work? Sort of. Badly.

On the other hand, flyers seemed to work well. I noticed that they brought in more business than they cost to send, and without the rejection and the physical wear and tear of calling and knocking. Flyers I embraced. Most important of all: I noticed that I was noticing, and thinking about what I was noticing, not just copying mindlessly.

This led me to formulate a key pillar of the Susiwala System:

Model Excellence Creatively

I got the 'modelling excellence' part from Tony Robbins. Back then he'd go on about this endlessly. Find someone doing something well and copy them. Not just their actions but their attitude, their state of mind, their beliefs. It was good advice, and once I started winning awards and hanging out with other award-winners, I began picking up their approaches and their attitudes as well.

But some of those approaches just plain didn't work. Or worked badly. Or could be made to work better. Or might work for them, but just didn't fit me. Cold calls and door-knocking worked so badly that people doing it threw in the towel and ended their careers, never knowing that success might have been waiting just around the corner had they changed direction. Flyers worked, but only so long as you kept at it. And yet people didn't seem to stick with it or put too much money into it.

I hated the very idea of cold-calling and door-knocking. I refused to do it. To this day I have never cold-called anyone. As for flyers, if it worked, why not do it consistently, regularly, constantly? Why not do more of it? If it got more business than it cost, how far could I take it? Gradually I took it to the max, and I've kept it at the max. I was not just running with a good idea, picking it up and dropping it when a buyer or seller called, but applying it systematically. I hit the 90/10 commission split in no time.

Yes: I'm telling you to send out flyers. Regularly. As many times as the market will bear, if that market sends you the business to cover it. Sending out flyers doesn't just mean physical flyers, either: nowadays these can take the form of e-flyers in social media and sponsored ads. Apply it, but apply it creatively.

Look at the results people are getting, yourself included, and use your head to try to figure out how to do better. It's not "Monkey See Monkey Do": it's "Monkey, Evolve!" Apply this principle to every single part of your real estate practice. If you do, you will be doing one of the key things that made my own real estate career take off.

What are the most successful people doing? How can you do it better? *Think* about it. Act on it. Look at the results.

Scale Down

Another huge breakthrough (that I had no idea I was making at the time) was the Susiwala System principle already mentioned: Scale Down, but this time applied to partnering and investing. Before, I had thrown myself into investing in a major commercial building with few personal resources, no prior experience, no backup plan, little attention to market trends, and multiple international buyers unfamiliar with local conditions. I got wiped out.

This time I called some college buddies in need of a place to stay. "Hey, why don't we pool a couple of thousand apiece and put a down payment on a two-unit residence? Maybe we can get a person to rent one of the units and put a little monthly cash in our pocket. Or better yet: pay off the mortgage?"

I'll get into this in more detail later, but you should know right now that this little principle has added millions to my net worth.

It didn't come about because I threw everything I had into it. It came about because I started small, with a few friends, buying a modest little property at an even more modest small cash investment.

I reached new heights because I scaled down, and started the journey as modestly, safely, and affordably as I could.

The biggest legacy of my Realty World years, however?

Heartset

Creativity, innovation, being inspired by 'rock star' recognition, developing social skills, being willing to lose a job rather than allowing oneself to be treated unfairly—all these are aspects of mindset: How you think. What you feel.

But mindset is a much bigger subject than any of these. It wasn't really till 9/11 that the full depth of the subject became apparent to me. And it should have been evident a long time before that.

Not long ago, as I was writing this book, I went through some of my old things. There were photos of me at twenty, sporting a bushy mustache so I could look older. There was the award I got at school for selling the most chocolate bars door to door. Finally, there was a lumpy box of toys from when I was a child.

I reached over to it, wondering what I'd been playing with when I was a boy.

Toy soldiers? Rocket ships? Cowboys?

I lifted the top off the box. What did I see?

Sketches of buildings and homes. Some pieces from Monopoly. Model cars and luxury magazines.

It's hard to describe the feelings that came over me. I looked around at the beautiful home surrounding me, at the sports cars parked outside the window.

My boyhood dreams had come true.

In that little box was my vision—a vision that had come true.

Of course, just daydreaming about sports cars didn't put one in my driveway, but is there really no connection between the things you dream about, the things that deeply move you, and the direction in which you eventually move?

It's important to be sensitive to your honest feelings. Our thoughts and attitudes surround us every minute, and still—even though what we think is what we are—we don't give it very much attention. Yet working on our thinking can help us do better in everything—our jobs, our relationships, our spirit.

When my family came to Canada, they thought they'd found everything they'd hoped for. My mother and father found a factory job; in addition to that, my mother took care of our growing family, the children went off to school—it was the same story that so many immigrant families have gone through—a new start, hard work, upward mobility. We didn't have a lot of money, but we were rich in a way that had nothing to do with money: we were together, and happy.

And then one day it all fell apart. I came home and learned that my father had had a serious accident in the factory, one so crippling that it could easily have been fatal.

I can't begin to tell you how hard this hit my family—how hard it hit a little boy like me. It wasn't only that we were shocked and heartbroken. The bills, the loss of our father's paycheque, the care and time needed for his recovery—all of it drained away our modest savings. Soon we were unable to make the mortgage payments for the house. Not long afterwards, our furnishings were moved out and a lock was put on the door. We had lost our home.

This section is about mindset. And I share this story because it taught me one of the most important lessons of my life—namely that the most important thing about suffering is not suffering, but how you respond to it. My father was not a victim: he was a tower of strength and optimism, determined to find a way to lead and support his family again. My mother didn't spend her days in tears, blaming God and being sorry we'd ever come. She spent it holding the family together, working full time, routinely walking miles to work, caring for my father, spurring her children on to do well at school.

We kids knew we had a part to play as well. We needed to contribute too; whether it was delivering newspapers or any other kind of odd job or tiny way to bring in something, we did contribute.

To this day, I can recall those days of feeling poor. That feeling still grounds me. I work each day to make sure it never happens again. That's why, however much money I make, I don't take it easy and relax. I can relate to the struggles I see my clients facing.

The feeling of poverty has never really left me, and I've never stopped refusing to be poor. As a young man, I began to feel something almost burn inside me—a protest or resistance, a determination not to accept this tragedy upon our family, not to accept any such injury, harm or threat to my family. We all felt it; we all pulled together. Each of us knew we would pull ourselves up from this dark episode and arrive somewhere much, much better, and if it took work, time, patience, and thought—so what?

The day I refused to be poor was the day I became rich.

People think mindset is a matter of cheap tricks—visualizing yourself lying in a solid gold Jacuzzi, or mumbling mantric affirmations a hundred times a day: "I like cold calls. I like cold calls."

No. That kind of shallow repetition isn't mindset. I'm talking about something deeper. Soulset. *Heartset*. It's about connecting your professional life to your deepest values. It's about honestly knowing yourself and what you want to accomplish through the career path you've chosen.

Though settling on my chosen career path wasn't easy, I chose it not to defy my parents but because I loved them and wanted to give them security; I stay on that path because I love my children and want them to live in safety and comfort. And then early on I walked away from a great job in hard times because doing the right thing mattered to me more.

This isn't a purely intellectual matter of learning tips and making affirmations, of 'faking it till you make it.' It's about getting rid of all the fakery, and really connecting with your deep self, your real self.

I call getting your mind and spirit into this space, 'Heartset.' Get into this space and success will not only follow, you'll be a success from the moment you're there.

Chapter 5

TAKING IT TO THE MAX

So, there I was. Age 23 (1994). Out of a job. In a recession. Money was tight. The real estate market was a disaster. The clock had reset to January so I didn't have any listings, and I would be making minimum commission even if I did—which I couldn't make anyway, since I didn't even have a licence! A broker needs to hold your licence for you to be able to work as a Realtor. I wasn't employed by a broker anymore.

I had done what I thought was the right thing when I left Realty World. Now I had no job, no listings, and no licence.

What was I supposed to do now?

I don't want to give you the impression that I was in a panic, or even terribly nervous, (OK, I was a little nervous), because I already knew what I was going to do. I didn't have any doubt in my mind, really.

I was going to go to RE/MAX.

Now if you know how RE/MAX operates, you may think that was a crazy decision. Especially given my situation.

You see, if you're an agent working at RE/MAX, it's not like working for a Mr. Menary who simply holds your licence and authorizes you to buy and sell without necessarily even charging you a fee. At RE/MAX you have to pay something called a 'desk fee.' And even then, a desk fee was not cheap. At the time a desk fee was around $800 per month—more than the amount of commission I left Realty World over.

On top of that, RE/MAX was pay-to-play. You had to pay for your own business cards, your own signage—your own advertising, on which I was already spending bigger and bigger parts of my commissions even at Realty World. Basically, you were leasing a little office from them for the cost of a monthly apartment, plus expenses. What did you get in return? You got the right to use their logo—their brand. There were other perks —their training, which was world-class, their networking, their awards system, their vetting, which was up there with Gerry

Faisal Susiwala stands proudly beside his RE/MAX sign. From his earliest days as a real estate agent with Reid C. Menary Real Estate agency, then with Realty World, he gained a reputation for representing his profession, and dealing with his many clients, with respect and dignity. *Photo by Dave Biesse.*

Stocks. But mainly what you got was a bill for nearly $1000 a month so you could say, "I'm with RE/MAX."

It was worth it. The brand sold itself. If people saw your face, they might call, they might not. If they saw a recognized brand next to your face, they'd call. Or at least they'd call a lot more often. It was my flyer principle at work: if paying for something got you more back than you put in, go for it!

Still, at that point, the fee hurt. If you're an experienced agent reasonably sure of a steady income, and you have savings in the bank, you may think, "Who cares? The brand will get me more business than the company fee." But I was unemployed. My car payment was $400 a month. My mortgage payment—don't ask! Health insurance, car insurance, phone services, utilities… How was I supposed to throw another $800 a month on top of that? I was out of work and I was expected to pay them to work?

I had other options. A short while earlier Century 21 had taken one look and turned me down, but the day the article about me came out, they were on the phone asking me to return. I didn't, because I had signed on with Mr. Menary, and I had no intention of walking out on him. But the calls and invitations kept coming, and the minute they heard I was a free agent, they called again. Coldwell Banker, Royal Trust, Royal LePage, independent companies—I thought I'd have to go out and knock on doors, but I'd built up a stronger brand of my own than I knew. I didn't have to ask for work. Offers came to me.

Most of these other companies operated exactly the same way Realty World did, too; they'd pay for your business cards, print your signs and put you on a split.

I said no. No to all of them, because I wanted to go to the top, and who was there at the top? Who sold the most real estate? RE/MAX. Who was the number one brand? RE/MAX. They were the market leader.

It might cost me more to work there, but would I make more working there? Could I do more business there? There was no question about it. Adam Contos, CEO of RE/MAX International said it best: "RE/MAX can be the most expensive company to work at, or the least expensive company to work at." It cost more, but you made more—if you made full use of the brand, the network and their resources.

They offered a lot. RE/MAX was more than a logo. RE/MAX was a brand. It took my principle of 'monetizing your licence' to the next level: when people saw that logo, they knew you were a top-flight professional.

In my opinion, RE/MAX was and still is the company that you go to if you want to be associated with the top brand in real estate. You did not go to RE/MAX as a new agent in those days. That just didn't happen. It was the best, and if they accepted you, it meant you were the best, or at least among the very best. People pay well for perceived quality, and when they saw the brand next to your name, they knew they were getting the best for their money. I knew that the RE/MAX brand would elevate the Faisal Susiwala brand to the top.

So I called a broker I knew at RE/MAX. His name was Bob Stephens, and he was not only a broker at the area RE/MAX office: he was the owner. I'd known him almost from the start of my career, and he was always encouraging me, but when I told him about my interest in working for RE/MAX, he didn't sugar-coat things. He was a realist. Times were tough for everyone now, and he was blunt and direct.

"It's not cheap to work here, Faisal," he admitted. "The bills add up. Some people here are into us for thousands of dollars."

This I knew. This was another RE/MAX thing. If you couldn't make your monthly desk fee or other expenses, RE/MAX would put them on your tab. That tab could get big. Very big. Some agents took out loans to pay it off.

I'd shown I could perform. Now I wanted to show the world that I could play the game with the very best. The very best was RE/MAX. Despite my age, despite the recession, I was ready to give it my best shot.

Bob nodded. "OK," he said. "Go see Louise."

Louise—now Louise Stephens, his wife—was the Office Manager at RE/MAX at the time. She had just come in from Royal LePage, and after Bob's hard-boiled talk about how RE/MAX worked, I was expecting negotiations to be blunt.

I couldn't have been more wrong.

"Look, Louise," I said. "I'm no longer with Realty World. I'm not licensed at all as of right now, but these are my numbers, this is my track record, and I really want to work for RE/MAX."

"Well, these are our fees," she said, "and this is what we do, and how we operate, and— "

"I'm not asking for any free rent or anything!" I said.

"No, no," she said. "That's fine. We'll give you a month to get started. We'll buy you your first 500 business cards, we'll pay for your first ten signs. Is that good?"

"It's good! It's very good!"

"We'll have to get some paperwork in order..."

"Where do I sign?"

As you can see, negotiations were not very complicated. I wanted to be licensed by the end of the day. It didn't happen quite that fast, but pretty close. She contacted the Ministry, got my licence transferred over, and that was it.

I'm very grateful to Bob Stephens, who remains a very close friend. Bob was an out-of-the-box thinker. He was the first to embrace the latest technology within our industry while others would resist. Championing new concepts, he would insist on the implementation, adaptation and most importantly the execution of systems. He was certainly ahead of his time. That technology was the catalyst for my peak performance and making our brokerage state of the art under his leadership.

Again, I find myself reflecting on some of the great mentors that came into my life, and Bob Stephens is undoubtedly at the top of the list.

That's how, in January 1994, I started my journey with RE/ MAX, a relationship that's still going on over twenty-six years later.

As usual, I was once again the youngest kid on the block. RE/MAX was as established a company as a real estate firm could be, and had been for many years. Everywhere you turned there were veteran agents, people with decades of experience, all the top producers, all the superstars. Everybody who was anybody selling anything worked at this brokerage. I was the new pup—people looked at me like I was the kid delivering pizza. Not that anyone there was rude. I wasn't completely unknown. They made me welcome, but they didn't roll out the red carpet. I was given a cubbyhole in the back with a bathroom down the hall, concrete walls, and no windows.

And—I loved it! At long last I had office space all my own. A desk of my own. Finally, I oversaw myself and my career. No one else. Me.

See, this is the thing about RE/MAX. They don't hold your hand. They do provide solid resources and training. When I got there, they even had two computers. That may not impress you now but compared to most real estate offices at the time it was like walking onto the deck of the Starship Enterprise. There was something about the atmosphere at RE/MAX; rubbing shoulders with the best and most experienced people in the business every single day just naturally brings you to the top of your game.

But how you do your job is up to you. If you want to knock on doors and make cold calls all day, that's fine. If you want to sleep late (like me), that's OK. Hate multiplexes, love single-family residential? Go for it. You do what you think is best. If you want to schmooze at parties and conferences, knock yourself out. If you want to focus on marketing, that's up to you.

I was twenty-three, but I had accumulated five years of boots-on-the-ground experience by now. I'd sold millions in a few months, and seen deals go bankrupt just as fast. I'd flipped, sold land, sold commercial buildings and partnered. At Mr. Menary's and at Realty World I had learned how to do what everybody else did, and how to do it right. Maybe even more than that: I had been learning best practices—"modelling excellence," as

Tony Robbins likes to say—and I was beginning to tweak that excellence into something even more exceptional.

But I was only beginning to do that. The training I received from Mr. Menary and Realty World was invaluable, but I was mainly copying, not putting it all together in a unique and creative way—my way.

At RE/MAX I was able to go beyond the basics and operate creatively. I was able to think about what I had learned and apply it in the most effective way. It was where I began to work out my own unique methodology—the Susiwala System.

What had I learned? That, at least for me, some things worked well, and some things didn't. Cold calling didn't. Knocking on doors didn't. Articles, advertising, and marketing worked. Taking advantage of the never-ending developments in technology worked. What I'd learned is that successful real estate was not about being intrusive; in fact, it wasn't even about real estate! The business of real estate wasn't real estate: it was marketing.

So I started marketing. Hard.

The first thing I needed to do, of course, was reach out to all my clients and contacts and let them know I was at RE/MAX now. So that's what I did. That alone was a major lesson.

How many clients and contacts and people who've done business with you, or who know people who might do business with you, do you know?

A handful? Hundreds? Thousands?

Well, guess what? If they don't hear from you, they don't give you any business. They don't send you any business either. Out of sight, out of mind. Out of social media, out of mind too. I wasn't trying to sell any listings. I didn't have any yet! I just wanted people to know I had moved on to a new firm. I needed to get attention, because attention gets you business.

Of course, this is an old principle. People don't like to be sold; they like to buy. You don't make a sale by pushing properties or anything else on people who don't want them.

But you can make a group of people aware, in a casual, respectful, non-aggressive kind of way, that you have something that some of them may want to buy. By interrupting a hundred people at home with a phone call during dinner, in the hope that one person out of that hundred might be interested? No way.

But an article about you in the newspaper? A blog where you talk about how they can build the value of their home? Or maybe about how you're helping a local charity in the community? Thousands of people may read that. Tens of thousands. Statistics all but guarantee that some of them are looking to buy or sell a home.

If they don't? Either way, you're doing people some good. Doing good is worth doing.

I hadn't quite formulated it that way yet. (I would later on, but I was already calling it my 'IOU' approach: "Do good for others and they'll look for ways to do some good for you").

But it soon became another key element of my system: "Never Be Closing" (NBC).

Haven't we all run into obnoxious salespeople who latch onto you even though you have no interest in whatever they're offering—salespeople who just keep bashing away no matter how politely you ask them to leave you alone?

In the olden days, you would just walk away, relieved to be free of them, and they'd be forgotten. Now, in the days of social media, every unpleasant encounter can turn into a poisonous online review that follows that salesperson till the end of their career!

I was slowly starting to realize that the best way of marketing wasn't to engage in this kind of hard-edge intrusive assault. The best way was simply to be present, like background music in an elevator, quiet enough not to intrude but pleasant enough to be noticeable and leave a positive impression.

Marketing is a little like deer hunting: make a lot of noise and chase the deer, and you can be sure it will run in the other direction. On the other hand, just sit there, quietly relaxed, and in a short while, the deer will come to you. Of course, you can do things to attract it, like put out food, or an attractive scent. And if you're out there all the time, the odds increase your paths will cross. But the trick is to never push. No aggression: no resistance. Eventually the deer comes up and eats out of your hand.

I wasn't busy working out such novel strategic approaches on Day One. Nor was I on social media either. Remember, this was 1994. That was the year the first web browsers were launched: Mosaic and Netscape. Social media? What the heck was that?

But you didn't have to be online to know that client contact works. So I went out and contacted potential clients with good old tried-and-true snail mail. I started a series of direct mail campaigns, with letters, flyers and post cards. I let people know I could help them get mortgages, show them affordable homes tailored to their circumstances, and provide market data. I could even help them with the banks. I wasn't calling, knocking, getting in their face. I just let them know I was there for them if they wanted to contact me. The goal wasn't to push my services.

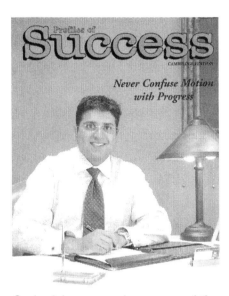

Susiwala's success has garnered the attention of magazines and newspapers far and wide.

That was the way most salespeople approach the public — and it's the wrong way. I was establishing relationships. For instance? Later that first year I took a trip to Pakistan. While I was there, I got an annual calendar made in Arabic. During Ramadan I sent it to the entire Muslim community in my area. There were only a few hundred homes, but did they appreciate it, and remember me? Of course they did. I'd get a call and visit their homes. And when I looked up — there was my calendar!

I didn't re-invent the wheel. I just drove it around a lot more.

Another example: at Realty World I would send out three or four thousand flyers. At RE/MAX I sent out 10,000 the first chance I got. Pretty soon I was sending out 25,000 flyers. Every jump in the number of flyers sent out turned into a jump in the number of people contacting me. I marketed more. I got more.

This isn't rocket science. If no one knows you're there, no one gets in touch with you. Isn't that obvious? All agents know this, and all of them try to get their face in front of their public.

The big difference between me and other agents is that I did it all the time, in as many places as I could. I drove those wheels consistently.

The real estate business suffers from a kind of boom-or-bust mentality. When the market is hot, everyone makes money — and so everyone slacks off. They go on vacations, spend their savings on new cars, move into a bigger place in a nicer neighbourhood, et cetera. In short, they put their newfound money everywhere but into the marketing that got them the money in the first place. Sometimes they even stop marketing completely. Why spend money trying to get business when you're flush, when you've already brought in all you can handle?

Because after a boom there's always a bust, a slump, and by the time you get the marketing machine going again, the bill for all the debt you've accumulated while riding high arrives, and wipes you out. Time and again I've seen this happen to agents. I still see it happen. It happened to me. I wasn't always prepared for the inevitable slump either.

But I've learned. And what I learned was to *always keep that marketing machine in motion*. Good times, bad times, it's all the same. What matters is consistency, constantly staying in touch, constantly letting people know who you are and what you do and that you're there for them the moment they need you.

Letting them know without being a jerk about it or disturbing them, I might add. As a kid back in public school when I'd gone door-to-door selling chocolate bars for a dollar, I remembered how diminished and rejected I felt when people slammed the door in my face. I didn't quit, which got me an award for selling the most chocolate bars in Grade 5.

But I hated it. You can't spend your career doing something you hate. And — if you're in real estate, especially in the age of social media — you can't irritate and alienate 99 people just to succeed with one. After all, every one of those 99 people will eventually need a place to stay. If they've had a bad experience with you, you won't get their next call. You won't get a call from their friends, either, after they pass their bad review along.

It's just common sense. If you're at home, relaxing with your family, or working, do you really want to get interrupted by someone selling you something? Something you could not care less about? Imagine that you're home at five or six after a long day at work, and you're sitting down to dinner with your family, and you're talking to your spouse or your children. Suddenly there's a phone call, or the doorbell rings. Even if it's something you might be interested in, having to stop what you're doing is just so annoying that you slam the door shut.

But what do they teach you at real estate training?

Knock on doors! Knock on doors!

Call a hundred people a day and get two appointments!

That's an *awful* way to do business. You put in a lot of time and effort for very small results. You bother and offend people in the community. You burn yourself out.

At RE/MAX I started thinking about how I could 'knock on doors' passively. How could I present myself to people without pushing myself on them? Without getting the inevitable pushback that leaves you nowhere? After all, Coca-Cola doesn't send salesperson knocking on your door to sell you a bottle of pop. We buy Coke all the time—we ask for Cokes, not for 'pop'—and there isn't a sales associate twisting our arm to make us do it. The most successful people and companies don't cold call or knock on doors. How many door-to-door salespeople have interrupted you over dinner to sell an iPhone?

Again, I was 'scaling down.' Coke and Toyota and Apple were doing something that worked all over the world. How could I adapt that and use it here? How could I narrow my focus down and apply it to Cambridge, Ontario?

Instead of just repeating clichés like 'call 100 people a day' or even 'focus on marketing,' at RE/MAX I began thinking about marketing. I started thinking about how to separate the most effective approaches from the less effective ones, how to take advantage of the new possibilities that technological change was starting to provide. It was the beginning of 'the Susiwala System.'

But it wasn't the finished form, just beginnings and bits and pieces. There was still a lot of work to be done. I needed to hustle, too. The recession was still on. Big time.

Moving to RE/MAX was not without challenges. In fact, 1994 was my worst year in real estate. It was a tough year for everyone, but especially so for me. I had to spend money to let all my contacts know I was moving over to a new brokerage. I had to change all my existing marketing to reflect the change. I had stiff monthly fees to meet. And the market was as dead as

I've ever seen it. All in all, I made less that year than I did my first year at Mr. Menary's.

But if I wasn't earning (much), I was definitely learning. RE/ MAX was rich in lessons, both positive and negative. Literally half my income in 1994 came as a result of the actions of a self-proclaimed superstar agent I won't name. He dressed sharp, looked good, and he had a much, much higher opinion of himself than of the peasants around him. One day an elderly gentleman walked into our offices. The man was wrinkled and dusty and rumpled, and looked almost like a homeless person. Mr. Superstar took one look at him and turned to me and said, "You take this one, kid."

Well, I took anything I could get in those days, and I was glad to take it. The man's rough appearance didn't bother me. I'd seen immigrants arriving off the train pretty rumpled too, and knew just what good people and good clients they'd turned out to be. I introduced myself politely, thanked the gentleman for coming, and asked him what he was looking for. It turned out that he was indeed a farmer, and had walked in literally from right off the field. He'd saved up some money, and he was interested in buying an apartment building. A particular apartment building. He gave me the address.

I looked up the property on the cool computer to which I now had access. I reached out to the listing agent and asked if I could book a showing. The agent got back to me quickly and said that I could show the gentleman a couple of the units immediately. So we drove out to see it. We made an offer later that day. The seller made a reasonable counteroffer, and it was accepted. I sold my first apartment building for 1.5 million dollars. It put roughly $40,000 in my pocket, most of my income for that year.

That was an easy lesson, and I've never forgotten it: don't judge a book by its cover. I've had more than one rough-looking client since, and they always look good to me!

The cherry on the cake from that client wasn't just the commission, but the fact that the commission put me over the top for my very first RE/MAX Award, the one real estate award I still keep on my wall: The Executive Club. It wasn't the top-selling award. In fact, it was only the first rung on the ladder, the bottom step for aspiring superstar sellers.

But it was the first step, and I had made it there, despite my age, despite the recession, despite my being the new kid on the block at a new job. I was among the best, and I was making my mark. I had made the transition to RE/MAX successfully, and I was performing ethically and with distinction even in the worst of times. Times would get better, and when they did, I knew my fortunes would rise with them.

It's funny, but when I see that award now, I think again of when I was a young boy going door to door to sell chocolates. Boy, I hated knocking on those doors. It was harder for me to make those sales than any other sale of my career.

When I got my Executive Club award from RE/MAX, I felt the same rush as I had when I won the award for selling the most chocolate bars in Fifth Grade. It was a wonderful feeling, like being a hero. I had struggled and persevered and not given up, and I had won.

I kept winning. The next year the market began recovering. I won the next highest award. I wasn't at the bare survival level anymore, and the year after that I was doing even better. Then the market began to take off, and so did I. Soon I was making $500,000. There it was, calling to me: the million-dollar award —Diamond! I could almost taste it.

Did sticking it out selling chocolate door-to-door, and then getting such a buzz from that award at age ten, put me on the road to the Executive Club Award, and to all the other awards that followed? I don't know.

But I do know that each time I looked at all those awards multiplying on my desk, I wanted to reach out to that ten-year-old boy and thank him.

Lessons

People come up to me all the time these days and say, "Faisal! You've sold more houses than anyone else in Canada. You're one of the leading real estate people in the world! Why on earth are you still working for RE/MAX? Why don't you start your own brokerage?"

I have to smile. They just don't understand. I'm not working for a company. I'm working with a company. They're not an employer cutting me a weekly paycheque. They're more like a franchise that gave me an entire business straight out of the box when I was starting out, complete with training and a worldwide community of support, all for a monthly fee.

More importantly, it gave me a brand. Associating your name with a strong brand, while you're building your own, was one of the best decisions I ever made, and one of the best decisions anyone starting out in real estate *can* make. Let me tell you why.

Building Your Brand

What attracted me to RE/MAX? The fact that it's the best-known real estate company in the world. It's a brand—a *great* brand, like Ford, McDonald's or Apple. Everybody's seen it, heard about it, and knows about it. And when you're associated with a major brand, it's like having a degree or a certificate to practice. It's an endorsement. People feel at once that if you're associated with that company, you know what you're doing.

Say you have to choose between two real estate agents, and the only thing you know is that one of them is an independent and the other one is with a major brand. The agent with the strong brand is going to get your business. Why? Because the label is an indicator of popularity and quality. High quality.

Why do people have a coffee at Starbucks, or wear a Rolex, or hire a Harvard-educated lawyer? The name. The name sells the product or service. If you're associated with that name, you get the business that it attracts. To monetize your licence fully, you need to enhance it, and working for a name brand agency does exactly that. Just having a licence is like having a college degree. You need it to get in the door. But putting a RE/MAX logo (or a Century 21, or Keller Williams, or Realty One logo) next to your name makes you a respected member of the company. It validates your personal brand.

Now you don't want to be totally dependent on just that label. In the long run you want the brand to be you. In Cambridge, Ontario, where my business is focused, when people think of real estate, they automatically think of Faisal Susiwala. That's because I've spent decades—and a great deal of money—on ads, flyers, busses, social media and so on.

That's not something you can do when you're starting out, or when you're struggling. When you're at the start of your real estate career, you haven't had the time or the track record to build a reputation.

If you're associated with a strong enough brand, though, it doesn't matter: your brand is your reputation. People who have never heard of you have heard of RE/MAX, of Century 21, of

Keller Williams, of Realty One. Sometimes that's all it takes for them to decide to pick up the phone.

Even for me today, that's still true. Suppose someone from New Delhi or Berlin or Hong Kong needs to relocate to Canada, and they've heard that Cambridge is a nice central location. Have they seen my face on the benches and buses in Cambridge? No. But they've seen the RE/MAX logo, and they know what it stands for. They'll Google for a RE/MAX agent in Cambridge—and find me.

I put a lot of money into advertising locally, but I can't saturate the entire world with my ads. I don't have to. The brand has already done it for me. It got me credibility with buyers and business when I started out, and it's still sending me business today.

The takeaway from all this is not that the royal road to real estate success is piggybacking on a Big Name Firm. The RE/MAX name helped, but what helped most was gradually developing and applying a System principle I call 'Return on Influence" (ROI). It's simple: be everywhere and become the brand. RE/MAX gave me a lift in terms of branding, but what took me to the top was me personally becoming a continual, nonaggressive but universal presence. I was everywhere! If there was an advertising spot to fill, an empty space, a niche, anything anywhere, I filled it.

There were two keys to making it work. First, I had to Scale Down. I wasn't Coke. I couldn't blanket the world. But I could blanket my target market—Cambridge. Yes, even that was expensive, but what it cost was a lot less than what it returned.

The second key was not being aggressive. I didn't hire a staff of cold callers or a crew of door knockers. I was everywhere, but in a subtle way--presence without pressure.

What I learned from Coke is that if you are simply there long enough and often enough with a simple message, people associate you with that message. My message was super-simple: "Faisal Susiwala—Real Estate Agent." People in my target market saw that message every day. Over the years they saw it tens, hundreds, thousands of times. And when the time came to buy or sell a house? My name was the first thing to come to mind because years of repetition made that association. No one resisted that association because it was so quiet and passive, so much a part of the background, that it was almost unnoticeable.

But once that connection in the public's mind was made, I became the first name people thought of when they wanted to buy or sell a house or invest in property. Yes, I gave them the best service I could give. But I didn't have to hustle for it. More business came in than I could handle.

Business In A Box

Beginning Realtors who are starting out often do a double-take when they first hear of the pay-to-play business model used by many top brand-name real estate firms.

"I become a company employee, and *I* have to pay *them*? I get hired and I have to pay for my office space and my marketing and pay *them* a percentage of what I make? Why don't I just open up my own office and keep the money?"

Because you don't keep the money. Go ahead! Start your own company. Now you have to pay for an office, a lease, leaseholds, office equipment, supplies, support staff and utilities. You still have to pay for your marketing collateral on top of that.

Sure, you can become a broker yourself. Eventually. But that takes time, and money, and you still won't get the buyers and sellers that you would have gotten if they had seen a well-known and well-respected brand logo and decided you were the professional real estate agent they were looking for. How much is 100 per cent of nothing?

How about if you just ride the brand for a while and then go solo? It sounds reasonable, but in my entire career, I've never witnessed one single agent leave a solid brand, go on their own, and be more successful.

The fact is, when you sign up with a really strong brand, the public regards you as an established reputable agent. You get calls. Period. Bang! It's done.

The Learning Community

"But—uh—what if I don't know much about running a business? In fact, what if I don't know all that much about real estate? I mean, I'm OK, I'm licensed and everything, but I'm not really a million-dollar pro…"

Not yet.

Trust me: take full advantage of everything a strong brand offers and you will be. Because one of the best things about the leading companies is their emphasis on continuing education. There are speakers. There are workshops. There are conferences. RE/MAX isn't alone in this, but their focus on cultivating talent and building skill is a model for any such company. There are lessons and trainings that cover every aspect of being a successful real estate agent. They're available online too, 24/7.

It isn't just a matter of going to your office space and shuffling paperwork and taking calls. It can be, if that's your preference; but meeting people and talking to people and being around people is the name of the real estate game. Every smart brand-name real estate firm knows this. It knows that the respect people give to that brand depends on the knowledge, skill and contacts of its agents. A strong brand will host events, foster meetups, arrange conferences, encourage everything from picnics to brainstorming sessions to holiday parties. You'll constantly be building connections, meeting people, multiplying your network and running into top performers.

Don't imagine that these sorts of gatherings are all small in scale. That's one of the benefits of being with a bigger organization: they have the resources to draw in major names to speak and educate.

There are international conferences too—the European Conference, the Canadian Conference (where I had the pleasure to speak in 2019). There are regular workshops at the regional head office. There's the RE/MAX Las Vegas Conference mentioned in the introduction to this book, an event where people from all over the world come together. Literally thousands upon thousands of agents get together regularly. Not just agents—CEO's, owners of companies, real estate affiliates, movers and shakers and rock star super performers, all coming together and exchanging ideas.

Oh, and did I mention that all this is fun?

It is. That's an important part of staying with the brand too. You have to like what you do. I don't like knocking on doors, but I like the people behind those doors. I wouldn't join a company that pressured me to knock all day, but I'm very happy to be with a company that gives me all the opportunities you can imagine to meet people inside the industry and out. A strong brand does what it can to ensure that you'll become part of the local community, but it also welcomes you into a real estate community—the company of your colleagues and peers.

Of course, that community isn't there purely for the socializing—it's there so you can use its many resources to build and develop your skills. Just signing up with a major firm doesn't automatically make you good or successful. You have to work at it—to take what you've learned and keep learning.

The point of aligning yourself with a major real estate company isn't to get event tickets, signage, office space or party invitations for their own sake. The point is to join a firm that gives you all the tools you need, and shows you how best to use them. I had the basics down when I joined the brand, but once inside I also found myself getting expert advice all the time from colleagues and peers and rock star agents and brokers, keeping me up-to-date with the latest developments. A good brand name real estate firm is more than just an office: it's a university. It provides a continual learning experience that moves you from good to great.

A Global Network

As for connections—well, let's just say that while local business needs to be your focus, global business is out there too, and out there for the taking. It's a lot easier to derive revenue from a global market if you're part of a global brand.

One of the core sources of income in the real estate business is referrals—someone is looking for a home, or looking to sell, and for whatever reason the real estate agent on the case can't handle it directly: he or she has to send the client to another Realtor. Maybe the agent is overloaded with work. Maybe the client wants a home in a region the Realtor is unfamiliar with. Maybe they're on vacation.

What does that agent do? They pick up the phone and send the business to another agent—and normally they get 25 per cent or more for the referral.

(25 per cent of the commission. For making a call. Does that get your attention, reader? It sure got mine. Keep reading. We'll talk more about this shortly).

Agents refer business. Need I tell you that those agents are more likely to send the referral to someone they know and like? That they're more likely to send the referral to someone in the same firm, someone they met at a class or seminar or event, someone they want to connect with, someone who gave the keynote speech at a conference? That they're more likely to send the referral to a star agent who—thanks to the core I.O.U. principle of reciprocity—will return the favour?

With a global firm, this kind of networking stretches all around the world. Does someone in China or Dubai want to buy a place near Toronto, but not too near it? Hmm. Cambridge looks like it's within close driving distance. Say, who sells real estate out there? The RE/MAX agent in Dubai checks out the RE/MAX roster in Cambridge, and there's Faisal Susiwala.

Don't get me wrong. Above all, you want to have a specific local area where you personally are the brand. If there's a reasonably-sized city, suburb, region or postal code where everyone thinks of you the moment they think about buying or selling a house, you will have an income stream that will support you and your family and your investments for as long as you want to cultivate it—for the rest of your life.

Becoming part of a strong brand is your first step in getting there.

But if that strong brand is also a global brand, your potential market is no longer only your backyard. It's the world.

The Awards System

All the major real estate companies have the same basic approach, and there are sound reasons for joining any of them. But for me, the one really brilliant thing about RE/MAX is its awards system. It sounds almost silly when you look at it from the outside. But despite all its many other pluses, I can't think of anything about the company that drives top performance and excellence more.

They have got people figured out really well. We as human beings are driven by rewards. Call it positive reinforcement, social reinforcement, whatever you like. We all like to get positive attention. We like it when we're looked up to and admired by our colleagues and peers. When all the other players in the game look at us and think, "There goes a winner!" We feel good. We feel proud. That's how we're wired. Sure, financial rewards mean a lot, too. But as people, we want to be recognized for our successes. We want that moment in the spotlight. That applause.

RE/MAX has really nailed it there. They've built an awards system into their operation that caters to that part of us like nothing else.

It starts with the Executive Award. You've joined the company? Well, if you make at least $50,000 in gross commissions in a year, congratulations: you're in the Executive Club!

True, that isn't really very much. In our industry, $50,000 a year is below the poverty line. You still have to pay your fees and your marketing costs and your taxes, remember? If you're only making $50,000 a year, you're struggling.

But RE/MAX wants to encourage you. To inspire you. And that's exactly what this award does. "$50,000? Wow! You're doing *great!*" And when you receive that award, you *feel* great. You made the cut. Maybe you're treading water, but you're not sinking.

During my first year at RE/MAX, I was struggling. The economy was scraping bottom. No one was buying, no one was selling, and things looked pretty grim.

Then I won the Executive Award. One single sale made the difference and put me just barely over the top. Still, *I won*, and when I got that award, I *felt* like a winner. I wasn't just another agent: I was an award-winning agent with the top agency in the region.

The Executive Award was only the beginning. Now I had a new goal. $50,000 to $99,999 makes you an Executive Award-winning agent. But when you do a little better, when you make $100,000 to 249,999 in a year, then you join the 100 per cent club!

The truth is, you're still barely emerging from poverty. But you're like that kid playing the video game: you've reached the next level. It feels good to reach the next level. People congratulate you. You see the award on your desk, and people see it in your marketing material. They mention it when you are introduced at conferences. You mention it, because you're proud of it, and proud of yourself.

And once you reach the next level, and you're making $250,000 to $499,999? Then you get the Platinum Club award! Now you're becoming a force to be reckoned with. Now you're in the company of people who are making a good living at this.

I do mean 'in the company' of those people, too. Because RE/MAX facilitates your association with them. Each award level has its own little gatherings and online forums specifically for the different award winners, all the people that reached the same bracket as you. Those people face a lot of the same issues as you do at that level, and guess what? As a member of the club, you get to share many of the solutions and ideas that work for people at that level. You have friends and peers who do their best to help you keep up your game so that you don't fall back to a lower level. They cheer you on so you rise even higher.

It sounds like a game, doesn't it? That's because it feels like a game. And games are fun. You're playing to win. And your friends are right there cheering you on!

What comes after the Platinum Award? The Chairman's Club: $500,000 to $749,999. Then there's the Titan Award: $749,999 to $999,999. And once you become a Titan, boy, do you ever want to reach the next level and become a Diamond! One million plus is Diamond and once you reach Diamond and make one million dollars in gross career commissions, you get another honour: you make the Hall of Fame.

It doesn't end there. Once you reach three million dollars in gross commissions, you receive a Lifetime Achievement Award. Once you reach ten million dollars in gross commissions, you become part of a group called The Circle of Legends. Once you reach twenty million dollars in gross commissions, you've entered Mount Olympus: you've become a Luminary of Distinction. There are only approximately seventy of us worldwide who've ever reached that.

Take my word for it. Inside the world of RE/MAX, once you're a Luminary of Distinction, people look at you at conferences like you're all four Beatles rolled into one.

There are all sorts of other awards—Broker Manager of the Year, International Broker/Owner of the Year, Top Office, and so on. These awards aren't just certificates that arrive in the mail. The company handles all this in a way that makes recipients feel like Elvis headlining Las Vegas. You get accolades after accolades at ceremonies resembling the Academy Awards. People are there in black tie. You receive your award dressed in gowns and ribbons. The lanyards you wear carry insignia of all the awards you've ever gotten. (Mine goes down to my knees, but then, I'm a short guy!) People stand back and gasp and smile and cheer and applaud as you walk down the hallway and pass by. It feels wonderful.

It isn't just about feeling good—though it feels *wonderful*. In the end it's all about performance, and what this system does is inspire you to stretch yourself—to do your best and be your best.

Once you reach Diamond, it forces you to keep your business up to that mark. You've made it to Diamond! Your friends and associates are there! You're a part of Diamond Club gatherings and conferences and online forums! You don't want to slip back.

The higher you rise, the better and more knowledgeable and skilled you become, and the better and more successful your social circles become. Those Luminaries of Distinction really are an elite group. You can't find better advisors or connections. No one knows more about the challenges and opportunities you're facing than your colleagues at that level.

The awards system is fun, it inspires, and it motivates. But at the heart of it is an educational and training process. You work harder and smarter and at performing better and better. It's a loop of continuous improvement and ever-rising revenues for everyone involved.

Maintain Your Core

I've been saying many nice things about RE/MAX, and why not? I couldn't think more highly of the company. Am I glad I joined? You bet I am. I'm still a part of it, and I'm proud to be a part of it. I believe in its model wholeheartedly.

But I don't want to leave people with the impression that RE/MAX is the only way to go. Are there other real estate organizations that follow a similar type of model and do a good job, too? Sure. Nothing I say here is intended to put down Keller Williams or Realty One or any other franchise. There's nothing wrong with starting your own independent brokerage either. Different strokes for different folks.

But I want to give readers the best advice I can, based on my own experience—my own successes. Doing it all on your own, especially in the beginning, is hard. Very few people are able to do it.

Joining a star brand has been a key part of my success, and I can't think of a better way of getting started in real estate than to start with a major brand and see how they do things. Yes, there can be a stiff entrance fee. Yes, some take a hefty percentage of your sales. But what the best can give you is way more than what they ask in return.

One of the crucially important things they can give you right from the start is a solid core business, a stream of income that can sustain you through good times and bad. You have to work to earn it, but once your marketing kicks in, it becomes a steady flow. That makes a critical difference. A successful real estate career isn't just a matter of working for a franchise. It's about building wealth. To build that wealth, you need to have a foundation.

The longer I'm in real estate, the more deeply I've gotten involved with investing. I wouldn't have been able to make those investments without the cash income coming in from my work as a real estate agent. That income is what allowed me to buy properties, build equity, and care for my family, without the stress and difficulty of building real estate wealth from real estate alone.

There's a terrible error in the thinking of many people breaking into real estate. They think that the whole goal of real estate is generating passive cash flow. Buy a couple of houses, put in some people, and once the rental income covers your bills and leaves you a little to spend, it's Game Over. Relax, live off the rent, and vegetate.

That's not a formula for sustainable investment success. It's a formula for going nowhere.

Yes, indeed: rental income and appreciation are wonderful things. They can give you the cash flow and equity you can put into investments and, by so doing, build real wealth surprisingly quickly.

But if you spend all that you make on bills and frills, where's the growth?

Having a source of income to cover your bills is fine. Having a source that makes enough money to allow you to invest is fine too. But that kind of income generation should come from your core business, not your investments themselves. Investments grow best and fastest when you feed them, not when you constantly leech off them. And real estate investments in particular are far from liquid. You can't convert them into cash overnight.

A good real estate practice—or medical practice, or legal practice—is exactly the kind of core you want. It's a solid income stream. It covers your bills, gives you the leeway to invest, and provides an additional pillar of support in slow times or times of crisis. It's a way to hedge your bet—and that's a central principle.

Your core is that part of your financial life that generates income. Not speculative or fluctuating or hard-to-liquidate income, like stocks, bonds, art or even property, but the sort of steady-stream income that covers all your day-to-day expenses and leaves enough left over for you to invest in truly wealth-generating opportunities.

Ensure that you have a sound income stream you can count on, from a profession or professional association that's reliably there for you, and all the rest will follow.

Be the Brand

So—what did I learn from RE/MAX? That a brand name alone can lift you up to success. Several large real estate firms have built such brands on the hard work and shoulders of their agents, and you won't go wrong if you join any of them.

But don't stop there. Realize that you use those brands as a platform to build your *own* brand, and sell your own brand, and enhance your own brand.

It's great to be part of an umbrella brand—part of a team. But that's where you want to start, not end up. Build your own niche brand in your own community.

To be your best, to be able to fully monetize your licence and your reputation, to reach the highest level of success, you must be the brand. Become the person people think of when they think of real estate. It is the same with any endeavour, be it law, or investment, or sports, or whatever profession you may be in. There's a lot involved in reaching that level. It takes time, money, marketing and regular, consistent effort. But once you do all that, you're at the top.

You can't reach that level at the start of your career. It's hard to reach it globally at any point in your career. Becoming the go-to person in your town, city or region is achievement enough.

Once you've done it, though, you've reached the true pinnacle of your profession.

When that happens, you've become a Luminary of Distinction, award or not.

Chapter 6

TURNING POINTS

For the first five or so years of my career, over 90 per cent of my business was working with buyers only. I didn't have the credibility, the audience, or the connections to get people to list their homes to sell with me. I didn't have the wrinkles. I mean, come on—who's going to let someone just out of high school, someone who started without a car, no less, sell their home?

"Hey, kid, here's my $900,000 mansion. Get on your bike and go sell it."

Yeah, right. In the beginning, very few people listed with me. Not the people with $900,000 homes, for sure. Not yet. But I had an immigrant community that supported me and wanted me to succeed. The people on my old paper route knew me and liked me. I did have a few connections, and a sphere of friends and contacts, and, as time went by, more and more professional ones.

So I hustled. I worked like a dog, labouring seven days a week, twelve hours a day, 9 a.m. to 9 p.m. I would have three to five sets of clients every single day. Saturdays and Sundays I would do open houses from one to three, and then from three to five. I put flyers in doors. I hand-delivered signed letters and post cards. I walked down streets before sunrise and after sundown. There wasn't a thing you could do that I wasn't doing. It was morning to evening work. It was what I did. It was all I did. That was my life.

I was still young enough to be able to handle it physically. And it didn't interfere with my private life. What private life? I lived with my folks. Mom cooked for me and did my laundry. Dad told me to clean up my room. I had no wife, no kids, no responsibilities. I worked, then I crashed, then I got back up and went back to work. I loved it.

Still, no matter how young you are, when you burn your candle at both ends, from morning to night, day after day, you burn out. I was burning out—burning out big time. I was exhausted. So exhausted, stuff was beginning to fall through the cracks. There were open houses where I was afraid I would fall asleep standing up. I was becoming like that mouse in the revolving cage, running over and over in the same place. But I couldn't stop: I was so focused and so driven that I needed a miracle to get me off the treadmill.

In 1997 it happened. A real miracle. Something that changed my whole life. I met my wife. As soon as I saw her, I said, "I need to fit this person into my daily schedule." For at least a few minutes a day, anyway.

It was a turning point in my life, but turning my routine around sure wasn't easy. We'd go out on a date, and I'd get a call. A client needed to see that house *now*. I'd ask her indulgence while I showed the property, and she would indulge me. A lot.

"I'll meet you right after work," I'd promise. Only—time and again—I had to go show a house after work. So she'd be sitting in the car, patiently waiting for me till the sun went down, after which we'd grab a late-night bite—if we could find an eatery still open—and then I'd drop her off at her home.

(Natalie, if you're reading this, thank you so much for your kindness and patience).

In a way, there were some good things about the crazy hours I kept. At least Natalie knew that if I wasn't home by 9:30 at night, I wasn't at a bar, or some club. I was out working. When we met I was 27 and she was 21. (We got married when I was 30 and she was 23.) But even at that tender age she could see what a struggle it was to make a good living at what I was doing.

It's still a struggle. If you don't have discipline, real estate can eat up your whole life. Realtors have a high rate of divorce, and it's no mystery why. They're gone all hours of the day and night. They're on the phone half the time. They eat and sleep whenever they can get a break. It's not the healthiest or most romantic kind of life.

There was another problem, too. Natalie was Catholic. Now that wasn't as large a problem as you may think it was. To Muslims, Christians and Jews are People of the Book, people who worship the same God. Marriages between people of our sister faiths are fine. However, my family background is not only Muslim but Indian, and among Indians the tradition of arranged marriage is really strong. It isn't the worst tradition either. Sometimes young people think with their hormones, while cooler-headed parents see a good match more easily than their children. My parents knew any number of perfectly wonderful girls of Indian heritage, and their radar was constantly scanning to find the perfect girl for Faisal.

The thing was, I'd already found her. I knew early on that Natalie was that perfect girl, But would my parents agree? How to approach them? What to say? It was like going into real estate all over again. *Uncle Rasheed, where are you? Help!*

Something had to give, and something did: me! I proposed to Natalie and she accepted. It was the best deal I ever closed.

Eventually I told my parents. They huffed and puffed but fell in love with Nat too and accepted her with open arms. How could they not? They gave us their blessing, and we got married soon after. As we were getting ready to make it official, I finally said to myself, "Faisal, it's time for a break." I sure wasn't going to take calls for listings on our honeymoon!

I mean, come on! By this time I was making $250,000-$300,000 a year. I was doing well. Really well. For once in my life—and what was more of a once-in-a-lifetime occasion than this?—I could take a holiday.

I did. That time with Natalie was heaven on earth. We were away for a solid five weeks, and it was the first five weeks, for as far back as I can remember, that I spent just living and not listing.

But the incredible thing was that doing nothing turned out to be one of the biggest business breakthroughs I would ever make. Without knowing it, our honeymoon got me doing business in a new way, a way that would make a big, big difference to my career later on.

You see, when I finally decided to take a few weeks off, I asked a local agent I knew and liked at RE/MAX to take care of my business till I returned. She did. She did a fine job, too. Naturally I didn't expect her to do all that work for nothing. The client might be my client, but because she was working with the client on my behalf, taking the time to show homes, answer questions and take calls, she deserved to make something too. So, we made the usual referral arrangement agents make: for any business that she managed to close, she would get a 25 per cent to 50 per cent fee. If the total commission was $4,000, she'd get up to $2,000.

Our honeymoon had been pure joy, but when I came back, I was scared. Five weeks, and I hadn't done any work. Five weeks! And I mean not *any* work. Nothing! I knew what no work meant. No pay! Homeless shelters. Debtor's prison! As I drove over to the office I was half afraid the windows would be boarded up. Walking in, I had visions of creditors moving my office furniture into the street!

Instead, there I was looking at a pile of cheques. Tens of thousands of dollars in commission income that I hadn't done anything at all to earn. I stood there and just kind of blinked at it. I did nothing, not a thing—zero —nada—and I was looking at enough funds and enough active listings and enough firm deals to get me through the next several months!

A light should have gone off right there.

Unfortunately, it took a few more years till the filament lit up. I took the money, but even with what would become a key component of the Susiwala System staring me in the face and waving thousands of dollars in front of my nose, I didn't realize what I'd just seen.

Instead, I soon went back to the same old same old. It was 2000 now and I threw myself into the new century at the same breakneck pace as the old. No, at twice the pace. I had to make up for the work I'd missed. Once again I was burning the candle at both ends. The middle, too. After all, I had a wife now! A house! (Much as I loved my folks, we weren't going to live with them).

The honeymoon had shown me how empty, in some ways, my life was prior to marriage. Real estate had taken up so much of my time and attention that when it was not there, it was almost like a shock. Marriage opened my eyes. Natalie brought a new breadth of humanity to me. I wanted to take time for my new life, to start a family, to spend more quality time with loved ones.

Luckily I picked an exceptional woman to marry. Natalie didn't ask me to give up my work life. Instead she made herself part of my work life. She'd walk up and down the sidewalks with me, and we'd drop flyers and magnets and fridge memo boards into mailboxes together. When people saw both of us like that, I think the community embraced us even more.

Thanks to Natalie more and more happiness was seeping into me day by day. It was almost distracting. Not that I complained! It was part of my evolution. I was becoming a more balanced and well-rounded human being.

We were already thinking about a family. In January 2002, our son Yusuf was born. In May 2005, our daughter Anisa was born. Once you have children, once you even think about having children, your whole view of life changes. I might have started out in real estate thinking about a yacht and girls in bikinis, but now I was an old man of thirty-one. An adult. A homeowner. A man with responsibilities. Deeper things were beginning to drive me, and they drove me to work not only harder but more thoughtfully—more meaningfully. I began thinking about what I was doing in new and different ways, ways that touched on more matters than just money.

Then, around that time, in September of 2001, something happened to make me rethink things almost as much as my marriage and the birth of my children.

It was the day that has since become known as 9/11. On that day, my wife—pregnant with our first son—and I were in New York City to have breakfast at the Twin Towers.

It happened like this. We were there because in June 2001 my brother Zeb decided to buy my wife and I an anniversary present. It was an all-expense-paid shopping trip to New York City.

After all, our son was going to be born in a few more months. What better way for a young entrepreneur and his wife to celebrate this than to enjoy a four-day package visit to New York City?

Zeb made all the arrangements and had booked us at the Marriott.

The Marriott at the World Trade Center, also known as World Trade Center 3. It had 825 rooms. Together with the twin towers, had its own zip code of 10048. It was an incredibly generous thing to do.

So generous, in fact, that when I looked at the room rate, my jaw dropped.

"Oh my God..."

Zeb was covering all the costs, but this was *too* generous. He was my brother and I didn't want him to spend that kind of money just to cover a few rooms for four days. The price was ridiculous!

Natalie took one look and completely agreed. We booked into a far more reasonable hotel called The Milford, several blocks away. It was just as elegant, and half the price. We were still going to have breakfast at the World Trade Center on 9/11. We had purchased a tour, and the tour included the Trade Center, as part of a tour package, and that wouldn't change. We would have breakfast at Windows on the World on the 107th floor of the World Trade Center on 9/11. We wouldn't miss a thing.

Now it so happened that the evening before, on the night of September 10th, there was an evening auction at Sotheby's. All the big stars were there, including Matthew Broderick and Sarah Jessica Parker. I was a big Matthew Broderick fan, so of course we couldn't miss that. We went to the auction, did some star-gazing, and enjoyed the New York City nightlife, as we celebrated our first year of wedded bliss.

But Natalie was pregnant, after all; and while we'd had a great time at the auction, we had a date for breakfast in the World Trade Center the next morning. I didn't want Natalie to over-exert herself or become fatigued. Besides, I was (and still am) notorious for sleeping in. I never get into the office before 11 a.m. I work late, but I sleep late too. So in the morning I like to chill. Everyone was always after me about it—my broker, the office manager, everyone. "Faisal, stop sleeping in! The meeting's at 9 o'clock. You can't show at 9:30!"

I'd totally agree, and swear I'd be there early. Then I'd show up at 10:30. (Out of pure kindness. I knew that if I *did* show up on time, everyone would be hospitalized from the shock).

I got away with it at work. After all, I was selling a lot of houses. Even so, my late morning schedule was a kind of inside joke of the office. Except it wasn't a joke. I really did like to sleep late.

But not on 9/11. On that day, of all days, for some reason, I woke up at 7 a.m. We were in the Big Apple, after all, and I didn't want to miss anything. Getting up early meant there was plenty of time to shower and stroll over to the World Trade Center for a breakfast we would be sure to remember!

Only this time, Natalie was the sleepy one. After all, it was New York. We'd been walking all over, staying up late, and she was going to have our child. She was tired.

I checked my watch. Almost time to go.

Breakfast at the top of the Trade Center overlooking Manhattan and Brooklyn. Not something to miss. We really should be getting dressed.

But did we really need to go over this early in the morning?

CAMBRIDGE

'Thank God we didn't go'

Cambridge couple planned to tour World Trade Center yesterday morning, but they slept in

By ERIC VOLMERS
THE CAMBRIDGE REPORTER

A Cambridge real estate agent says a last-minute decision to sleep in yesterday morning, rather than tour the World Trade Center during a New York City vacation, probably saved his life and the life of his pregnant wife.

Faisal Susiwala, 31, and wife Nafisa, 22 – who is five-and-a-half months pregnant – are stranded in New York City today with thousands of others after terrorists hijacked two airliners and crashed them into the World Trade Center yesterday morning.

In a telephone interview with The Reporter from a delicatessen in Times Square at 1:30 p.m. yesterday, Susiwala said he was still in a state of disbelief.

"Thank God we didn't go," said the Fairview Road resident. "I have a tendency of sleeping in. For once in my life that paid off. I can't believe we were saved from being down there."

Susiwala said he and his wife had been at the centre Monday and were planning to take a 8 a.m. tour but they slept in.

Susiwala and his wife are staying at the Milford Plaza hotel at 8th and 45th streets, roughly 30 blocks from the World Trade Center. The couple has been in New York City since Friday and was originally scheduled to come home last night. The trip was a first-year anniversary present from his brother and sister-in-law.

The couple was in the hotel room when they heard the explosion.

"We heard a loud bang and fire engines and we didn't even know what was going on and all of a sudden we turned (and looked out the

window) and saw this cloud of smoke," he said. "The people working in the hotel are just terrified because they haven't heard from family members who were over there."

Susiwala, who spoke to The Reporter on his cellular phone, said the streets of Manhattan were chaotic yesterday afternoon. Sirens sounded in the background as he spoke on his phone.

From the deli at Times Square he could still see smoke billowing on the horizon against the azure sky. Thousands of people flooded the streets, including many from New York's closed subway system.

Small pockets of angry and dazed New Yorkers were gathering in Times Square, some listening to doomsday speakers on street corners.

"You are hearing all kinds of people on the street corners, a lot of interesting figures who are preaching," Susiwala said. "There's a lot of angry people, pointing fingers and placing blame on certain groups, but again, nothing has been confirmed. There's little gatherings on street corners preaching and saying it's an act of God."

Susiwala said he had been planning to check out of the hotel before he left for the World Trade Centre. Since he didn't, he was able to extend their stay by one day but it was unclear how or when the couple will be coming home.

Hundreds of stranded people were lining up outside the hotel hoping for a room for the night, he said.

"We haven't checked out, that was our original plan," he said. "We were going to leave our luggage in storage. Fortunately, that wasn't the case. We are just basically here right now staying close to the hotel."

Susiwala said he tried to phone out of the hotel to his family immediately after hearing about what happened. He reached his parents in Cambridge between 10:30 a.m. and 11 a.m.

Susiwala and his wife had toured the World Trade Centre Monday after buying into a two-day tour package.

> ### 'You just can't believe that it's totally gone.'
> FAISAL SUSIWALA, CAMBRIDGE REAL ESTATE AGENT

Monday night he and his wife enjoyed the New York City night life, including a stop at Christies auction house. When the couple spotted actors Matthew Broderick and Sarah Jessica Parker getting out of a limousine at the famous New York auction, they decided to star gaze for the rest of the evening.

"We figured we'll watch the stars at these auctions and we ended up staying quite late," he said. "We were going to pack our bags last night and we just felt lazy."

They decided to go to the World Trade Centre for lunch yesterday rather than make the 8 a.m. tour.

Susiwala said he and his wife had taken a tour in a double decker bus through Times Square over the weekend and had clearly seen the World Trade Centre.

"In the distance we had a clear vision from Times Square," he said. "Today there's nothing there but a cloud of smoke. You just can't believe that it's totally gone. We can't believe the fact we were scheduled to go out there. Thank God somebody was looking down on us."

Zeb Susiwala, Faisal's brother, was at work at Babcock & Wilcox Canada in Cambridge when his parents called him to say his brother had contacted them.

"We haven't had enough time to really talk to him. It was just a quick call to let us know he is OK," said Zeb, who is a engineer at the Coronation Boulevard plant. "We know now that he is safe."

Zeb said he and and his parents were shocked about the news and worried about Faisal, but they didn't know how close he came to being at the centre during the attack.

"When he called us that's when we found out," Zeb said. "He is fascinated with the markets so it was something he really wanted to do along with other tours, like the Statue of Liberty and the Empire State Building."

At Re/Max Twin City Realty, where Susiwala works, employees were "glued to the TV set" this morning, said broker Bob Stephens.

"I contacted his mother right away," he said. "And his mother lives with his brother. I told them to phone as soon as they hear. I knew he would be calling home."

Stephens said he had no idea at the time that Susiwala was scheduled to tour the building. He assured Susiwala's mother that he would sleep in.

"The standing joke around here is that Faisal works very late and evenings and mornings. I assured his mother because it was in the morning he would be fine. And that ended up being the case."

Faisal Susiwala

This 2001 article was published shortly after 9/11 and chronicled the Susiwala's brush with the disaster. They were in New York on that date and had a reservation for breakfast in the restaurant on the top floors of the World Trade Centre. At the last minute they changed their reservation to lunchtime. That small change made a world of difference.

Couldn't we maybe do lunch there later on?

I stretched.

"Natalie," I said, "let me call and see if I can switch it over to lunch. Then we can sleep in a little longer."

She murmured in agreement. That would be a great idea.

I called.

"Guys, would it be possible to change breakfast to lunch?"

They checked.

There was a second set of tours at 12:30.

"Sure," they said. "No problem."

Great. We could see the World Trade Center and tour the Twin Towers then.

Except by then there wouldn't be any more World Trade Center or Twin Towers.

The 22-storey steel-framed Marriott we'd just left would also be destroyed. Sadly, the people making the change for us, as well as all the people having breakfast and in the upper floors of the towers, would be gone too.

The thought of that—all those innocent lives lost—still overcomes me with indescribable emotion.

Around 8:45 a.m., Natalie awoke and took a shower. I tossed and turned, then grabbed the remote to see what was on TV. Nothing very much. Voices sort of chattered away in the background. The usual stuff: news, weather, talking heads.

Then, around 9 a.m., there was a little box in the upper corner of the screen. It said, "LIVE."

A stream of words passed across the screen, like a stock ticker.

"World" "Trade" "Center" "Hit."

I was still a little sleepy and didn't quite register the headline or even the "LIVE."

Trade Center hit? What was that about? I knew a military plane had hit the Empire State Building some years earlier. Maybe it was the anniversary, and they were playing back some old footage.

Or maybe it was a trailer for some new disaster movie. I yawned and squinted at the screen. Wow. Sure looked realistic.

And then I heard—boom!

It didn't come from the TV. It shuddered through the air around us.

Suddenly the "LIVE" registered.

Natalie rushed out of the bathroom. "What was *that?*"

"Construction, maybe?" I said. I was still trying to put it all together. "It's New York. There's always construction going on."

But why was the TV saying the World Trade Center had been hit?

Hit by what?

We got dressed and went downstairs to find out. There was all this hustle and bustle on the first floor. Outside, people were running down the street. So we stepped outside too.

A row of fighter jets roared over our heads.

The jets shot low through the air up and down, again and again, so incredibly loud you could feel the sidewalk vibrating through your shoes. We could feel the wind, smell the jet fuel as we got closer to the towers.

We stumbled toward Canal Street trying not to get caught in a sudden crowd of screaming running people as smoke began curling around from nowhere. I put my arm around Natalie and we returned to our hotel.

Natalie and I would be stranded in New York City for several days. Unimaginable days, with military and firefighters storming through the streets, lockdowns on every side, fear that more attacks might come, longing to be back home with family and friends. For hours upon hours those people nearest and dearest to us had no idea whether Natalie and I and our expected child were alive or dead. Communications were down—there were no smartphones then, no Wi-Fi, not even phone service.

But we were alive. Thanks be to God, we were saved.

Many others weren't that lucky.

For me, 9/11 changed everything.

Staring out at the wreckage of the Twin Towers, reflecting on how we had come so close to losing everything, yet coming away with Natalie and our child alive and whole, was a major turning point in my life. It really put everything into perspective. I felt like we had been spared. God, spirituality, call it what you like—I was grateful for simply being alive. But ,I also felt something more.

In the wake of so many people perishing that day, and coming so close to death ourselves, I found myself wanting to do something more with my life, something that mattered. It gave me a boost, a desire to do something extra with the extra days God had given me. I wanted to show my appreciation, to make my life count; to make something good come out of something so tragic. I felt I owed it to myself, and to all those who had not survived.

People think tragedies and crises are things to be feared and avoided. Well, they're certainly not things to chase after foolishly. But a crisis can focus your mind, and your values. It can burn away the noise in your life and help you realize what really matters. It can help you see how precious life is and inspire you to make something exceptional and even magnificent out of it.

As I was writing this book, another crisis caught the world's attention. The global pandemic, COVID-19. Mass deaths mounted globally. It forced much of the world into lockdown. Fear of the unknown and uncertainty about the future, especially the future of the financial and business world, was followed by protest and rioting.

I pray and hope that by the time this book is published and in your hands, that you and your loved ones will be safe and in good health. But I also hope that you emerge from these harrowing days the way I learned to after 9/11, taking time to reflect, assess, support one another, see the future in positive, not fearful, ways, and calibrating your mindset toward personal and professional growth.

After 9/11, when I looked at my life from those perspectives, as grateful as I was for all I had, I wasn't very happy. The truth was that I hadn't accomplished all that much, at least, in a meaningful way. Before 9/11, I was a successful real estate agent. A good one, an honest one, a hard-working one, but I wasn't at the top of my profession. I hadn't come up with any new ideas, much less any industry breakthroughs. Sure, I had some quirky ways of doing things—I never made a cold call, or knocked on doors, and I put a lot more into my advertising and marketing than my colleagues did. I tried to do more of what I saw working well for others, and less of what didn't seem to work. But that wasn't leaving a legacy, or making a mark.

My life came within an inch of ending. If it had, what would I have left behind? An insurance policy that would benefit my family, and some property to pass along; that was pretty much it. Yes, that mattered. A lot. But it wasn't enough. A person's life should amount to more. I felt a new responsibility to make it amount to more.

And that's when my life, personally and professionally, began to change. To truly evolve.

It evolved professionally in three major ways.

First, I stopped wanting to be just 'good enough' in my line of work. I wanted to be great. I wanted to be number one in my profession, and I wanted to understand how and why I could manage to achieve that, if indeed I could. I wanted to be remembered for passing that information along to my peers and colleagues. This book you're reading is a part of this bigger plan that arose from the 9/11 tragedy.

Throughout my career I've seen people get into real estate and fail, or underperform. Some burn out. Some hold themselves and their profession in such low esteem they go nowhere. They weren't good, and they weren't happy. They weren't *succeeding*. Why not? What were they doing wrong, and how could I help them to go about things in a better way?

If I was more successful than other agents, it wasn't because of blind luck or charm. It was because I was consistently doing things differently. I analyzed what I was doing, I thought about what was getting me the results I was getting. I thought about how I could make it work even better. I didn't stop working hard, but more and more I focused on working smart, on developing a systematic approach to my professional life and my business activities.

I hadn't come back only to do business-as-usual. I was consciously focused now on achieving professional excellence — not just buying and selling more properties but understanding and defining what professional excellence meant, and how anyone could achieve it.

The more clearly I did so, the more success I personally achieved.

There was a second big change. A change in the way I saw my profession.

The truth is, many people who get into real estate do so because they think it's easy money. I did too. There was Tom Vu, sitting on his yacht having a mint julep, and throwing hundred-dollar bills around. Sure, who wouldn't want that — or so I thought as a teenager.

But even from the days I met Mr. Menary as a child I could see how much impact a real estate agent could have on a person's life. Getting someone to buy a property they couldn't afford just to get a few hundred dollars more commission could set that person up for foreclosure, divorce, even suicide. But talking to a home buyer and explaining to them how a home gave them ways of leveraging equity, of turning a monthly payment into a lifelong investment resource, a retirement fund that could put their children through college, and support their entire family in wealth to the end of their lives—*that* was not only honourable, but incredibly meaningful.

I began to see how much a real estate agent mattered. He or she wasn't simply just a salesperson taking a quick commission. Agents like me were more like a valuable investment consultant, an expert professional no different than a doctor or an attorney— as well as someone who needed to present himself and his services as such. A broker's or Realtor's licence, and the years of experience behind it, was a form of specialist expertise that an agent could not only monetize but use to develop his or her personal brand. A brand that could not only supercharge their own income, but also do a tremendous amount of good for their clients.

I also started thinking in terms of retirement—of an exit strategy.

You may find that strange, coming from a then-thirty-year-old. But 9/11 got me thinking in terms of my legacy. I didn't think of myself as immortal anymore. I knew I would leave a legacy behind one day, one way or another. 9/11 helped me realize that the time to start building it was now.

This was a bigger breakthrough than you know. Because in the world of real estate—even now, but especially at the time— no one thinks in terms of retirement. You buy and sell homes till you're too old to cold call, at which point you just sort of disappear. Doctors pass on their practices. Money managers pass their funds along to new managers. But Realtors, like old soldiers, were expected to just fade away; and when they left, vultures descended as they pleased to pick away at their client list.

I thought of Mr. Menary. What was his legacy from all he had done; what had he left behind after a lifetime of work?

Me.

I wanted to make that count. For his sake as well as mine.

How I could develop an exit strategy that could preserve something of what a Realtor built up over his or her long career? Preserve it and monetize it in a way that would support him or her financially all throughout their retirement. How could I leverage that exit strategy into an investment resource for the agent retiree?

Over the years the result became something I now call the LEXIT Strategy: a series of steps that, properly carried out, provides the retiring real estate agent with a rich ongoing stream of revenue. By understanding the steps and carrying them out from the very beginning of your career, you could retire a great deal earlier. The more I worked the details out, the more I kicked myself for not having started putting them into effect from Day One of my real estate career.

I'll be talking about LEXIT in more detail in a coming chapter, and the steps will be laid out in detail, but to give you a few key points:

From the start, the agent needs to think in terms of building a unique brand—a unique *business*. That means marketing themselves, but it also means developing their business practices and operating model into a standalone business-in-a-box: a systematic blueprint of operations and processes that an agent can sell to a successor.

From the start, too, the Realtor needs to build up a database, and develop the people in that database. Even today there are agents without a database. They get a call, sell a house, get their commission, enter a name in a company record, and forget the caller. That's insane.

And also from the very beginning, the Realtor needs to begin building a portfolio of properties. It's just plain ridiculous to spend your entire career working with properties continually rising in value and generating income for investors, and never invest in any of the prime properties constantly passing under your nose yourself.

The great lesson I took away from 9/11 was that I needed to make my life matter, personally and professionally. I wasn't just going through my daily routine anymore. I was looking for ways to make my life count. To find meaning.

I found it by deeply and systematically re-thinking what I was doing as a real estate agent, and where it all was going. I also found it in spending more time with my family and my community. I found it in charitable giving to hospitals and schools and my place of worship. Professionally, I found it by striving to have a long-term positive impact on my clients' financial lives, and by working not just hard, but in thoughtful and efficient ways. I work less hard nowadays than I did when I started out because I started thinking. I began to systematize, experiment and tweak to evolve a clean new understanding of my ever-changing profession.

Gradually, what I worked out and applied brought me to the very top. Which is why I wrote this book—to give others the knowledge I wish I had had when I began.

But I also learned is that pure knowledge, alone, isn't enough.

After 9/11 my career rose to a new level, because I, as a person, rose to a new level. It wasn't an easy process: what had happened shook me up, But it shook me up enough to make me re-examine not only my professional practices, but what it was in life that I most valued.

It wasn't money. It wasn't getting my face on billboards. It wasn't winning awards. I became an entrepreneur because, as a young boy, my father was horribly injured, and our home was lost. I knew then that if we were going to survive, our family had to pull together, and all of us had to contribute as much as we could. I had to do my best, not just for my sake, but also for their sake. For everyone's sake. Lifting myself up lifted everyone I loved with me. If that meant me knocking on doors, selling chocolate, peddling T-shirts, selling cheap watches at public markets, or delivering papers door to door, so what?

Where I began didn't matter. What mattered was the direction in which I was going, and what I could do when I got there.

I didn't know then that the day would come when I could take those streams of income generated by my profession and

After marrying and becoming a father, and in the aftermath of his brush with death on 9/11, Susiwala gained a broader appreciation for family and humanity, as well as his ever-evolving role as a Realtor and philanthropist.

transform them into funds for charities, hospitals, education, community developments and global ventures—into things I haven't even yet thought of. Larger, greater and more meaningful things.

All I knew is that, in coming to care for and appreciate life so much more deeply, in being inspired to reflect and to think, I was also learning to dream.

Chapter 7

TO THE TOP

Before 9/11, I was a good, honest and competent real estate agent. I wasn't anything special; certainly not a Diamond-level million-dollar agent. If I had gone to breakfast at the Twin Towers that morning as planned, I wouldn't have left behind much, save for a few insurance policies. No children, no grandchildren, no book. My family and friends would remember me, but in the end, all that would be left would be a few photographs and people's memories. 9/11 changed everything. After 9/11, I became someone determined to leave a mark. A legacy.

But what kind? And how?

The first days back at work after that tragedy were a swirl of phone calls and journalists and friends and families coming over. Soon the dust settled and I began asking myself some hard questions. I felt like I'd been spared. But if my life had been saved, then why? For what? What did I want to do with what amounted to this second chance I had been given?

Well, I did not want to spend it showing houses to people from nine in the morning till nine at night. I wanted to spend at least some time with my family—with my wife, and with my son, who would be arriving any day now. I wanted to do those things, but when I finally got back to my office, forget it. There was a desk stacked impossibly high with an avalanche of papers comprising stacks of printouts, flyers, legal documents, Post-it notes and listings. I felt crushed. I wanted to sit down in the office chair and put my face in my hands. But the chair was stacked with six feet of paperwork, too!

One of the big lessons I want to pass on to you is this: *take the time to look at what you're doing*. I was making nearly half a million dollars a year in real estate, and yet only at that moment did it really sink in that I was carrying it all on my own breaking back—no assistant, no staff, no help, nothing. Aside from Natalie walking beside me as I stuffed flyers into boxes, it was literally just me doing everything: emptying my own wastebasket, getting my own coffee, answering my own phone. I

Being successful means being able to give back to the community: In 2017 the Susiwala Family made a major donation to Cambridge Memorial Hospital's Trees of Caring campaign. The donation represented one dollar for every resident of their community.

handled every detail, from the most critical to the most trivial, and I was burning out. It didn't make sense. *It didn't even make money*, since I was spending so much of my workday doing things others could do, instead of the things I'd spent years developing the professional expertise to do.

I couldn't keep living like this. I went out into the lobby, and there, sitting behind a desk, was a young woman who greeted visitors. She had worked there since high school. Her name was Jennifer, and she was nineteen or twenty years old.

"Say, Jen," I asked. "Do you work here full-time?"

"No, just evenings."

"You think you could put in another four hours a day working for me? Twenty hours a week maybe?"

She thought about it. "Sure."

A revolution was about to take place in my business, and it started at that very moment, though it took me a full year to realize what a monumental step forward I had just taken.

Jen's first task was to clean up the desk and put together a desk for herself, then go to my house and put some patio furniture together. In no time my office was meticulous, but that was time enough for a couple dozen other things to crop up. She got right on it. All in all, that part-time twenty hours of help took up over sixty hours of her time. Jennifer hasn't worked less than sixty hours a week for me since then, and that was 17 years ago. Looking back, I feel nothing but gratitude. There's no question that my wife Natalie has been my greatest source of strength and support, but without a doubt, Jennifer has been the foundation and structure of my business. Above all, she has been my most trusted and loyal friend. Thank you from the bottom of my heart, Jennifer.

What I felt at the time wasn't yet gratitude, though. It was my familiar old companion: fear. I was now responsible for an assistant, someone who would be counting on me. It was new territory for me. Now I had an employee—a person who needed to be compensated, whose benefits needed to be covered, and around whom various regulations needed to be observed with which I would be obligated to comply. Not the least of my concerns was that I had to meet her salary every week. What if I ran out of clients, or cash? What if the market crashed—again! I'd already gone bankrupt once. How could I be sure to meet that salary regularly? Sure, hiring an assistant would make my life a little easier, but how much was it going to cost me?

A year later I found out.

My total income for the year *doubled*.

Now, in retrospect, it's kind of obvious why. I wasn't sitting around figuring out whether to file listing A into drawer B or drawer C. I wasn't taking out the wastebasket. I was out there *listing*. I was doing more of the things that brought money in. So, more money came in. *Duh!*

The more money came in, the more I put into marketing my services. The more marketing I did, the more listings I got. Soon it was Jennifer who became was overwhelmed, not me.

At that point, the same old dread came over me.. I realized I would need to hire yet another assistant. Again, I went through the same old drama. How could I afford two assistants? An inner voice told me I was setting myself up for disaster.

I needn't have worried. My Gross Commission Income (GCI) doubled once again. (Yes: I soon got a third assistant. Real estate is nothing if not a learning experience).

I don't pretend to be a real estate genius, but I do think I have enough intelligence to see when something works. What I had done clearly worked. I'd done things that worked before, but this time the difference was that, after 9/11, I started to take the time to sit down and reason out why. I began thinking about my business process—my system.

And that led to the next big change in how I did real estate.

Multi-Level Partnering

Success in real estate depends on leads, and on converting leads into sales. Marketing alone can generate leads. Printers and advertisers and social media could help get my face onto flyers, buses, billboards, Facebook and so on. It cost money, but the numbers told the story: the amount of leads it generated made much more than it cost.

But what do you do when you get more leads than you can handle? One person can't handle more leads than they can service, not if he or she has to manage each one alone.

Once I started analyzing what I was doing, I soon realized I'd been kidding myself about being a 'hard worker.' Yes, I worked long hours, but most of my time was taken up doing things that brought me the least income, not the most. Necessary things, sure, like paperwork, or showing homes, but not the things that generated serious returns.

It hit me that I didn't need to do more to make more money —I needed to do less.

Take Jennifer. By lifting a tremendous amount of office work from my shoulders, I could now spend the day talking and presenting to buyers and sellers—actually making sales, instead of writing them up, sending documents to attorneys, and putting duplicates into files.

I built on that insight. What else could I do that would focus my time on those actions that brought in the most business?

One thing immediately came to mind: buyers. Dealing with buyers took a massive amount of time, and took it away from other, more profit-generating activities.

So I stopped doing that. Totally.

The eyes of some of you reading this are probably popping out of their sockets right now. What? You're the top-selling agent in all of Canada and you don't deal with people who want to buy houses at all? What? Showing houses is all you real estate people do, isn't it!?

Most real estate agents, yes.

Not me.

I don't show houses to people who want to buy houses. Period. For the first ten years I did. That was why I worked from dawn to midnight and beyond. (And I'll admit: some experiences with buyers could be a real pleasure. It was great settling a young couple in their first home or seeing an immigrant family find a safe and comfortable place after a very long journey indeed).

But the fact is, buyers can call you at any time, day or night. They may have you walk them through (and research) dozens, maybe *hundreds* of properties, and then just shrug and change their mind, leaving you with no compensation whatsoever for your time. Sellers require far less time (and hair-pulling) than buyers. Strategy and marketing are the keys to working with sellers, not constant physical attendance. List a home for sale, and buyers come to you. Other agents can show them the property, while you're busy working with more sellers.

For the first ten years of my career, because of my age, it was all buyers. No one gives a high-school kid a million-dollar property to sell, but as soon as I became known, it was a different story. The amount of commission income I made from selling homes, relative to the amount of time needed to do it, absolutely blew away the amount made from buyers when you factored in the enormous time investment. Focusing almost exclusively on sellers not only supercharged my income, it allowed me to finally spend a decent amount of time with my family and friends—and write this book.

Don't misunderstand. People who want to buy a house can still come to Faisal Susiwala, and they should. I have the most competent buyers' agents around, and those agents are ready to find them the property they want. It's just that I don't need to be there, in person, to walk someone through a home. I have associates (not team members) who can do as good a job as anyone when it comes to researching properties, helping them find the perfect match. The long, time-consuming process of actual home showings—that's done by others.

All the buyers who call me still want Faisal Susiwala, and they get what matters about me: my business process, my listings, my network, my oversight—the things that give them the result they *really* want, along with (no less importantly) handpicked, personally trained, trusted buyers' agents. The only thing I'm doing differently now is that I'm letting a trusted and qualified associate give them a home tour and handle a few simple aspects that don't require me being present. That opens up my time enormously.

I should have understood this much sooner. When I got back from New York I felt the same dread I felt when I went on my honeymoon. I'd delegated all my business out to other agents, and paid 25 to 50 per cent of the commission to those who agreed to take up the slack. I thought I'd get nothing, but so long as my marketing kept rolling, the leads kept coming in, and that's all that mattered. When I looked at the results, I saw that I'd made 25 to 50 per cent of my annual income as my system continued to do what it's supposed to do. When your annual income is over a million, making 25 to 50 per cent of that amount from delegating, and from implementing a system that continues to generate business for you no matter where you are, is an absolutely amazing business model.

After all, those buyers have come to Faisal Susiwala *the brand,* not Faisal Susiwala the person. What they want is a good property at a good price. If they can get that from an associate, with me in the background, providing oversight, isn't that better than having them go somewhere else and getting less value?

So I made an arrangement with a new associate—Robert. And I said to him, "Robert, run your own office, handle your own business. But if you want buyers, I'm going to give you my overflow. We'll make it 50/50, OK?"

Robert made $250,000 that year from our arrangement.

He was more than OK. He was ecstatic!

I was ecstatic too. *I* made an additional $250,000 that year simply by generating steady leads for him, while freeing up time for me.

Then he got too busy. After all, like I said: buyers take time. Did I ditch this model, and start showing houses again? No, by now I had learned from my experience with Jennifer. If something works, makes more money, and asks less of your time and involvement, it's a no-brainer. Do more of it! So I brought on a second person using the same system.

I'm now up to six people. They're not my 'team.' They're my professional equals. I think of them as my network. They're still independent. I get nothing from the business that they do on their own. But *I do* I get 50 per cent of the commission from the business that I send to them. All the business I send to them are buyers.

Why are the buyers coming to me, and not to them directly? Because I've spent years, and hundreds upon hundreds of thousands of dollars, branding myself. I've marketed myself so well that, in my target region, I've become the go-to guy. I'm the man with the listings. People see the listings, call, and say, "I want to see this house." I introduce them to someone who can show them the house, and, if they don't like that one, who can show them another house that's right in line with what they're looking for? My buyers' agent!

Let's say that this week, I have five such buyers. I send five of those buyers to five agents. Those agents show them the properties and sell them homes. Meanwhile I'm at my cottage, collecting 50 per cent of each sale.

This is my 'big secret.' (Not the only one. Keep reading.) This is how I'm able to sell so many houses. It's not because of what I'm doing—it's because of what I'm not doing.

I call this 'multi-level partnering,' because what I've created is not a *team*. I don't employ these buyers' agents. We partner. I have six people available that can show houses, do the legwork, and the paperwork, and sell properties. When they do, we split the commissions 50-50. But—unlike a team—I don't have to feed those agents regularly. I send them business when I have more than I want to handle. If I hired six people as my agents and put them under the Faisal banner, I'd have to make sure they get fed properties every single day and that they have business every single day.

Many growing agents create teams, which is why many such agents don't succeed. If you have a network, you don't need to manage a team. All you need to manage are listings. Listings are manageable. I can have twenty homes with my sign on it, no problem. But I can't work with twenty buyers. I can't work with five buyers. Because to work with five buyers, I may have to show twenty, thirty homes a day. There aren't that many hours in a day.

Thanks to my constant marketing, I'm getting *more* than five buyers. What I've built is a lead generation machine. I need to handle that stream, though, so I evolved a key element of the Susiwala System: 'multi-level partnering.' I still handle all my own sellers, but all my buyers are handled by independent buyers' agents running their own businesses.

Multi-level partnering is a little like multi-level marketing because it's scalable. You can focus on getting all the buyers you can, more buyers than you can possibly handle as a solo agent, because you have an elastic network that can accommodate them.

It's like multi-level marketing in another important respect: everyone wins. I give you business. If it results in revenue for you, you pay me a percentage. If you don't make any money, I don't get a penny. Why is that better than being part of a team? Because if you're part of a team, you may do all the work of landing the buyer, all the work of showing him or her dozens of properties, and all the work of negotiating price and working out conditions. Even so, much of the compensation—in some cases most of it—goes to the team leader. Why? Just because his or her name is on the banner.

I don't operate that way. The people I send business to are not my employees, or under my "banner." They're my referral network. If you need a home in Toronto, or in Buffalo, I call up an agent I know and trust, someone I'm sure will do good by you. I say to him or her, "I have someone who's interested in buying a home. If you find one the person likes, and they buy it, send me 25-50 per cent for my sending him to you."

It's win-win for everyone concerned. Once again, you're giving to get.

I've been doing this literally since 2002, and I make no secret of it. Yet it's a system that almost no one seems to be using, much less using consistently. Well, to each their own, I suppose.

The bottom line is: if I have I buyer and I sell him one home, I've sold one home. Whereas if I have ten buyers, and I refer them to my referral network, the network sells ten homes. True, I may get 'only' 50 per cent of ten homes, but I still make five times as much as if I were to sell one home at a time. And every such sale counts as a partial sale both for the agent in my referral network and for me. I haven't shown one home, but I've still shared in the sale of ten.

That's what's let me sell more homes than anyone else in Canada.

"Why are you sharing this with us, Faisal? Aren't you worried that other people are going to cut into your business?"

No, not at all. I'm happy to share. The reason is, I have so saturated the market with my marketing, I'm so well known in my target area, I've been so entrenched as part of the mental landscape of people here for so long when it comes to real estate, that I've become the default go-to real estate person. When you want a pop, you ask for a Coke. When you want to buy or sell a house in Cambridge, you call Faisal. It took time, money, and consistently great service to get to that point. But once you reach it, you're there. My business is all listings now, and people applying my systems are not going to take away my listings any more than smartphone makers who make Apple look-alikes are going to replace Apple.

RE/MAX has asked me to give talks about my system to its agents, even around the world. I'm glad to do it. It's not an especially difficult system to work. Really, it's only a question of how to pass the buyer along courteously, and what's a fair compensation package. After all, why *wouldn't* an agent want to use it? If you're having a slow week, and you *know* there's a steady stream of business available from a referring agent, why would you turn it down? You don't have to cold call or knock on doors or pay a fortune in advertising to get it. Faisal Susiwala is putting it right in your lap! Isn't 50 per cent of a $10,000 commission better than 100 per cent of nothing?

Moreover, my system encourages entrepreneurship. I encourage my network to build their own brand, unlike a team system, where you're forbidden to do so. I encourage my partners to use the extra money they make from being in my network and put it into marketing and self promotion to build their own business.

I even go so far as to allow them to keep the client on their own database as well. (I put them on mine without a question.) Most of those buyers have never directly met me, but they'll be getting my flyers and post cards. I don't want them to feel that the buyer's agent abandoned them right after the sale.

My referral network contract specifically deals with compensation if the buyer contacts my buyer's agent sometime in the future. It's a legal contract which is enforceable even if they leave my referral network or the brokerage under which they currently work.

Could my network send referrals to me? Sure, why not? This is what happens when you work in good faith with people, and you come from a place of abundance and not from a place of fear. Somehow everything just works out. You create abundance together.

Lesson: Scaling Reciprocity

The time I freed up by no longer working 24/7 with buyers; my growing ability to focus more attention on getting listings, thanks to assistance from my growing office staff; the network referral system I slowly engineered; my consistent and continual

For Susiwala, success has been a family affair.
Photo by Stan Switalski

saturation marketing—all of it shot my sales (and my income) through the roof. Fast. I grossed over $1 million within a year.

My scalable system generated more sales the larger it grew. I soon hit the next level, and then the next. By 2010 I had hit the top: Circle of Legends, at the time, the highest RE/MAX career award of them all.

Chapter 8

GETTING THE LISTING

There are professions where you have to study for years on end before they let you practice. Real estate isn't one of them. In real estate, you study for a few months, and then they throw you into the real world. There, a broker or an agency may or may not take you under their wing. If you're smart and ambitious, you'll learn from the people around you. If you're really smart and ambitious, you'll do it creatively, trying to come up with better and more effective approaches.

I did things creatively. I started by mastering the basics, like everyone, and I listened to and read and copied seasoned mentors, slow, and I made mistakes. But even from the start I looked at things in new, different, and unique ways. Not just small things like showing houses or filing documents. Things that got major results in terms of income and career. I kept asking: what are the key elements that made up my day-to-day actions, my work process, my services. What key activities made the most difference? What was I focusing on, what *should* I focus on, to generate the greatest rewards?

The answer was simple: getting listings and making presentations. By getting the first, and becoming good at the second, success would follow. So, that's where I began applying my thinking and new creative approach the most.

Now getting listings begins with marketing. I don't mean hard-sell marketing, the kind that intrudes and twists people's arms. I'm talking about the kind of marketing that has a simple goal: to get people to think 'Faisal Susiwala – Real Estate Agent'. To make my name and what I do part of their mental landscape.

When I market on buses, benches, scoreboards and social media, it's intended to get people to instantly associate me with real estate. When they think 'real estate agent,' they should think 'Faisal Susiwala,' and vice versa. No other option needs to come into their minds at all. They should simply pick up the phone. I want my name to be so synonymous with real estate in the

Susiwala embraced marketing and advertising early and often, but today, most of it is online and via buses and billboards.

public mind that they think of me first, and they call me first.

It's obvious why. If they don't get in touch, I can't sell their home! But what most agents marketing their real estate services don't realize is that this needs to be done *softly*—almost subliminally. If I bang away so hard and so loud that it puts them off (remember the deer that runs away when it hears the hunter approaching?), they won't get in touch either.

The trick is to be everywhere, but to apply pressure nowhere.

This non-invasive approach—call it face marketing, passive marketing, branding—is a key part of what's made me a success.

But when they call, is it Game Over? No! Just getting the call isn't the end of the story. If someone wants me to sell their home, they need to actually sign me on as their agent. As a rule, that only happens after we have a meeting where I make a case to them for that—a presentation. Getting a call and making a successful presentation are two very different things. Doing the presentation properly is what makes or breaks the deal. There, too, I slowly evolved some very unique strategies.

How exactly do I do it? What does Faisal Susiwala do differently from other real estate agents to get that listing and sell a house?

A lot of things.

In the beginning I followed what other agents were still doing, but it didn't take much reflection to see that some of it worked and a lot of it didn't. So, I began separating the two, doing more of one and less of the other. Again, I started asking myself how I could do what worked even better. Soon enough I came up with my own custom way of getting listings. Which, as the record shows, works darned well.

Prepare Beforehand

The process usually starts with a call to my marketing team, to or from my network, or from a lead generation service. Often, it's a request for an evaluation. My staff asks the caller a series of questions about the seller's home. What style is it? What's the square footage? Are there any notable upgrades? If there's any information the seller wishes to share, we want to know it. Each item helps me get ready for the presentation that my staff then schedules.

Once that's done, the staff gather all the information they can on the property beforehand. The first stop for that is the MLS, but they also check the Internet and use industry-specific proprietary software and look up older listings too, if available. My staff fills out the listing paperwork ahead of time and uploads it, then prepares any other documents I may need for the presentation. Electronic signing software is already in place.

Before you go see a seller, what you need more than anything else is knowledge. Product knowledge. You need to know the neighbourhood you're going into. You need to know the background information and details about the house. You need to know when they purchased their home, what they paid for it, what similar properties in their neighbourhood sold for and sell for now, what the general comparables are in the area.

What you don't need are preconceived ideas. That's where too many agents fall down. They go in thinking, "I already know what homes around here are worth: $500,000! So I'll do a range of $425,000 to $500,000."

Not me. I research comparable properties listed and sold and what I find are prices between $400,000 to $600,000. Why wouldn't I? After all, I haven't toured the homes. I haven't seen what the owners have done to them. They may have gutted their home. They may have the best home on the street, a house that's been improved in every possible way.

The condition and maintenance of a home can make all the difference. If a mould-infested home with a decrepit roof down the street sold for $500,000, it doesn't matter if it's the same size. That isn't a fair comparable.

Home sellers are more intelligent than Realtors give them credit for. They typically know what their neighbours have sold their homes for. A lot of times they even know something about the condition. So you're just shooting yourself in the foot if you leave out comparables that don't fit your presentation. If you're telling them they can't get more than $475,000 and they *know* that a home far inferior to theirs got more than that, it's over! Your presentation is toast.

Now here's what *I* do: I show them the highest of the high comparables and the lowest of the low. Then I do a comparison at the table in real time with them.

"OK. *This* home got top dollar, true. But the owners completed a $150,000 renovation. On top of that, they did this, they did this, they added that. That's why they got that great price. Now let's look at *your* home. What upgrades have you done? What improvements have you made?"

It's not a matter of telling them their house isn't so great. It's a matter of explaining what the real comparables are. If you tour their house and you see that, yes, their home is comparable to the one they're telling you about, then fine: use that home as a guide for valuation.

But if not, you need to provide them with as much full, accurate and relevant information that they need to make an informed choice.

Here's the key. You're not there to *sell:* you're there to *educate*. You're there to answer questions and be perfectly transparent, because the facts are what sell. You can't leave any facts out, because the minute you leave something out, the seller is going to call you out on it.

Being prepared and having knowledge before you walk into a presentation is an absolute necessity.

First Impressions

No less important than preparation is professionalism. So many agents try to be 'friendly' and cozy up to people. Come on, be serious. You think they're going to trust a $500,000 property to you just because you have a cute smile?

When I arrive, I do my presentation with maximum efficiency. I'm not there to schmooze, socialize or spend the evening getting to know them. I want that presentation to be done within 30 to 45 minutes. Max.

We give ourselves too much credit. We think people enjoy our company. OK, some of them do. My friends enjoy my company (or so they tell me). But people who call a real estate agent aren't looking for companionship. They want to know what they can expect to get for their home. They want to see that number!

What do weak agents do? They weasel out. Weak agents think that if they give a number the seller doesn't like, they're out, so what they try to do is distract the seller with big smiles and small talk and avoid the subject for as long as they can. The seller knows what's going on. He or she is not getting the information that they want to hear, and so the agent just comes out and asks the seller what they think their home is worth.

Not me. I get there on time. I say hello, I place my briefcase down in their foyer, I take off my shoes, and when they invite me to come into their kitchen and sit down, I say "Thanks. But let's have a tour of your home first."

The All-Important Tour (And How to Do It)

I never walk in and go straight into my presentation. I always ask to do a tour first. I need to do that tour (and so do you) to properly set up that presentation for maximum impact. But also because what I'm really doing is gathering more product knowledge. I'm learning more about what the prospect wants and expects, and about how to best deal with them as individuals.

Suppose I just come in and sit at the kitchen table, and I haven't walked through their home. The seller starts asking me questions. What am I supposed to say? Sure, I've done my paper research. But I need to actually, physically see their home. Is it well kept up or not? Are there strange smells? Is it musty? Worse, mouldy? Is there dampness in the basement? How will it feel to a buyer who comes to the showing? Clean, elegant and well lit? Or dark, mildewed, and stuffed with ten years of hoarded whatnots?

Google Earth doesn't have a nose. Google (and Zillow and Trulia and all the rest) can't replace your senses. (Which is why computers and artificial intelligence will never be as big a disruptor in the real estate world as some think.) They can't tell you if a house feels comfy or creepy. You need to actually go there and look. Because when the buyers actually walk into that house and look, it's going to make all the difference to that sale.

You walk through that home because your product knowledge needs to be complete before you start talking. But you need more than product knowledge to get the listing. You need person knowledge. Buying or selling a house may be a rational decision. Buying or selling a *home* is a personal decision. That's why there'll always need to be a personal element—you, the real estate agent. Not just to provide information, but to provide judgment, support for their decision, feedback, reassurance.

When someone walks me through his or her home, I'm doing my best to understand them personally. I'm picking up things about them as people—their personality, their expectations. I don't interrogate them: I stay silent and let them do the talking. How long does a tour take? Usually only 10 minutes. But it's enough to give me insight not just into the house, but into the owners' expectations and mindset. What I learn during that time helps me frame the whole presentation.

For instance?

They'll show me a doorknob that I know cost $9.99 at Home Depot. Yet they go on and on about how amazing this doorknob is, and how it makes the house look just incredibly elegant! They'll say, "We did this, we did that, we added such-and-such." Sure, it tells me something about the house, but it also tells me what's going on in their minds before we ever sit down. I'm assessing and observing not just what they've done, but what they think. It shapes what I'm about to say. When I hear comments like that, I know the person is expecting me to name a high price—a price that's higher than the home may be worth.

The seller may even state point-blank the value they have in mind. Some Realtors even make that their first question! Not me. I never ask a seller what they feel their home is worth. I'm shocked at how many agents do. If a seller knew what their home was worth, they wouldn't be calling you over to ask for your opinion!

But knowing *their* opinion matters too. Because when I have to tell them their home may not be worth quite what they think, chances are they'll object. I have to be prepared beforehand for their resistance, and I have to be able to help them see why the best price I can get them is the best price they're ever likely to get.

That short tour isn't just me gathering information and impressions, either. To get their business I have to get their trust and confidence. The presentation is the key to doing that, but the tour prepares for it. It helps me determine how I need to best shape my approach, what sort of language, personality and behaviour I should deploy.

I learned a good deal about this using techniques from people like Robert Cialdini and Tony Robbins and NLP (neuro-linguistic programming). That sounds complicated, but really, it's simple common sense. Mirroring, for instance. As we do the tour, along the way I pick up on things that the prospect and I have in common, or thoughts we share. It only takes one or two such items for you and that person to click.

Once you do—and once you have all the information you need, and once you gather the feelings, the impressions, the expectations you will never learn from Google or Zillow— you're ready to present.

Now let's explore the process of winning that listing.

Structuring the Presentation

After the tour is complete, I sit down with the sellers. It's time for me to take them on their journey to success, and describing that journey is what makes the difference. It's like Robert Frost's poem, "*The Road Not Taken*," in which "Two roads diverged in a wood, and I— / I took the one less traveled by / And that has made all the difference."

In almost every case, the journey I am leading them on comes down to the four questions all sellers want to know:

1 – What can I get for my house—how much is it really worth?

2 - How are you, the agent, going to sell it for me? (In other words: what is your marketing strategy for this house?).

3 – What do I need to do to get my home ready? (They're looking for feedback and recommendations.)

4 - What's your commission going to be?

I address those questions as quickly and directly as I can. Many agents don't. They schmooze. They try to be charming and make friends. They show you their Rolex to impress you with what great agents they are. They avoid mentioning their commission for as long as they can and try to pressure the prospect into signing as early as they can and as hard as they can. They usually blow the deal, and deservedly so.

I make the presentation straight and simple by going through these four steps.

Getting to An Agreement About Value

First, I have three lists in my presentation package:

1 - Homes sold on their street.

2 - Homes sold in their neighbourhood.

3 - Homes listed in their neighbourhood (so I can show them what their competition is in that market).

I have a book that outlines my recent track record and sales throughout the region. I show them the price homes were listed for and the final selling price that I got. I also show them how long it took me to sell the homes. The book features over 300 homes that I sold in the past year.

Next I show them what the municipality says their home is worth—the official assessment. I start by using this as the base reference when presenting the assessments of comparable homes, as against the actual selling price.

Then I show them what the municipality record is on the square footage of their home.

Square footage is an important point! I always include the official square footage because owners typically think their home is bigger than it is. In real estate, exact size matters. It matters because you always want to come across as knowledgeable, informed and authoritative, and you never want to become argumentative.

When you've got the official documentation in hand showing the square footage and assessment value of their home, you never have to argue. The official statement makes it a done deal; and believe me, you will need to have that kind of statement.

Because the minute you say this 2500 square foot comparable home sold for $500,000, they're going to come back and say, "My house is 2600 square feet. *It's worth more!*"

The first house may have all the upgrades in the world. It can be perfect in every way. Meanwhile their house may have a leaky roof, a cracked foundation, and a basement half underwater. It doesn't matter. To a homeowner, a larger square footage means more money. When you pull out that official municipal assessment, there's no need to disagree. If the paper says '2500 square feet' in black and white, the argument is over.

Your Marketing Strategy Sells You

It's amazing to me—shocking—that there are agents who don't present their marketing strategy. They don't bother to tell the seller at all how they intend to sell the house. They don't tell the seller why he or she can expect it to sell quickly. Some agents don't even *have* a marketing strategy. All they do once they get the listing (if, incredibly, they do) is to enter the house on the MLS multiple listing service, put a sign on the lawn, and hit the couch! They actually believe sellers will be so charmed by the agent's personality that they'll take his or her selling ability on trust.

It's true, a few sellers—very few—do. Since they don't know or ask how agents sell houses, they expect the agent to sell their house using some kind of magic. Sellers like that get frustrated very quickly. When they don't get the instant results they want, they hop from agent to agent

But here's a news bulletin: *most* sellers don't want to *hope* that you'll sell their home fast at a good price. They want to know it. They want to feel sure that their home will sell fast at a good price. They want to believe in you, but they need to have reasons to believe.

That's what this next part of my presentation supplies. I show them how I intend to market their house.

First I tell them about myself. Here's who I am. Here's how long I've been doing this. Here's my track record.

Next I show them where I'm going to list their home, and where I'm going to be advertising. This includes Google, Facebook, Instagram, Twitter, LinkedIn and all the leading social media platforms.

The key element, the number one hook that I have, comes the minute I say to them, "Mr. and Mrs. Seller, I don't intend to sell to your neighbours. They're good folks, of course, and we won't turn down a top bid if they present one. But they already have preconceived ideas, and they don't understand the true value of your home. I'm going to sell your home to an expanded marketplace that does understand value—a market where people have bought similar homes for 30 to 40 per cent more than they pay here."

What's that all about? The tried but true real estate axiom: location, location, location. I operate in Cambridge, Ontario. It's located sixty minutes west of Toronto, thirty-five minutes west of Milton, and forty minutes from Oakville and Burlington. All these marketplaces are priced at least 30 to 40 per cent higher than my region. I explain this to the customer, and then I show them a sample of my advertising: the one that says, "Drive 35 Minutes and Save $350,000!"

I put this ad on Google. I tell them that when a prospective buyer clicks on this ad, they'll see a picture of their home, their floor plan, a virtual tour, and a statement that tells them that for a little commute the buyer could save up to 40 per cent on a home just as good as one in the slightly closer high-ticker area.

Now if you had a million to spend on a home and you could get pretty much the same home and keep $350,000 in your pocket, be honest. Wouldn't you take it? If you saw an ad pop up on your feed that said you could drive a half hour and save $350,000, wouldn't you be curious to find out more?

At this point, I've got the sellers' interest. They're more than interested. They're riveted. Next I take out my smartphone and show them my social media feeds. I scroll down, and they see how my sponsored ads keep popping up, and popping up. I explain to them that when prospective buyers—by the thousands, by the tens of thousands—go about their day scrolling through their social media feeds, ads for their house are going to pop up endlessly, exactly the same way.

Guess what? They see the power of this approach immediately. They're impressed. They're convinced! I'm not just putting up a sign on their front lawn and going home and taking a nap. I'm not hoping and wishing that someone's going to miraculously drive by his or her home and call me with an offer. I'm putting their home in front of literally tens of thousands of potential home buyers 24/7, and I'm doing it exactly where people go to get information: on Google, Facebook, Twitter and all the other major social media.

On top of that, I'm putting their property in front of the faces of people who pay 30 per cent to 40 per cent more for homes just like theirs. It's pretty much game over at this point. But I don't stop there. List their home on the local real estate board only? Not me. I'll list their home on the local board, all right, but I explain that I also plan to list it on every real estate board outside of the region: a marketplace where home values and home buyers operate at far higher price levels than ours. I make sure to add that I work with agents in those marketplaces

Yes, I'll show their home to consumers browsing the web. But I'll also put their home in front of agents who may not have homes that fit their clients in their own marketplace. I'm providing those agents another option, new inventory and a solution. It's like having multiple agents out there actively working to benefit my seller.

What I'm creating is buzz. An environment where people will not only want to buy this home but will compete to buy it. I then build on this idea. The social media marketing and the expanded market listing approach has usually convinced them that I'm their agent of choice, but this next part takes it to the next level, absolutely nailing it:

I show them my plan to get multiple buyers sitting in my office fighting to get their property.

Instead of jumping at the first offer, I arrange a buyers' auction.

You know what happens in an auction: when one person raises their hand, the next person wants to outbid them. It stops being about the house. It becomes about who wins. Bidders don't want to lose! Just by showing up they've already committed to buying the property. Now that they're actually there fighting to get it, they don't want to miss out. If that means paying my client a few thousand dollars more, or even a few tens of thousands more, so be it.

A Word About Open Houses

In the first ten years of my career, I held open houses from one o'clock to three o'clock and from three to five every Saturday and Sunday. That was worth doing at the time. It was a lead generator for me, and not a bad one. Everyone who stopped by got my business card. Showing the seller's home let me promote myself to all the nosey neighbours. It didn't sell many homes, though, but then I still hadn't worked out my System. Now I do things differently. I'm an open house skeptic.

What's the problem with open houses?

For one thing, many sellers can't stand them. They hate having perfect strangers walking through their home. They don't care for the disruption to their schedule. (And, of course, given the coronavirus upheaval, now there's a lingering fear of germs and infection too.) This level of discomfort is no small matter to an agent. Sellers can drop an agent any time, and few things get under a seller's skin more than a string of seemingly endless open houses.

Agents who want to use open houses to generate leads like I once did, or team leaders who want to attract buyers' agents by hosting open houses, still play it the old way. That's why sellers heave a sigh of relief when they hear me say that I don't. I keep showing to a minimum.

In the Susiwala System, open houses are just not the most efficient or effective way to generate good quality leads. Showing a house, and holding regular open houses, isn't the same thing. If all you want to do is distribute business cards, you can do that at any group get-together. True, an open house may help sell that particular property, but the vast majority of people passing through aren't going to buy it; and from the agent's perspective, it isn't the best way to generate business. Random people strolling in to browse simply don't compare to targeted social media marketing putting your ad in front of hundreds, maybe thousands, of high-likelihood buyers.

From a personal perspective, if I do an open house, it takes time away from friends and family; from a professional perspective, it takes time from stronger business operations, like presenting, or like generating leads through marketing or technology .

So what do I do? I tell the seller that when I get a call from someone asking about the open house, I say the open house is in thirty minutes. The phone usually goes silent on the other end for a few seconds. That's not what the caller was expecting. Often they mumble about needing to check with their spouse and promise to get back to me. Typically that was a nosey neighbour just wanting to get into the house and snoop.

A serious buyer doesn't back away like that. A serious buyer doesn't want to wait till Sunday from two to four, either. They book an appointment, and a serious agent shows them the home.

I show the house to individuals on an appointment basis only, and I facilitate all showings for agents to show their buyers by appointment. What I do is set up a presentation date to review offers after I list the home, typically one week after listing. During that first week, agents and buyers are invited to come in and see the home. A time is set for each visit, some individually and some in small groups, and this way the sellers know that the people looking in are serious buyers and not just curiosity-seekers off the street. They also realize the showing is not a weekly feature for however long it takes to sell.

My staff follow up on each viewing to get feedback. If there's interest, we keep the person in the loop on prospective offers.

More Marketing

By this point the deal is virtually sealed. But I don't stop there. I continue showing more ways I plan to market their home. I'll tell them that I plan to do a coming-soon video and show them that I typically get over 10,000 views per video. I tell them I'm going to do a virtual tour of their property and put it on YouTube. I plan to put their home on every available popular real estate sales platform there is so as to ensure the maximum number of viewings.

What I'm not doing is saying, "Trust me." I'm showing them my approach, I'm showing them *why* this is my approach, and I'm showing them example after example, proving that it's worked. They can see why marketing their home this way will succeed. They can see the numbers. They can see that it's worked for others time and again.

What are other Realtors doing? Often not much more than posting the property on the MLS. They may say to the seller their house is going to be on the MLS; they may say it'll be on the World Wide Web (on page seventeen of Google Search?). But agents *not* on the local board won't have detailed information on your listing; and without that exposure, they just plain won't get as many high-quality bids.

Why not market to agents who work in higher surrounding markets, like I do? Doesn't it make sense that this will bring in more money? I tell the seller that I cooperate with all agents, especially higher market agents. I'm showing them that I'm committed, that I'm taking what Tony Robbins calls 'massive action.'

By explaining my approach, I'm also showing the sellers that I'm partnering with them. That I'm being completely honest and transparent. I'm doing everything I can to get multiple offers and sell their home for top dollar. How can they not want that?

And yet I'm not pressuring them to sign. I'm showing them why it's in their best interest to work with me. Yes, there's profit in my getting the listing, and there may be more if I find the right buyer. But I'm not trying to land just one specific transaction. I'm building advocates. Evangelists. I want to build a growing sphere of people who are going to tell their friends, family and neighbours that I'm the guy to go to because of the spectacular results I got for them. This is how long-term sustainability, at its finest, is built.

When there are a lot of eager, interested buyers, it's almost guaranteed the home will sell above market value. How do I drive up the value of the home even higher? By bringing the buyers and their agents together in an auction-style framework.

How do I convert that framework into an exciting bidding war that gets my clients top dollar?

Read on.

Chapter 9

BIDDERS NOT BUYERS

My marketing will get buyers and offers for me and my seller. I've explained it clearly by this point in the presentation, and the sellers have gotten it. I've taken them on the journey, and they can see how happy and satisfied they're going to be by the journey's end.

But then I explain how getting those buyers to compete is what really gets them top dollar, and what lands them the best possible sale.

I start by applying reverse psychology. If the home is worth $525,000 or $550,000, I'll list it for $500,000.

The seller's jaw drops!

They almost panic. "We don't want to sell that low!"

I tell them, "Relax. We're not going to. That price is there purely to gain attention and drive interest. Sellers aren't required to sell properties at the list price."

I show them the clause in my listing agreement: "The seller has the right to decline ANY offer at their sole discretion."

They almost melt with relief.

"The lower price is there to attract multiple interested buyers," I explain. "I'm bringing them together into a competitive bidding environment. When people compete, they know they'll have to present their best offer, not their lowest. They also know they won't be able insert many undesirable conditions (if any). And they're likely to pay more in the heat of the moment when the bidding is happening, just like at an auction. Yes, we ask less at the start to prime the pump. But you, the seller get more at the finish."

I don't ask them to take my word for that. I show the seller the book I bring along. It's about four inches thick and shows every sale that I've had in the past 12 months, each one of which sold for more than asking price. (In fact, the title on cover of the book says: "Homes Sold Above Asking Price"!)

"Here's a home just like yours, Mr. and Mrs. Seller. Here's another, and another. This one here? It sold for $30,000 over asking. These? They sold for, $50,000, $75,000, even $100,000 more than asking."

What I'm doing, of course, is continuing to lead the journey. I'm helping them see the results they could get, and are likely to get, if they choose Faisal Susiwala and the Susiwala System.

Now the traditional way is to list high, let the buyer come in low and you both meet halfway—in the middle, where no one gets all they want, and everyone is unhappy.

What I do is show the sellers is that each time I started with a lower list price and opened it up to bidders, the sale price exceeded expectations.

"The numbers speak for themselves. I've done it time and time for hundreds of sellers. See for yourself," I say, and invite them to turn the pages.

Now if you're an agent who has never employed this type of strategy before, and you don't have a book, that's not a problem. Create a book and fill it with sales in your region where similar results were obtained. You don't need to have a track record of personal success to use a successful strategy. It's the strategy that generates the prices, not you personally. All you have to do is know the strategy and put it into practice. Once you know it and use it, especially after you do it a number of times, success follows. Then your own successes can go into the book.

What if the seller says, "What happens if we don't get multiple offers?"

You can expect sellers to ask that. So I turn to the very next page I prepared beforehand, and say, "What happens if we don't get multiple offers? Look at this. Here's a house I listed at $500,000. It didn't get the $550,000 we expected. We received offers but not our target price. So, what did we do? The next week we came out again, with our target price. We showed the market what we were prepared to sell for, and we stayed firm on our price. We got it."

I show them ten or twelve examples of homes that sold exactly the same way. It worked. We got the sellers their firm asking price and sometimes even more.

Why exactly does the market fluctuate this way? It could be any number of reasons. Buyers who were only thinking of buying last week may have finally decided to get serious this week for myriad personal reasons.

The seller doesn't really care. Because I've shown the seller that one approach gets them their asking price, and the other gets them more than their asking price. I'm ready to go ahead with both. And when I show them examples that they both work—especially when I show them examples that they both work—they're happy either way.

Why do I show them examples of the times that didn't result in a bidding war? Because I'm being honest. It doesn't always work. It *usually* works, and works beautifully. But nothing works perfectly 100 per cent of the time. Why pretend otherwise? If it doesn't, you go with your backup plan. I show them a dozen cases where the backup plan delivered all they were asking for. They're good with that.

They're also good with my honesty, and my confidence. I don't list high and go lower. I list low and get higher. A lot of agents will give the seller the price they want to hear, regardless of how high it is. Then, after they've locked them in for 60 or 90 days, they'll work on them to reduce the price. Talk about poisoning a relationship and inviting bad word-of-mouth for yourself!

Remember: the first question buyers ask is, "How much are you asking?" The second question they ask is, "How long has the home been listed?"

The longer the house has been on the market, the less likely it is you'll get your price, let alone a bidding war. "Why is no one buying this house? What's wrong with this home?" That's what buyers think when a house just sits there for months.

I'd rather tell the seller the truth and risk losing the listing. Because eventually, when the wrong strategy doesn't work out, and the dishonest agent fails them, they'll remember—and come back to—the honest agent.

Up Close

Let's look at how this process works up close and in detail. What *exactly* are the steps? Where do we bring the bidders and the buyers together?

I start by listing the house and setting a date to review offers. Usually it's quick. If the listing date is on July 31, the offer date may be scheduled for August 7. I set a time of 7 p.m.

I have the seller sign a seller's direction form which states that the seller's instruction to me, as their agent, is that they will only entertain offers on a specific date at a specific time.

Now I'm not excluding consideration of pre-emptive offers (or 'bully offers'). The bully offer rules are that if a buyer wants to bid now and not wait until the bidding date, they're welcome to submit their offer right away—but the offer must be significantly higher than the asking price; it must be accompanied by a bank draft; and there must be zero conditions attached to the offer. Upon receipt of such an offer, I require up to 24 hours to alert all the agents who have been patiently waiting. If they wish to compete, they can try to beat the early price, but it will be on the same terms—a significantly higher price, a bank draft, and no conditions.

This sometimes ticks agents off. We said the bids would go in a week, and we're not waiting. But my job isn't to make other agents happy—it's to make my client happy, to serve my client the best I can. I'm preserving my seller's right to consider all offers at any time. Why shouldn't they? After all, it's their home!

If we don't get a bully offer, everything proceeds as planned. As the bidding date approaches, agents call and tell me they plan to make an offer. As soon as I get and register an offer, I immediately broadcast the news to the entire network, including any and all agents and buyers who have seen the property. I don't disclose the terms of the offer, or where it came from. I do maintain strict records as required by law throughout. It's very important to be transparent in this process and maintain an ethical environment.

When the offer date arrives, I encourage each agent to bring their buyer with them. I facilitate this by giving each of the agents a space within the office where they and their client can sit in a private room, and discuss developments as the process proceeds.

It always surprises me how many listing agents don't allow buyer's agents to be present at these things. I do it the other way around. The buyer isn't permitted to meet with my seller, but I give the buyer's agent the opportunity to come in for a few minutes and tell us a little bit about their buyer and their offer. This way, they can honestly report back to their buyer that they made the offer and made the best case they could to get that offer accepted.

The bidding rules are simple. Anyone who shows up must have a bank draft or a certified cheque in the deposit amount along with his or her offer. (We don't want to confirm a sale and find out the next day the buyer can't pay for it.)

I also make it known there are no special arrangements between myself and the seller on commission reduction, or any incentives to accept an offer from a purchaser who's asked me to represent them and make their offer. That's just too close to conflict-of-interest for me to feel comfortable with it. I couldn't do auction-style bidding if I even appeared to be acting unfairly and unethically. I don't want a buyer's agent thinking, "Whatever we offer, Faisal's going to beat it by a dollar." Every offer is registered, recorded and open to later review to ensure legal transparency.

Now here's where it gets interesting.

Only the listing agent—in this case, myself (and of course the seller)—knows what all the other offers are. Let's say, for instance, that we're asking $500,000, and the top offer is $550,000, and all the rest are $525K or less.

We don't simply take the best offer on the table and stop there. We go back to the agents who offered less and tell them we're considering another, stronger offer. But if they want to stay in the running, they can. We simply ask them to make a better offer—to do better.

We don't go back to the best offer. We don't want to risk losing that offer. We've received their offer, and it may be the best offer we get. We leave it where it is. Why would we throw away the top offer? We have it in hand along with the draft, and we can secure a sale the moment the client agrees to it.

But I advise the client to let things roll, because we've arranged things to allow the other agents to come back with a better offer. That's exactly what I tell those agents "We have an acceptable offer. You can walk away, but if your client still wants the house, you're welcome to make a better offer and come back for another round."

The goal, of course, is for us to beat the best offer with one that's even better (and maybe beat that one with an offer that's even better than that). And that's what happens. A rejected bidder who had initially offered $525,000 suddenly comes back with an offer of $560,000. Now we go back to the best offer we didn't touch, and ask them to do better. If they come back at $565,000, we go back to the offer that came back at $560,000 and ask them again to do better. We do this until everyone who has less than the best offer on the table decides to walk away.

This works. It's obvious why it works, isn't it? The moment the buyers are there with a draft and offer in hand, it signals that *they want to buy*. They haven't come simply to be told that we accepted some other offer. Mentally too, they know how competitive bidding works. They come prepared to bid higher. They may not be prepared to bid that offer up to the moon. But if paying a few thousand more, or even tens of thousands more, gets them that property, many buyers will go for it. So what happens? The price of that home shoots up!

Now price alone isn't the only consideration. We also look at the terms of the offer. I may recommend to my seller that he or she take a lesser offer if no conditions or contingencies are attached to that offer. Say we got an offer that met our target price of $550,000 in cash, with no conditions and an acceptable closing date. There's another offer for $555,000. It's slightly more, but that slightly higher offer is dependent on a home inspection, or the sale of the buyer's property, or the buyer getting bank financing, something she or he hasn't secured yet. Sorry, the risk is just too high. We've met our target price. There's no good reason to let the deal possibly fall through.

And sometimes it's not a 'risk' at all, but a scam. An unscrupulous agent may make a ridiculously high offer planning to withdraw it whatever the result of the home inspection. After all, by then the auction is over; the competing bidders have all gone away. The agent and buyer say that the results of the inspection don't justify their earlier offer. The agent reduces the price to $525,000. This time it's the only offer on the table. Take it or leave it.

That isn't a gamble I advise my sellers to take.

Leading the Journey

Everything I've said here I say to the seller at their kitchen table.

Trust me: they're spellbound.

Why wouldn't they be? Most sellers have no idea what a real estate agent goes through to sell a home. When you actually sit down with them and explain the things you're going to do for them, why it's needed and why it makes sense, and most of all why they're going to get better returns than they ever imagined, all because of this unique process they've never heard of, they're amazed. More importantly: they're sold.

They get it—they understand how and why all of this is designed to get them the maximum price. Of course they go for it!

My brand marketing gets them to pick up the phone and call Faisal Susiwala. But when we sit down and they decide to hire me, they're not buying me: they're buying my process. My system—the Susiwala System. And they *should* buy my System. It works!

Why does the presentation approach I use to present that System work? Mostly because it makes rational sense. The track record is there, the logic is there. My presentation is not one long-tired repetition of "List with me, list with me, list with me, I'm so-o charming." It's about what I'm going to do, about how I'm going to market their property, about why my strategies work and have worked, about what kind of results they can anticipate, and what sort of time frame they can expect. I'm not pressuring them to close at all costs. I'm not pressuring them at all! I'm simply showing and explaining why my System will get *them* what *they* want in the fastest, best way possible.

But there is a special twist I give in my presentation, and it's critical when it comes to making it a success.

I've mentioned it before. I call it 'Leading the Journey."

When I go through the comparables with a prospect, when I talk about how many people will see their advertised house, it's numbers. Numbers matter tremendously, but if all you do is recite numbers, you'll strike out. People want to see themselves making a successful deal. They want to see themselves going through that process and coming out on top. So when I present the process, I do it in a way that lets me walk them through a story—*their* story, a story featuring them, in which we both go together through the whole thing, till, at the end, they have a good deal more money than they ever thought they could get.

At the end of my presentation, what are the sellers thinking? Not, "Hmm, that makes sense." They're thinking, "My God! We're getting $50,000 more than we expected! We could go on vacation! We could put a down payment on a second house and become investors!"

In the beginning it's the seller who initially leads me on a journey, a journey that starts when they take me through a tour of their home, and tell me about their property and its history, and show me everything they've had done to it, and share with me the hopes and expectations they have for that sale—and for their future after the sale.

I follow that lead. I show them a picture in which they've gone through the home-selling process faster and more profitably than they ever imagined, in a way that's met their every expectation—and exceeded it! I tell that story from the very beginning, from the first social media ad to the final high bid. I trace them through this story every inch of the way, and I build myself into it at every step; I'm at their side throughout the journey. I'm an irreplaceable part of that story. I'm with them throughout the journey until their home is sold.

It's a good, honest, compelling story, and at the very end of it, they're the winners. We both are.

The story is so compelling that they want to go on the journey. So they take the first step. They make me their agent.

Then together we go on to make the story real.

A Word About Commissions

Commissions.

For most agents that's the worst part of the meeting. They go to great lengths not to bring it up at all. They play this scenario in their head:

Seller: "So what do you charge for commission, you gouging little worm?"

Agent: "Uh—um—ah—five percent, maybe? But I'd be happy with four. Or three. Or even…"

Seller (roaring): "*Five percent!* You bloody *thief!* Get out of my house! *Get out!*"

The agent flees as the seller, brandishing a horsewhip, chases him out to the curb, while the seller's children and the neighbours throw stones from the windows.

As usual, I do things differently.

Seller resistance to agent commissions happens for two simple reasons.

The first is that the seller doesn't know what the agent is doing to sell the house. Five per cent of $500,000 just to stick a sign on the lawn? Of course a seller who gets service like that is angry. He or she should be angry. I'd be angry too! There really are agents who don't do much more than that, and if agents who do more don't explain what it is exactly that they do to earn their commission, the seller can't be blamed for assuming the worst.

The second reason is that, even if the agent is active and skilled and clearly gives his or her very best, a percentage of the sale of a house can amount to a lot of money, and no one likes to say goodbye to a lot of money. People like to make money, not wave farewell to it.

My system addresses these problems directly and perfectly.

I describe what I'll be doing for the seller from start to finish. It's a lot; it's smart and effective, it's complex and it takes skill. They know beyond a doubt that they're getting value for their dollar.

More than that: they know the value they're getting will get them more money than would otherwise have been the case. This part of it is a no-brainer if you state it clearly. If I can sell their house for $50,000 over asking, are they going to cry if I get $10,000 or $15,000 of that? I've just put $35,000 they never expected to have into their pocket! Agreeing to my commission doesn't cost them $15,000. It makes them $35,000. Ask a seller if they'd like to make $35,000. They'll say yes!

Now how do I time that during a presentation? Early on. I never wait for sellers to bring up the matter of my commission. I do it, and I do it before the seller asks. I take charge of the presentation from the start, and I raise the issue as soon as I see the sellers see how much effort will be put into selling their home, and how much they will profit from it.

It doesn't generally come up until after they see themselves making that extra $50,000, and at that point you'd be surprised how smoothly it goes. Blowback is rare. Why should they resist? I've already shown them I can do it, that I've done it many times before. I've led them on their journey, so that, in their mind, they've already gotten $50,000 more than they thought they'd have. It's funny how, with that kind of money, a single percentage point difference from another Realtor becomes almost a moot point.

In my region, listing commissions have gone steadily down, from 6 per cent to five per cent to 4 per cent, even to three per cent. People often don't realize the agent may not receive even that. When an agent receives a commission, he has to pay the cooperating broker. The broker usually takes half, sometimes even more. Out of that the agent also must pay his or her marketing costs for the property, travel expenses, taxes, office fees, professional fees, and so on. That half becomes a quarter. Maybe less.

That doesn't leave a lot; and let's be honest: no one wants to work for next-to-nothing.

A buyer's broker or cooperating broker wants to see two per cent minimum going to them on every deal. If they don't get that, they don't even want to show your listing.

So put yourself in the shoes of someone who is charging three per cent commission, giving two per cent to the cooperating broker, and then only gets one per cent—and then has to split even that with the buyer's agent, who's invested no money in marketing, done no strategic planning, and has spent none of their own money.

Less than one per cent to do something that can involve weeks, maybe months of work, that requires steep cash expenditures on the agent's own part, and that sometimes may not pan out at all.

What kind of motivation does an agent like that have to do a good job? None. Zero. That's why agents put up a sign on the property, and do next to nothing else. They're not even trying to make money on the deal. They want to use the seller's lawn to display their advertising. Maybe it will get them a lead actually worth servicing!

I explain the commission process to the seller. I don't do it to complain about how little real estate agents make. I do it so they'll understand that what they think is a 'great' low commission all but guarantees them poor to no service and, in the end, far lower returns.

My commission rate is five per cent. I maintain that five per cent by demonstrating value. If the buyer's agent is satisfied with two per cent as a cooperating broker, that's what I'll pay them. I get three per cent of that, which allows me to allocate even more to marketing and overhead.

Agents ask me how I can get away with a five per cent commission. "Faisal, you're so expensive!"

Most sellers don't even bother to ask. Why should they? I've already shown them the value I'm bringing them. I've already shown them what I will do for them and how my unique marketing and strategy will get them superior results.

If a seller asks why my commission is so high, I'll joke and say, "Because I'm worth it." But it's not a joke. I *am* worth it: my presentation has shown them exactly why I'm worth it. I'm better, period, not because of who I am but because my *system*, the Susiwala System, is better. I've shown them where their money is going: into advertising their home, into getting their property on all the social media platforms, into connecting with buyers throughout the region. What they're paying out when they pay me is less than what they're getting. *Way* less!

It's simple math. Do you want to get an extra $50,000, even if it means paying me an extra $5,000 more? Or do you want to *not* get $50,000, and pay an additional $1,000 or $2,000 for worse service that may ensure you *never* get your target price?

Wrapping It Up

The case I make to sellers is bulletproof. I've done everything in my power to make sure the results they get from me are the best results possible. It's all so clear and transparent they can't possibly miss it. I don't want to put a seller in the awkward position of having to ask questions about commission, or about any stage of the home-selling process about which they're unfamiliar. My goal during the presentation is to anticipate and make sure I've already answered any questions they could possibly have.

So finally I proceed to the last step in my presentation: I package everything that I've shown them, put it neatly into a folder, slide it over to the seller, and thank them for inviting me to their home.

I tell them all the information in the package is for them to keep. I tell them that I've appreciated the opportunity to present to them. I add that I respect their privacy, and let them know I've been on the receiving end of pushy salespeople too, and haven't liked it either.

"So, respectfully," I conclude, "if you have any further questions, please feel free to call. Otherwise you'll never hear from me again, unless you wish to contact me."

What???

This is exactly what I do each and every time. I call it the NBC approach: Never Be Closing. It makes my real estate colleague's heads explode.

What are we told in real estate from Day One? A.B.C.— Always Be Closing. "Mr. and Mrs. Seller, if I give you a number you're happy with, will you sign with me today? Right now, this minute? If I tell you what you want to hear, will you cancel the other agents? Will you cancel the other appointments you have scheduled? Will you sign with me right now? This second? Here's the paperwork, Mr. and Mrs. Seller! Here's the pen!"

I've actually heard of agents who will drop their pen so the seller will pick it up and be that much closer to signing. This kind of—I won't use the word I'm thinking of—is a pathetic, awful, manipulative, coercive way of doing business and, worst of all, it doesn't work. It alienates sellers. It irritates them and puts them off. Who falls for an approach like that? I've come to think the only reason it ever works is because all the agents the seller sees act the same way. They don't have a choice. I suppose they pick the least awful agent of the bunch.

Never be closing. Never!

When I've made my case to the seller—my air-tight, bulletproof case—I don't go for the close. I thank them for their time, and I wrap it up on the spot and go.

In most cases this is the point where the seller jumps up and says, "Where are you going? We're ready to sign!"

Well, of course they are. That happens so often that I've come to expect it. In anticipation, I've already had my staff prepare a hard copy of the listing agreement in my briefcase.

I thank them for choosing me and take out those forms and present them to the seller.

I tell them we have everything all filled out, and I review the terms of the contract with them.

I fill out the form that outlines the critical dates, including the listing video, photos, the offer date, personal information, et cetera.

I thank them for their trust and confidence and we begin our journey.

Sometimes the sheer shock of me thanking them and packing up everything and telling them they'll never see me again creates a situation where they don't ask me to sign the listing that very moment. They're too stunned. Sometimes I actually walk out the door before they run out and call me back in because they're ready to sign.

But if I'm already in my car on the way to the next presentation, I call my listing coordinator Alicia and ask her to send them the document and have them e-sign it and send it back. In anticipation of a successful presentation, I've already had Alicia electronically upload the entire listing agreement to a DocuSign file, which she can simply email to the seller and have them execute.

Listing secured. Thanks, technology and thank you Alicia!

Remember, though: the signature is only the first step on the journey. The journey really began earlier, when you described it to them, and when they visualized the journey's end. Again, that's something I picked up from Tony Robbins. He'd look out at a gigantic audience and tell all of them to close their eyes, and then imagine being where they wanted to be, where they really wanted to be. Soon the faces in that audience would be ecstatic. Tears would be falling from their eyes. Their faces would be lit up with laughter and joy.

That's what I do. During the house tour I let my sellers tell me where they want to be, and during my presentation I show them how and why I can take them there. Then I describe the picture of them being there, and let them take pure joy in the feeling of having arrived.

I never put them on the spot. I never pressure them to decide. I present the decision as already made and show them the journey they're about to take and how happy they are that it's worked out so great for them!

But that's *after* I make my case, and *after* I show them that I can deliver. No, it's not about giving them a rosy best-case scenario. Just drawing a pretty picture's not enough. You must make it happen. You also must be honest about the potholes along the way. Nothing goes perfectly. If you raise their hopes too high, then even a great job disappoints. That's why the presentation is so compelling: it's not fluff, it's a step-by-step realistic roadmap, a blueprint for their success. The vision inspires. The blueprint convinces.

Set a mark you're sure you can hit. Better yet: set a mark that you can exceed. Because when you do even better than expectation, that's when they really start singing your praises.

That's when you create not just customers but advocates— and more than advocates: evangelists.

Lessons

I won't spend too much time summarizing the process I've described above. It's all there in precise detail. Put it into practice, and you won't be sorry.

As for the overall picture? If you want listings—market, market, market. Target a tight, specific location, one you know and one you serve. Don't market intrusively, but do market everywhere: effective marketing is saturation marketing. Put your face and phone number and what you do every place you can. Build referral networks—what I call 'multi-level partnering'—so it's win-win for everyone. Utilize competent staff to do the research and prep work for you, so you can free up your time and focus on your most profit-generating activities. List low, not high. Cultivate bidders, not buyers. Lead the journey: make the sellers feel like they've already chosen you and gotten the results they dream of, instead of twisting their arms and pressuring them to close.

These techniques work. They made me successful. Very successful.

But once again: it isn't *me* getting the results: it's the *System*, the actions, the principles behind what I do.

I've taken the time to go into really fine detail in this chapter because there's nothing more important to real estate success than getting the listing, and I want you to see how my System works in practice.

The main takeaway for you, though, is something I said at the very beginning: take the time to look at what you're doing. Ask yourself what works, what doesn't work, and what you can change to make it work better.

I went from being a good real estate agent to being the top selling real estate agent in the nation not because I did what everyone was telling me to do. If I did, I'd still be planting signs on lawns, cold calling, door knocking, and trying (and failing) to close.

I became a success because now and then I was willing to do things differently, and sometimes I noticed that it worked. When it did, I kept doing it. I kept tinkering with it too, constantly trying to make it better.

I've given that approach a name and made it a key element of the Susiwala System: "Modelling Excellence Creatively." Don't think I'm bragging when I tell you how much applying that principle has made me. I'm embarrassed—embarrassed that it took me so much time for it to sink in.

For some people it never sinks in. They take something that doesn't work, and just keep doing it over and over anyway. That's the wrong way to do things. Look at what works and build on that.

Each agent's situation is different, and I'm sure there are ways to improve on what I've done. Please share them with me when you discover them—share them with everyone. Those who are sharp will take them up and give you back something even better. Remember: "Give and you will receive." A thinking network is the best way possible to build a lifelong profit-generating one.

When I started seriously thinking about what worked for me and how to do it better, my business took off. In this chapter, I've tried to give you a tight, detailed, crystal-clear description of how those different approaches work in practice.

Study them in detail. Put them to use. Believe me: they work.

Chapter 10

ON THE EDGE

I attend a good many real estate talks and conferences. Often, I'll run into fellow Realtors from the United States. Like most others, they're good people, but they have one quirk: at some point they'll always bring up 2008.

"Oh, just before 2008, prices were exploding. Homes were increasing in value every month. Banks gave mortgages to anyone with a pulse. Everyone was buying. We were all on top of the world. It was incredible!"

Then: "2008! What a disaster. Homes foreclosing. Banks failing. Commissions dying. You couldn't pay a buyer to buy. Getting a mortgage from the bank? Impossible. It was the end of the world!"

Then they'll tell you about their heroic struggle, and how they crawled back up from the edge of the cliff by their bleeding fingernails to post listings once again.

Eventually they'll look over at me and say, "So—how did you handle it?"

And I'll say, "Great. Couldn't have been better. Wonderful years. The year leading up to it was a little challenging. But once 2008 came, I made a bundle."

They look at me like I dropped from Mars.

Let's be clear; 2008—to be precise, two days after Christmas, 2007—was a major turning point in my career. I came as close to going over the edge of a cliff as I had for a long time. My approaches to marketing, getting listings, cultivating bids instead of just offers, building referral networks, emphasizing sellers over buyers, had all come together to make me one of the leading Realtors in the entire nation—and yet I finished the year curled up overnight in a sleeping bag in an empty apartment, wondering if I was about to lose my own house!

It sounds grim, but really it wasn't. I had taken a reasonable risk. Yes, the market had turned around and might yet knock me flat. Whether it did or not, though, whether my investment panned out or not, I still had my career. I still had my reputation, my networks and my brand. I had a system, and financial crisis or not, it was humming like a well-oiled machine. Whatever happened, I'd make it all the way back, and then do even better.

When I was twenty, I didn't have that confidence, and I didn't have my System. The market went down, and I went bankrupt. The next time the market went down, only one sale that year kept my annual salary from being lower than a fast food cashier's.

But that was then. Good times or bad, I now knew how to deal with both, how to keep moving up, spotting opportunities and taking advantage of the situation, whatever it was. That's what this chapter is about.

So how *did* I deal with 2008?

Well, in the first place, I had the great good luck of living in the great nation of Canada, where there are checks and balances. In many ways, Canada's financial system was the envy of the world back then, at least among the G7. There are lot of real estate people who absolutely hate all government, and see it only as a source of mindless regulations, petty interventions and horrible fees. There's some truth to that, but there's also value in orderly rules and reasonable oversight. Especially in times of crisis.

The Canadian government applies several limits and a lot of restrictions when it comes to banks. You can't finance a deal 100 per cent. You can't over-finance a deal. There are verifications that have to happen. You can't fund everything with borrowed money. You need to have some skin in the game, which I think is a very good principle.

As a result, Canada didn't get hit all that hard in 2008. There were buffers and insulation in place to soften the blow. Prices did drop—12 per cent to 15 per cent over the course of a year. That hurt, of course, but it wasn't fatal. And it was short-lived. By the end of 2009 and into 2010 prices started bouncing back.

Interest rates began going up too. That was a problem. But then I have a theory about interest rates—I see a kind of cycle happening every four or five years where the banks fear-monger and start edging interest rates up quite deliberately. Why? Because it starts a knee-jerk reaction among frightened homeowners. It scares them into wanting to lock in their mortgage payments at that higher rate before it goes even higher still. When enough people lock in their payments at a higher rate, the banks have secured their money at that higher rate. They're happy. So, they drop the rates again.

Personally, I think a homeowner is better off riding through the storm on a variable rate. It's very rare that rates hit double digits before they sink back.

The bottom line, though, was that things weren't so bad here. They were a little scary at times, but that was more media panic than anything going on in the Canadian market. So, far from seeing the 2008 housing crisis as a disaster, I took it as an opportunity. From a marketing perspective. I saw the real estate scene during and after 2008 as a prime time for me to kick things up a notch.

If you do what everyone does, you'll get what everyone gets —average results at best. If you want extraordinary results, you must do things extraordinarily differently. Of course, you need to keep a close eye on the results you're getting. What you're doing has to work! But when what everyone else is doing doesn't work, applying a little thoughtful creativity to your own contrarian response can do wonders. Everyone runs for cover when there's a storm: I ran against the grain, like I generally do. Everybody saw prices falling and tamped things down: I ramped up my advertising and shifted it into high gear.

You see, good times or bad, some people will still need to sell their homes and other people will still be looking to buy them. You have to make yourself visible to those people—you have to make yourself known by them, either personally or through your marketing and your brand.

What do you need to get you through a recession? More than anything, you need branding. When times are tough, people shift to the experts. So when you brand yourself as the go-to person in an industry, you're the one that will get attention during those times. You're going to be the person getting business.

That's why it's important to market yourself as an expert—as *the* expert. And not just market yourself as the expert, but to actually be that person. To be that brand. To be the person who could provide solutions, especially when times are challenging, I

had marketed myself as exactly that, as one way of monetizing my licence. I'd made a point of presenting it as a mark of expertise.

In 2008 and 2009, when times were rocky, talking to an expert could make a huge emotional difference to people. I'd get calls saying, "I just lost my job. Can you sell my house?" That's not a call I ever want to get. Home ownership should be a positive experience. Speaking from experience, no one should ever lose their home. That home should be the basis of your financial future. But if you buy a house with a five per cent down payment, and it drops in value 12 per cent, you're upside-down in debt. You'll be in debt even *after* you sell your house. That's crippling.

My expertise made a difference. I was able to show some people how their homes could be refinanced, not lost. I could talk to banks on their behalf. I could get some of them enough money to have a good solid base to start over.

I could also have sold fast and cheap, and taken the money and run. But no—no, I couldn't do that. I knew what Mr. Menary would have thought of me if I'd done something like that, and I knew what I would think of myself deep down if I'd behaved that way. I honestly wanted to give every person who called on me the best outcome possible. I tried my best.

In the end, I benefitted more. That's the thing about core principles like reciprocity and 'giving to get.' Once you help people in a desperate bind, they never forget. Sometimes I took on customers that other Realtors wouldn't touch, and put in more work than my commission really justified. My friends in the business constantly dumped on me for it.

"Faisal, you're crazy," some of my colleagues would say. "You're not making money."

Not at first, true. But the people I helped went on to give me future business and to recommend me to many other clients. When you're doing the right thing, you're doing the smart thing.

But there's a way in which people in need are just like people who are flush with income: they both need to know who you are, and what you do, and that you're an expert—the *expert*, the person to go to. For that to happen, you need to market yourself.

But when there's a recession, business dries up. To most Realtors, less business means less money to put into marketing. Their advertising dries up. That's exactly the wrong thing to do.

Every market situation, good or bad, has opportunities. In 2008, opportunities were everywhere. So if I saw an advertising spot that wasn't filled, I filled it. If there was an area that was under-serviced, I serviced it. I took ad space wherever I could get it—and suddenly there was a lot more available, and at lower prices, too.

When everyone hunkered down, I pushed to become even more of a name. When other Realtors retired, or let their licence lapse, I picked up their business. The public responded. And why not? I was there. I was unobtrusive but I was available, and I let people know it.

Now, if my system had been a little further along at the time, I wouldn't have just picked up an abandoned client or two from Realtors who decided to throw in the towel: I'd have been buying those Realtors' full databases left, right and centre, collecting them like cherries off a tree. But I wasn't quite there yet.

So instead I went off on a tangent and ended up staring over my personal cliff's edge, but not after experiencing some incredible highs, and a few disheartening lows.

Maintaining a positive attitude, along with a willingness to act and even dare, meant that over Christmas 2007, I had to sleep on the floor of a plaza/apartment development that was nearing completion. I can smile at those three memorable days, which were followed by one of the best New Year's of my life. Read on to see why.

Here's how it happened:

Back in January 2002, I was in Montreal with my wife and son when I saw a listing come up on a property at 685 Myers Road. That address won't mean anything to you, but I knew the land well and had been keeping an eye on it for years.

It was four acres on the south edge of Cambridge where I just knew a lot of growth was destined to happen. But although it had been on my radar, I knew the owner wasn't interested in selling. He had a little garden centre there, and a kind of dilapidated old barn that he'd turned into a convenience store. He was willing to sell me half the acreage, but he wanted to hold on to the garden centre.

Well, I wanted the whole thing, and said so. He said I could have it—for a million dollars.

A million dollars? Though I hated to do it, I walked away.

But suddenly, there in Montreal, I saw the listing pop up, and it was for the whole parcel. Price: $550,000. What was up?

I called the agent.

"Angela," I said. "Is this for sale? The whole thing?"

It turned out that it was: the owner had passed away, and his wife had no interest in keeping the property going.

I sent in my offer for $535,000 immediately, and it got accepted.

There was only one problem. I didn't have enough cash money to buy the whole thing outright. I had a little cash, but not enough; and in Canada, you can't get a mortgage on land.

You see, when it comes to land, the banks, being risk-aversive, always ask themselves, "How is this person going to service the debt?" If it's a duplex or triplex, there's always a potential source of rental income. Money's going to be coming in. That's acceptable. Even physical property all by itself is worth something. You can sell a house or a building. But land? It's just land. It's empty. What are they going to do with that if you can't make the payment? So, in the case of land, you need cash.

The problem with holding real estate is liquidity. You may own a lot of properties, and they may amount to a lot on paper, but property isn't the same as cash. You can't buy a Big Mac with a duplex. You have to sell that duplex first. And your Big Mac can get very, very cold before you finally find a buyer, and close, and get the cheque in the mail.

Still, I wanted that property. It wasn't just that I wanted it for its own sake, which of course, on one level, I did. I could almost see the development that could be built on it. I knew the profit it was capable of generating. But more than that, I wanted to take the step of becoming a developer—a serious real estate investor. I was already a successful agent and broker. I didn't think I would ever put that aside. But I had reached the point where I wanted something more, I wanted to round that achievement out —to expand into new areas, new horizons. Acquiring this property could be the beginning.

So I called a friend, Shaheen, a physician who had only recently started out. He didn't have a lot of ready cash either. His dad was a physician as well—but Dad was putting three children through college. There went his money! Once I explained the situation, both gentlemen could see the potential in the property. They got together, talked, and between the two of them, they figured they could put up a third of the funds needed. Me? After a lot of scraping, I was able to get $200,000 together.

That still left well over $100,000 to go. So, I kept looking.

I called my brother-in-law, Shoaib

"Hey! It's Faisal. Listen, a great real estate opportunity just turned up. It's a $535,000 property. You interested in a piece?"

"Well," he said, "not really... but I could put in 5 per cent."

Every bit helped. I took it. But it still wasn't enough. I just didn't have the funds. Yet with all of these investors coming together, I could feel us getting close. I wanted that property badly.

Then I learned that another developer had bought property surrounding the land I was interested in. He was planning to build 500 homes there. (There are 2,000 homes on the site now). That set me on fire! There were no commercially zoned lots nearby. My four adjacent acres would be the perfect spot for a grocery store or a plaza, even a mini mall with a salon, convenience store, pizza joint, doctor's office or daycare. All those things would be right next door for those new families. All I had to do was build it. Commercial tenants would flock.

I scraped together the last few tens of thousands of dollars any way I could. I borrowed on other properties I had. I took money out of my lines of credit. I pulled together funds in any way possible.

In the end I succeeded, and we managed to buy that property —cash.

Of course, that wasn't the end of the story. It was the beginning. Now I had to develop it!

So I began putting that ball into motion.

I would need tenants for those commercial units to come. I called grocery stores. They were enthusiastic:

"Put a grocery store out there in the middle of nowhere? You're nuts!"

"The people will come," I said.

"Yeah? Call us when they do," they said.

I kept on regardless. I called Victor, a planner who was a neighbour, to plan the entire plaza.

"OK," I said, "here's what I want: I want to build a plaza on this property, but only in the front area here, not the back. I want to leave some space in the back for townhouses. Plus, I want to build a horseshoe around in the back so I can put in a street there later."

Victor, a mild-mannered gentleman looked at me and said, "Well... "

I could tell he was trying to work with my crazy idea, but was quietly thinking "The man's cracked." When he'd mulled it over for a few seconds more, he asked the big question: "Who's going to want to live behind a plaza?"

It was this honesty that's made him my trusted planner, consultant and friend.

"There's always a need for town homes, and for bungalow townhouses," I replied.

"Bungalows?" he said.

"There are a lot of Portuguese people in this area, including seniors. Trust me, those parents and grandparents are going to want to stay near their families and grandchildren, and they aren't going to want to climb steps."

"*But—bungalows?*"

"Bungalows. Do it. Draw up the plans."

He drew up the plans. He also drew up plans for a second floor on top of the plaza for offices, as per my request. He wasn't crazy about the idea. "Nobody's going to want office space over a plaza in that location Faisal," he said. Because he's a creative guy, he added, "But apartments—now that's another story. Let's draw up plans with apartments on the second floor."

I gave him the OK and he did so. When he was done we took the plans to Cambridge City Hall and submitted it to the city planner.

He laughed in our faces.

"Are you serious? *This* is what you want to submit?"

"We're here, aren't we?"

"No, sorry, there is no way the staff are going to recommend this."

"Look," I said. "I'm offering a full commercial area that'll attract businesses and add to your tax base. I'm creating more residences. I'm creating a lot for developing future townhouses. Everybody wins!"

"A mini-mall with apartments on top? Are you serious? There's no way this will get through Council."

"Well, we're submitting it. Present it to Council, and we'll see what they say."

He presented it.

Council approved it.

Hooray! Game over! We won!

Except for one problem.

I had used up all the money I had to buy the land, draw up the plans, and get them approved.

Now I didn't have any money left to build the place!

But, like I've said, you have to have the proper mindset. There's no point in dwelling on a problem. What you need to dwell on is the solution to that problem.

What was I missing?

I let the back of my head work on it while my body ran around and got everything lined up properly. I got the property. I got approval. Now I wanted to build a plaza on the property. How much exactly was the price tag? I needed exact estimates. I called builders.

The best estimate came in at $2.3 million dollars.

That was exactly $2.3 million more than I had. I didn't have a cent. All my funds were tied up, all my properties were tied up, all the cash I had (and extra money from lines of credit, which I now owed) had gone into buying the land and paying fees.

So, what were my options? The banks wouldn't lend me anything.

However, the banks *did* say they'd give me construction financing.

But only if I had tenants.

"I don't have a plaza yet, how am I going to get tenants?"

"We don't know, but if you build it and get some leases signed, we'll think about giving you a mortgage."

This was kind of like *Field of Dreams*; I knew that if we built it, the tenants would come.

"If I can get the tenants to sign leases before the plaza is built, will you consider giving me the loan then?"

They thought about it.

"If you can get the tenants to commit to sign leases, yes. We'll give you the loan."

Now I had a new challenge—how do I get people to sign a lease for a building when there's no building?

Well, I leaned on my knowledge and experience. Big time. I remembered that when I was starting out buying properties, I would send people flyers.

"Hello neighbour! Looking for a home? Looking to sell? This choice little duplex could be just the thing." Or: "I've got buyers looking for a home in this neighbourhood. Are you interested in selling?"

I sat down and designed a flyer. At the top it said, "Wanted," and underneath was a beautifully rendered artist's conception of the finished plaza and apartments, and prominently displayed underneath that, was a list: Day Care. Pizza. Physician. Pharmacy. Hair Salon. Convenience Store. Veterinary Clinic. Any service I thought might one day go into that plaza.

Then I sent it to 3,000 homes—not businesses, homes— inside a three-kilometre radius of the plaza. There were seven commercial units to lease. I sent the flyers out on a Monday.

By Friday all of the commercial units had been reserved. A dentist had spoken for one of the commercial spaces immediately. A Day Care called and wanted to take one quarter of the whole plaza! (Naturally: there were thousands of homes in the area, and more to come, and not a single day care centre. It was a no-brainer. Would I put aside some open garden space for a play centre too? Done.). A variety store came in, and a hairdresser too—and all these people signed leases. It was January 2007, and I told them their spots would very likely be ready by summer.

I went back to the bank proudly with the signed reservations.

"Well..." said the banker with a shrug, "we've sort of reconsidered. No loan."

"*What?*"

"But tell you what. We'll give you up to 50 per cent financing on it, but you have to get the other 50 per cent first. And you also need to sign letters of credit. Additionally you'll have to sign this, and sign that, and, oh, did we mention you'll have to pay us $25,000 just to look at your deal? We have to do appraisals, as well, for an additional fee, of course, and we're going to have to take a two per cent management fee from you, yada yada yada..."

I rolled my eyes. What had I signed up for? This was a nightmare. It was nothing but red tape, at $1,000 an inch. All I wanted to do was build a little plaza! Was it necessary to go through all this just to find someone to start knocking some hammers and nails and boards together? Even if I somehow got through all these fees and hassles, I still didn't have the funds I needed. Where was the money going to come from?

I lay in bed that night turning the deal over and over in my mind.

And suddenly it hit me.

Builders.

What did I need the money for? To pay builders to build the plaza. But did they absolutely have to have it up front? What if I could find a builder willing to wait till the project was built before collecting his cheque?

I'd have to make it worth their while—I might have to pay a bit more or take on some conditions. But if it got the plaza built, once rental and leasing income started streaming in, it would be a win.

Brilliant! What a great idea!

I called my attorney.

"That's a bad idea," he said.

"I've got the land. I can put it up as collateral."

"I've never heard of a builder doing anything like that."

"Look. It's the same principle as a mortgage lender. I'm giving you my home as collateral. You're putting a lien on my home. If I don't pay you, you take my home. It's the same thing. I'm saying to the builder, I'll give you my land as collateral. You build on the land that I have signed over to you, and when I pay you upon completion of the plaza, you hand me the keys and remove the lien. I'll even pay you more money than you would get otherwise. If I don't make the payment on time, you get the land and an entire plaza-apartment complex, complete with signed tenants waiting to move in."

How could the builder say no?

The first three builders I approached said no.

"They build houses," said my attorney. "They don't hold rental properties. They'll never go for it."

I wouldn't give up, however, and approached a fourth builder who was intrigued. (They were probably thinking: "This kid is biting off far more than he can chew, and we're going to end up scoring an entire plaza.")

The builder went and talked to his partner. They came back and gave me a list of prices for the various things they could do. I handed it back.

"Look," I said. "I don't want a monthly invoice from you. I don't want to see a stream of bills saying I need to pay for all these separate items. I'm going to sign my land over to you right now as collateral. You put a lien on it. If I don't pay you by the appointed time, it's all yours. Till then I want you to agree to cover all those items and details."

I did that to take all the stress and pressure and nagging details right off my shoulders. I could then focus on the plans and getting everything done.

"And," I added, "I also want you to build this."

I took out my plans and rolled them open.

"Here are my leases and letters of intent from people already set to move in," I said. "I'm also planning to build five apartments atop the plaza. I'll have them signed before you're finished. Can you build this for me?"

They left and talked privately some more.

When they returned, they spelled out the details. The cost to build it would be $2.3 million, but they also had to factor in their interest and a few other things. My premium meant another $200,000, and on and on it went.

In the end the total cost came to $2.5 million.

If I was good with that, it was a deal.

"Oh, and you'll have to pay us out in full upon completion. If not, we take it over."

"It's a deal," I said, and we shook.

Soon construction began and my plaza was on its way to becoming a reality! Every day more and more of the units started going up. As I checked out each one, part of me was in heaven. It was more than the money I knew the project would bring. This was my biggest development to date, and I felt heroic, like some great Ayn Rand architect, a builder of communities.

Of course, there were glitches. Things took longer than expected. They always do. The date kept being pushed further back, and soon it looked like the builders wouldn't have it ready till December.

But when it was finally ready, they'd hand over the keys. On that day, I had better be prepared to hand them the money. Or else I'd be facing a total loss.

By December, though, the banks were getting nervous. We were nearly into 2008, the year the housing market collapsed in the U.S. and the Great Recession began. American banks were teetering on the brink. Some would shortly be going entirely out of business. Even Canadian banks, strong as they were, began feeling the oncoming tremors. They were no longer lending money quite as readily. My future tenants were enthusiastic, ready and waiting to move in, but the sentiment throughout the financial world was turning darker and darker.

I needed their financing to pay the builder at the end of construction, and I thought I had nailed it. With the builders building the plaza, and the tenants all signed, I had worked out a deal with Toronto Dominion Bank. They had agreed to fund me. That, I thought, was that.

Then the bank took another look at those residential apartments above the plaza, and decided that, at such a delicate time, funding one too many residential properties was just a tad unwise.

Out of the blue they contacted me. "Sorry. We initially agreed to finance a commercial property, but those apartments mean your property is now mixed-use, commercial and residential. We don't want to do mixed-use right now. Goodbye."

"Are you kidding me?" I said.

They weren't kidding me. The microscopic fine print in our contract let them out of our arrangement. I was left high and dry.

I couldn't believe it. I'd been working on the project for a year. I'd pulled in partners, secured tenants and signed leases. I put every spare penny I could into the project.

And now, just when it was at the point of being finished, I was going to lose it all?

No way!

Now this was at the end of November. The builders had finally settled on a day when they would be 100 per cent finished: December 27. On that day I would get the keys, and they would get a cheque.

Or not.

I had less than a month to scrape up $2.5 million.

Well, I was *scrambling*. $2.5 million! I called everyone I knew. Every mortgage broker I knew. Every lender I knew.

Finally, I reached out to a friend of mine, Naveed, who worked at Royal Bank. He heard me out and said, "Listen. We have a commercial lending branch. It's not a bank, it's an insurance company. It's called Royal Bank Insurance. They may charge you a hefty premium. In fact they will charge you with a hefty premium. But, I'm sure they'll at least look at this deal. Mind you, they may hit you with bond rates and not bank rates…"

I didn't know what that meant. I didn't care.

"Sign me up!"

The next day I met with gentlemen from Royal Bank Insurance. My friend was right. They said, "We may be able to work something out. But first we need to see full occupancy and a final occupancy permit from the city stating that the building is completed and passed inspection."

"I've got tenants and full occupancy," I said, "I've got all these units rented."

"The commercial units aren't enough. We want to see the five residential units rented as well."

"Well, how am I going to do that? I can't give people the keys. I don't have occupancy yet. The builders haven't signed the apartments over to me yet."

"That's up to you. Give us a full occupancy permit, and full occupancy, and it's a deal."

"But—"

"And one more thing."

"There's more?"

"We want you to put up your personal home for collateral."

"My home?"

"The plaza isn't a going concern yet, Mr. Susiwala. Some of your tenants may cancel or try to get out of their contracts. We need to be sure our loan is covered."

Back then my personal home was worth around 2 million dollars. All my other holdings were in land. I was financed up to the hilt. I literally had no other cash.

So, what could I do?

I took their offer and put up my home as collateral.

By this time, it was well into December. At this point I was tearing my hair out. Where was I going to get five people to rent an apartment they couldn't yet occupy, in the middle of December, with the holiday season around the corner? I pulled out all the stops, sent flyers everywhere, marketed myself blind —and got five people.

By then it was the 23rd of December. I had to have the money by the 27th or it would be all over. Four days to go and I still hadn't gotten the advance from the bank. But it was in the bag. All I needed was to get full occupancy approval from the city.

I went to talk to the city inspector in person.

"What do I need to get occupancy? Tell me." (If they'd have said, "Give us a pint of your blood," I'd have given them two).

Instead, what they said was: "You have to have an approved interconnected fire detection system connected, and it has to be monitored. Your fire detection system is not connected right now. Until you connect it, we can't give you occupancy."

And so, because the fire alarm wasn't connected, I couldn't get occupancy; and because I couldn't get occupancy, I couldn't get the advance; and because I couldn't get the advance, I was about to lose the half million I'd invested in the land and the entire $2.5 million development project. (I'd already lost a good deal of my sanity).

"Hmm. Say," I said. Why don't I get someone to go over and just connect it right now?"

"You have to have a monitoring company to set it up properly and set up monitoring and surveillance. You have to connect to the fire station as well."

I called one monitoring company after another. It was Christmas. No one was available.

I turned to the city inspector.

"Is there any other way of monitoring a possible fire that the city would accept?"

The gentleman with the city pursed his lips and considered. "One way, yes."

"What?"

"Place a 24-hour-a-day security guard on the premises to monitor the property and make sure the fire alarm isn't going off. That's sufficient. If you don't, we can't issue you the final occupancy."

"Sir, it's two in the afternoon on Christmas Eve. Where am I going to find a security guard at a time like this?"

"No security guard, no occupancy."

I buried my face in my hands, and took a deep breath.

"Look. How about this," I said. "The security guard. Does he need to be specially licensed or anything?"

"No."

"Could I do it?"

"You?"

"Me."

He left to confer, then returned.

"Yes."

As I was thanking God, he added, "But—even if it's you, you must occupy the property around the clock."

I agreed. They issued an interim occupancy permit, I raced to my office and faxed it to RBC to get my funding.

Then I went home and got a sleeping bag and a pillow. I went to the plaza, picked a unit, and spent the next three days of the Christmas holidays sleeping on the floor.

(And the city did check. They sent some guy around regularly. Every single day he would push the buzzer to make sure I was there, my tax dollars at work!)

It wasn't the vacation holiday spot you'd expect for the #1 earning Realtor in all of Canada, but it was memorable.

I didn't care. I was so near the finish that I could taste it. I counted down the final minutes.

Finally, on December 27 at 8 a.m., the security system installers arrived. Soon after, I advised the city inspector that it was connected and monitored, they confirmed and signed off, and gave me full occupancy. Then I went to my solicitor's office and provided the proof of occupancy, which I had already faxed to RBC. He confirmed that they'd received it. They funded the deal later that afternoon. My solicitor issued full payment to my builder.

That was it.

The deal had gone through.

I was now the proud owner (along with my partners) of the land, the plaza, and the apartments.

I thought of the disappointed expressions on the faces of the builders as they received the cheque, and was almost sorry for them. They came so close!

Never have I lost more sleep or had a more stressed-out holiday season than the one I lived through that week.

But I had the happiest New Year imaginable.

Lessons

I never shared this story with my partners in this venture until very recently. They had trusted me, and I wasn't going to let them down, and I didn't. But I had no reason to stress them out, either. I'm sharing this story with you because the next chapter is one of the most important ones in the book if you're a real estate agent—and even if you're not. It's about investing in real estate.

I've said before that, to monetize your agent's licence fully, you need to stop thinking of yourself as a one-time salesperson, and start thinking of yourself as a consultant and advisor—as an investment advisor specifically. Because a house is not just a place to stay: it's equity. It's a means to grow wealth, a way to open lifelong opportunities for the owner. A real estate agent can help shape peoples' lives for the better—provided he or she knows the full range of what property ownership can offer.

I went into detail about my experiences developing a plaza not just to show you a road map, or introduce you to some of the traps, problems, challenges and frustrations you'll encounter along the way on a major deal, but to point out that despite all of these things—it worked. In the end, I became the principal owner of a terrific plaza property that's been generating wonderfully steady profit for everyone concerned.

Was it worth doing? Yes, absolutely! Is it something you could do? Yes! If you're willing to expand your horizons about your skills, knowledge and your profession, and what you personally can do and be.

As I lay there those nights in that sleeping bag, I thought about a lot of things. Was I about to reach the next level as an investor? Or would some last-minute glitch come out of nowhere and shoot me down? At moments I felt like I hadn't come very far at all. After all, there I was—about to have the building and land taken away from me, just like when I was a boy.

Back when I was twenty, I had lost just that kind of big deal. All the money I'd invested vanished. I went bankrupt. Was it coming around full circle? Was I about to take another beating?

No. It wasn't the same thing at all.

I wasn't scared. I wanted that development to go through, of course. Badly. If it didn't, I'd regret it.

But would I go and jump off a cliff? Would I quit real estate? Heck no. It wouldn't be the end. It wouldn't even be a terribly big blip, all things considered.

Sure, losing the plaza development would hurt. But I had other investments. I had a network now, skills, expertise, a reputation, a brand. Taking a loss wouldn't destroy me.

After all, I had a constant stream of income coming in from my real estate practice. That was part of my system: Maintain Your Core.

My system was in operation in other ways too—surrounding me and protecting me like a shield. I had Hedged My Bets: even if the deal went sour, my brokerage and my brand would still be standing. My other investments would still be there. I had backup. After all, I had Leveraged My Licence: that's what had given me credibility with the builders, the banks and the tenants.

What I had done and learned over the course of my real estate career all came together to lift me up to new possibilities, like the plaza development, and at the same time gave me a measure of protection if my first shot at being a developer failed.

If, in the end, the entire venture did fail, I'd just sell more homes, accumulate more capital, and try again. My experience had given me the knowledge, reputation and the connections to let me analyze this deal, assemble the funding, arrange to hire the builders and find the right financial backers. I saw that the deal would work, and how and why it would work, and I was able to put my vision across clearly enough to assemble a team of people to help me make it a reality. If the deal had failed, it would set me back, but it wouldn't knock me out. And what it had taught me—good and bad—fed my experiences and knowledge. These experiences and knowledge would only open new doors in the future.

It was a marked contrast to what I'd faced when I was twenty. Then bankruptcy had knocked me out. I had no backup funds, no other investments, no brand. But that was when I was starting out. No longer was I that inexperienced vulnerable kid. I was active, innovative—hustling, playing the game creatively. Compared to when I was twenty, I was on a whole other plane.

So when, right after that entire year of struggle, the Great Recession hit, I took it in stride. So what? It didn't scare me. To me, it wasn't a disaster. It was a string of great opportunities. For many others, it became the worst of times. For me, it was the best of times, or close to it. I was ready for it, personally and professionally.

For me, when prices dropped 10 per cent to 15 per cent, it was time to buy! I did, and the properties I bought appreciated all the more once the crisis passed and values quickly went back up. My business grew as well in tough times as in good times, because in tough times, people go to those big-name Realtors they believe can get them top dollar in that kind of environment. I had more sellers approach me during the crisis, not less.

For a lot of people those were frightening times. But I was beginning to see the connection between fear and courage, between fear and inspiration. I learned that what really mattered was not the fear but how you responded to it. I was learning to see whatever came in terms of the opportunities they presented, not just the dangers. The more I analyzed those opportunities, the more creatively I thought about them, the more opportunities and success I could see and create.

The real estate market and I had both come to the edge of a cliff, but instead of throwing in the towel and leaping off, I'd pushed even harder—and won.

Chapter 11

YOUR REAL ESTATE INVESTMENT PORTFOLIO

I went into so much detail in the chapters on Getting the Listing and my first major development deal because I wanted you, the reader, to get a really concrete sense of what it's like actively doing real estate. You see so many books saying, "Buy and Flip!" and "Rent, Rinse and Repeat!" They make it sound so easy! In some ways, it is easy—once you get the experience, assemble your network, find the right resources, accumulate a little capital, learn to think ahead, exercise a little self-discipline, and start working smart instead of hard.

Working smart, however, doesn't mean that you spend all day looking at calculators and spreadsheets. Numbers matter, but in the end you need to look at the results those numbers are getting you.

That's why I think you'll find this chapter to be a bombshell.

You see, the Susiwala System is everything I've done that's worked, condensed and put into principles. Writing this book gave me the opportunity to go over my entire life in real estate and examine my total net worth, and to ask myself where it all came from.

I got quite a surprise No, more of a shock! My total net worth was more—twice as much more!—than my total lifetime earnings. The total value of my properties equaled in value more than double the money I'd made working over the course of my entire life!

Think about that. For every dollar I'd ever earned, I now had two! And I've earned millions. It's like a copy of every cent I ever earned during my whole life went into the bank, waiting for me to spend it.

How is that *possible?* Where did that money come from?

The amazing thing is that I really wasn't paying all that much attention to it as it was happening. My workday was spent pretty much like it is now, earning commission. That was my focus, and still is.

But at the same time I was investing between 20 to 25 per cent of those earnings into real estate, and other investment opportunities. The remainder went toward life and its expenses —food, clothes, restaurants and entertainment, charitable giving, day-to-day living. You know—stuff. I didn't deprive myself. I've lived a full, blessed life, travelling the world, enjoying every moment. I just did it on 75 to 80 per cent of my retained earnings.

The remaining 20 to 25 per cent, I invested. That has made me as much as every penny I ever earned over the course of my working life.

(Actually, it's made me more. I spent much of my commission earnings. What I spent is gone. What I've invested is still there. Still there, and growing more and more every day.

How?

I don't pretend to be an investment counsellor, in general. If you're looking for advice about buying silver, or a Van Gogh, or first editions, I'm not your guy. My personal opinion on those matters is probably about the same as the next guy's.

But I approach investing through one of my core principles: Scale Down. I know real estate. So real estate is what I invest in. I also know Cambridge and the land immediately surrounding it. I've worked in local and regional real estate here for thirty years, and I can spot and develop good investment properties here. Period. *Excellent* investment properties.

Yes, I own a few stocks and the like. There's a case to be made for diversification, and I've diversified my investments a little. Diversification's a good thing. But concentration is an even better thing—if you know what you're doing. I do know. If you're an experienced real estate agent and broker, you probably know too.

I've talked about monetizing your licence. The key part of that is leveraging your knowledge. As a real estate agent, you're privy to information, and trained to develop insight: you learn to accurately assess the value of homes and properties, you have your finger on the pulse of demographic trends, you see the movements of jobs and businesses, and you know that properties and property values follow them. You work with property buyers and investors and you have a stream of choice investments continually passing under your eyes.

No one is better positioned than you to discern a good real estate investment. No one is exposed more often to the sight of properties constantly rising in value. No one is better able to predict which properties and which areas are most likely to explode in value the fastest.

Yet I am constantly running into agents and brokers who own no properties whatsoever! Who live in apartments, blow their commissions on trips and sports cars, and retire on what's left in their bank account. They're nuts!

Why don't such agents do for themselves what they do (or should do) for their clients? As I see it, it's one of the prime responsibilities of a real estate agent not just to buy and sell property for their clients, but to advise their clients about the investment value of that property.

It's so important to a person's future, to their children's future, that these days I touch on it whenever I give a talk or make a presentation.

Most people buy houses purely in order to have a place to stay. They

Long a top agent, Susiwala has been featured in numerous real estate industry vehicles through the years.

have no idea that property ownership is one of the best ways imaginable to build wealth, and no idea how to go about it. Well, a house is not just a home. The properties we live in are a financial investment—one of the best possible investments. An affordable home today can provide for a couple's retirement in some not-to-distant distant tomorrow, or ensure their children's education and future. It can even make those people wealthy. It helped make me wealthy, and when I speak to clients, I want them to know that they have a chance at that too.

It's just like Mr. Menary said: doing the right thing by others returns good things back to you. Exercising your responsibility to advise others on the investment value of their home purchase gives an agent an unexpected, but priceless, gift: the agent learns almost automatically to analyze and weigh properties for their investment value. Yet some agents remain totally ignorant of the precious skill they've developed, and what it could mean for their own prosperity and future.

How did I go from being Faisal Susiwala, real estate agent, to Faisal Susiwala, real estate investor? Same as a lot of other people. I started by buying a house. Actually, I started by paying off a house—my family's. Then, when I got married, I got a house of my own. Along the way I listened to tapes, went to workshops and conferences, and dabbled in flipping a property now and again. It wasn't a big deal. Here was a modest house someone was selling cheap because the roof leaked and the yard was a mess. I bought it, added a roof, did some updates, cleaned up the yard, and sold it for a modest profit. I didn't think of myself as any kind of mogul or guru. It was just a modest and obvious way to make a few extra dollars.

Then one day a friend of mine, a client who bought a house from me, asked me a question.

"Faisal, you know real estate. What other properties around here would make a good investment?"

"Well, obviously, this property here, and this one, and this, one" I said.

Why was it obvious? Again, because when you're a real estate agent, you have access to information that most people don't. Trends and bargain properties and motivated sellers' stream by you every day. Your colleagues know the market and talk about it. It isn't hard to figure out which homes in what areas are likely to appreciate fast and high. How much brains did it take to realize that if hundreds of houses were being built in an area with no shops, building a plaza there would make money?

My friend nodded. "So," he continued, "if I put in some money, and you put in some money, and we got a couple of other people around here in on it too, you could find a good property and we'd all do really well, right?"

I thought about it. "Yes. We would. We'd do very well."

"Well?"

He was right. I got cracking. I went through all the available properties I was aware of at the time, sent an email around to people in my database who I thought would be interested and had the funds, and invited them all to a presentation. Once we all got together, I explained why such-and-such an investment made good sense, told them I planned to put my own money into it, and asked them if they'd like to take part. If enough of them did, we'd have enough money to put together a deal. Why not? The numbers were there, and we'd all make a profit.

All this came about naturally. Because I was an active and alert Realtor, I found myself exposed to good investment properties and advice daily. Because I bought and sold properties for people, I made connections and built trust. By assembling a database of clients with enough income to invest, clients who had expressed an interest in investing, I found myself with a body of interested investors I could contact by a simple email.

I didn't go beyond my abilities. I didn't and don't advise people on stocks or gold or cryptocurrency. Real estate is what I know, and I stick to it. I stick to the people I know too—all my partners and fellow investors are people who've bought properties from me. They know I've treated them well, that I'm trustworthy, that their property has risen in value and made them money. They've gotten a good deal from their association with me. I know them to be people of fine character and sufficient resources. They know the same about me.

I don't want to give the impression that I run some sort of consortium. I've built up a successful portfolio of investment properties all by myself over the years. The fact remains, people call me regularly nowadays, asking me to help them invest, or asking to partner with me on some investment that I'm making. It wasn't something I planned on doing. It just evolved naturally.

That's one of the lessons I want you to take away from this book. When you brand yourself, when you become the go-to person, the subject matter expert in your industry and your area, opportunities open. You don't have to chase them. They come to you.

Of course, partnering with others— 'multi-level partnering,' as I've come to think of it—wasn't why my investments today make up half my net worth. Partnering has been profitable, and even fun to do, but that's just gravy.

What I'm about to share is my big secret—my key to generating real estate millions with minimal costs.

How? Through simple appreciation, and by going against the grain and the gurus on one of the most repeated, and silliest, ideas in real estate investment.

Cashflow.

Chapter 12

20 to 20

Many years ago I began adding a new word to my marketing material.

My material once just said, 'Buy' and 'Sell.'

I changed it to, 'Buy. Sell. Invest.'

Copycats in the local industry soon took over the tagline. Drive around Cambridge today and you'll see *Buy Sell Invest* on every business card, postcard and flyer.

If I go on to ask them to explain their investment strategies, I'm often surprised to learn, they don't have one. They typical response: " There are good reasons for people to buy property, right? Like—um—an extra few bucks from rental income, maybe? Cashflow, right?"

I want to *scream!*

If you happen to be skimming through this book and you read nothing else, I want you to read the next few pages closely, because, if you put cashflow aside, building wealth through real estate investing is so easy and so simple that I barely know where to start.

I'm about to share a simple formula with you, a formula that, if you understand it and apply it, will not only allow you to build wealth, but help ensure that your retirement is as comfortable and secure as you would like it to be.

Here it is:

Let's say you're starting out, and that you get a job—ideally as a real estate agent, since that will put good investment properties in front of you every day, and give you a solid sense of home values and property market trends like no other profession. But any job will do. That part is up to you and depends on whatever field you're passionate about. For me, of course, it was real estate.

Put away 20 per cent of every pay cheque you get at that job till you can invest in a property. If you become an agent, it shouldn't take long for you to get good enough to generate a decent enough commission income to allow you to put 20 per cent away comfortably.

Remember that magical number: 20 per cent. Because in most every case, 20 per cent down will get you bank funding to buy an investment property. That $400,000 home you're thinking of buying? $80,000 is what you need to acquire it.

I don't mean just you personally, either. What if all you can afford is $20,000? That's fine too. If you know three friends who can also afford $20,000, you can pool your funds together and use that.

Either way, whether you save up personally or whether you partner, once you bring together enough funds to buy a property, what you do next is find a bank or other entity that will give you a mortgage. That bank will tell you what the monthly mortgage will be.

Here's the formula to remember. If the monthly mortgage, plus property tax, plus a little put aside for upkeep, is roughly equal to what the estimated rent is for properties like the one you're considering, buy that property. Then find a tenant, start generating rental income from it, and use the rent to pay off the property.

That's the key. You're not buying and renting to get rental income so you can have more cash. You're not buying for cashflow. You're buying that property for capital appreciation over time.

Cashflow is not your goal at this point. It is not what you want. What you want is to pay down that mortgage as quickly as you can comfortably manage to do so—and you can do so very comfortably indeed, since you're not the one paying it down! The mortgage can be entirely paid down by the income from the tenant, and the property value appreciates, rising in value each year.

Let that sink in; over time, the property pays for itself!

Over time, the property rises in value!

You're actually paying only 20 per cent, and at the same time you end up with 100 per cent over time.

Is that great or what?

Now it's true that increases in property values aren't a perfectly smooth upward curve. There may be yearly fluctuations, market volatility. Property can even go down in value, though (if you do your due diligence) that's the exception, not the rule.

But why even argue this point? Open any newspaper from twenty years ago—or even ten years ago—and look at the real estate ads. Nothing's more obvious than the fact that that real estate values rise over time.

Even if the value of the house does go down—so what? Say you buy a $400,000 property for 20 per cent down. If your property bucks the historical tide to the point of utter disaster and is worth only $300,000 at the end of the term, the tenant's rental income has paid for it all. That's not only put your down payment back in your pocket—you've landed a $300,000 property *for your original $80,000 investment*. And that's a *worst-case* scenario. (I've never seen this happen in my career.)

True, the process takes time and you do have to invest and tie up some money—which will eventually be returned—up front. But look at what's happening. On the right column your equity is appreciating. On the left column, your debt is decreasing. The spread in between grows larger and larger over time. As it does so, say around year 12 to year 20 (depending on amortization and payment frequency—and even earlier if you pay it down quicker), you're going to reach a point where your property debt is zero, where you have an income-generating asset worth several hundreds of thousands of dollars, where you have rental income coming in from that asset providing monthly cashflow at retirement, and where you eventually have an asset that you can take to the bank as equity to secure a loan allowing you to re-invest those hundreds of thousands of dollars into even more properties. (Remember. As you approach retirement, you don't want to leverage or borrow against those properties anymore because that's when the cashflow will replace your day to day income.)

Congratulations. You've just created your portfolio.

Now you can start building it.

It's an incredibly simple formula that I call '20 to 20.' Put 20 per cent down, and wait 12 to 20 years. You'll have your original down payment back, a property that's fully paid off, and regular cashflow from that asset—cashflow from an asset that's risen in value during that time and is *still*, constantly, rising in value.

Repeat that every two years (or a couple of times annually in my case), repeat it however often you can secure a mortgage to buy another such investment property, and in each case by year 12 to 20 you will have an income stream that may be able to keep you going financially, job or not, savings or not, all by itself.

If you have multiple such income streams from multiple such properties, you may be able to replace your present-day annual career earnings *completely* and still maintain the same lifestyle you enjoy right now.

You will have a legacy—a portfolio for you to leave behind for your family and loved ones. An asset that will not only give them monthly income but create ever-growing wealth for them. An asset that will allow them to invest further and build secure wealth all on their own.

To me, the single most incredible thing about this process is that I had no idea what I was doing until I had done it.

I bought a property because I had built up some savings as a real estate agent.

I wanted it to grow in value, as opposed to losing value in a bank account owing to inflation.

I knew that houses appreciate, so I bought one.

I found a tenant and didn't really need the rental income immediately, so I applied it toward paying down the mortgage.

Every now and then another great investment property would catch my eye, and I knew I needed cash to make a down payment. Hey, why not use the equity in the property I already had?

One day I looked around and—boom!—I owned dozens of properties, and I had millions in equity.

I realized that not only did I own all these properties—all of them had been paid off by tenant rental income.

I had secured a full portfolio of fine properties valued in the millions. The total cost to me? 20 per cent of my regular income — that 20 per cent, too, had been paid back to me by my tenants.

I had acquired an income-generating real estate investment portfolio worth millions of dollars—for a fraction of my income.

Chapter 13

INCOME AND WEALTH

When I see how all this operates—and see the wealth this simple formula has given me—I find myself just utterly dumbfounded at people who don't invest in property, or who buy property and immediately spend the rent revenues. They may literally be a decade or two from nearly becoming millionaires. Yet they throw it away to blow another one to two thousand a month now.

The mistake they're making isn't just falling for the trap of instant gratification. They're failing to see the difference between income and wealth. There's no more important distinction to keep in mind.

Income is what you spend—it's how you arrange to get enough cash coming in to pay for your bills and necessities and a few luxuries now and again. *Wealth* is all that you have that you do not spend—all the things you have that *grow in value* so long as they remain unspent.

Your paycheque is income: it pays for the gas and fills your refrigerator and allows you to live life—but in the end, once you spend it, you have nothing. You have to work to generate enough to let you keep running through the cycle time and time again. If you only aim at generating income you're like the mouse in the cage, constantly running but really getting nowhere.

Your house is *wealth*: you don't use your house to buy a hamburger or a new suit. But as it sits there, even while you're sleeping in bed, its value is growing year by year from the $400,000 you spent buying it in January to the $425,000 it may now be worth in December.

If, like Rip Van Winkle, you fall asleep for a few decades? You wake up in a house that may be five or six times the original home value. Or more.

Income fluctuates. Wealth grows. That's the question that intelligent investors have to constantly ask themselves: "What can I acquire that consistently grows in value, that consistently provides me with more and more, instead of less and less?"

The answer isn't only real estate. There are many forms of wealth. Stocks grow in value (sometimes); a good market index fund that includes many stocks will rise over time because the market, as a whole, rises over time. That's not a bad investment at all. That money in your bank account making 1.5 per cent interest? That's wealth too. Compound interest over a lifetime may even make it impressive. But it'll take a very long time to do so.

Property investment? That takes time, patience and self-discipline,

But in my experience, the returns are at least as secure, and exponentially higher.

Once upon a time people knew this. They knew that wealth was intimately connected with property. Own enough land, houses and big buildings (and OK, maybe a few thousand shares of Berkshire Hathaway and Apple, just to diversify), and Game Over: you're rich.

Then along came Robert Kiyosaki with *Rich Dad Poor Dad*.

Now there's a great deal of very good advice in his books, including *Rich Dad Poor Dad*, but many people interested in real estate came away from that book with the mistaken idea that the key to wealth was building immediate passive income. Get enough rental income fast and use it to cover all your bills, and overnight you'll never have to work again.

From this perspective, cashflow is king. Buy four rental houses and an apartment house dirt cheap (so you can buy them all the faster) and retire on the spot. The rental income will give you a livable income stream. Collect it, spend it, and relax.

This was a bad idea for a lot of reasons.

First, as anyone who's ever tried knows, managing five low-rent properties, (and especially low-rent multi-units) is anything but passive. You'll be babysitting tenants and dealing with their issue's day and night.

Second, if you're not using that rental income to pay off the mortgage, your equity stays where it is for a long, long time. You can't go to the bank to borrow more for other investments. You don't have the equity to justify it. That isn't growing wealth; it's retarding it.

Making enough cash to cover your immediate day-to-day expenses doesn't build wealth. You need to make more than enough money to cover your needs if you want to have extra money to invest.

Third, that approach propelled many a real estate agent to stop being an agent and go into the lone-wolf world of foreclosures and wholesaling and power of sales properties. After all, if the goal is to buy cash-flowing properties for yourself fast and cheap, and stop working, why buy and sell homes for a commission percentage for others?

The answer, of course, is that working as an agent for commission provides the regular income you need to invest, and connects you to the information and networks and other resources of the real estate profession. 'Alternative' real estate investing can work out on occasion, but sometimes foreclosure properties are junk properties with severe issues, both structural and legal. Sometimes properties at auction have stiff liens or clouded titles. It's buyer beware. Investing like this isn't pleasant, it isn't regular or consistent, and it doesn't build a good reputation, good brand or good will. It doesn't even make very much money. It certainly doesn't help you network with trustworthy friends and investors.

The real problem with this alternative cashflow model is its timing. Today, I have passive income: if I stopped working entirely, I'd receive enough income from the investment properties I own to let me maintain my current lifestyle. I've reached that point by waiting till the properties in which I chose to invest were paid off.

If I were starting out today, I wouldn't have the money to invest. I might not have even enough money to pay my bills. (When I did start out, I didn't. I had to live with my parents!). Sure, it's a good idea to aim at building passive income—after you've established a steady flow of active income. If you try to build it immediately, right out of the box, you end up taking the no-money-down other-people's-money low-quality property route. That sort of thing may create flamboyant gurus, but it doesn't create a brand you can be proud of, and it doesn't create genuine wealth.

My core business is being a real estate agent, and I follow my system: I maintain that core. It's the income from being a Realtor that gives me the dependable cashflow that I need to invest in more properties quickly. It's also what covers my bills, fees and all the other things people need to cover.

Living off existing wealth reduces the capacity to grow that wealth; it can even eat away at that wealth directly. That doesn't mean you need to live like a miser. It does mean you need enough self-discipline to step back from immediate gratification long enough for your wealth to really take root.

"But doesn't waiting ten years, or twenty, for cashflow mean twenty years of no cashflow?" Not if you have a business model that uses part of the cash from your income to contribute to your investment, rather than a model in which your income depends on your investment.

Making your income dependent on your investment can lead to disaster. If your day-to-day survival depends on your cashflow from a single property, you're going to be a nervous wreck. If the tenant walks out, and you can't fill that slot for months, how do you pay your bills?

But if you have a good overall business model—if you have a job, if you're in real estate and you're generating leads and marketing and selling—you don't need property cashflow for survival. You can let that property pay for itself. Like I have.

I've bought properties with *negative* cashflow. Why? Not because I felt like taking a loss (A loss with significant tax advantages, I might add).

I did it because it's not a loss! I'm not just talking about the tax write-off, though that alone is reason enough. It's not a loss because the appreciation outweighs the negative cashflow— it far outweighs it.

I cannot understand why even people in the industry simply don't get this. The value of any property I buy, even taking negative cashflow into consideration, is likely to increase annually, and increase by much, much more that the $100 a month that I'm supposedly 'losing.'

Think about it. If you're losing $100 a month, you're losing $1,200 a year. But if the value of your property has gone up $10,000 that year, you've made $8,800 that year!

So long as the value keeps rising, your net worth keeps rising too. This is a problem?

We're in an amazing industry. It's not like automobile sales. The moment you drive a car off the lot, the value of that car plunges. Not houses. Houses are an appreciating asset. They go up in value while you just sit there. People hung up on cashflow fail to appreciate the power and the beauty of appreciation. That's why their net worth fails to appreciate too.

They also forget this other marvellous thing called 'debt repayment.'

What is debt repayment? To me, it's using other people's money. Rent is other people's money. *Their* rent money pays down your debt.

Again, people—even people in the real estate industry—just don't seem to get this. They have tunnel vision: "You want me to invest in a property that costs me $100 a month? Oh, no way! I'm not going to lose money. I'm not going to be down $100 a month!"

I want to grab them and shake them.

"No, no, look at the bigger picture! You're not losing $100 a month. You're making $8,800 a year!"

I got so frustrated once trying to explain this to someone that two years ago I created a PowerPoint slide and a full presentation to clarify it once and for all. It showed, in real time, the progress of a negative cashflow property I purchased that 'lost' $150 per month—while at the same time it grew $200,000 in value over the course of two years.

'Loss': $3,600. Profit: $196,400!

The people who didn't get this property because they didn't want to lose money through 'negative cashflow' managed to 'save' $3,600—and lost over $196,000 in equity.

Granted, this was in 2016 to 2019, a very good time for property values. At the time those values gained 40 per cent. But suppose they only rose 20 per cent. Or even 10 per cent? The return in value still far outstrips the tiny amount paid out.

(And this doesn't even touch on matters like debt repayment, or tax advantages, or your ability to better leverage those returns for further investment equity).

You don't have to be an investment genius to get these results. You don't even need to be conscious! You could be comatose the whole year and still make money. Why don't people get it?

That's why I continue to buy properties, and people don't get that either. "Faisal, why are you still buying all these $300,000 townhouses? You've got a house. You've got lots of houses. You don't need to buy more."

Yes, I do! How can you not want to buy properties that over time will put hundreds of thousands of dollars, *millions* of dollars, into your pocket as they pay for themselves? At the end of the day it's literally free money.

I won't dwell on this point. It's too simple. Your money's not going to grow making 1.5 per cent in the bank. It's going to grow through appreciation, and getting that appreciation by applying my formula is easy. Yes, you'll need a little discipline. Feast or famine, you'll need to make and put away enough income to cover the 20 per cent you need to buy a property.

If you can't put 20 per cent of your income away? Look for other assets you may have that cover at least 20 per cent of the property you want. If you want to buy a property for $250,000, maybe you have $50,000 in your personal residence. Maybe you have a small business or some other holding that a bank may consider collateral. Whatever you have, leverage it, and buy some properties. As they appreciate, extract from those properties to invest in more. When, in ten or twelve years, you've paid that $50,000 down, and the value of that property is $400,000 or $500,000, extract it again, and re-invest.

Let it all just keep on growing.

What to Buy?

Now some properties are better investments than others. What sorts of houses do I personally like to put in my portfolio?

Well, as I said, I don't generally like foreclosures and power of sales. If a property is for sale cheap, there's generally a reason. I don't like surprises, or properties that take a lot of work. I also don't like babysitting. Multiplexes and apartments make money, but they will have you tearing out your hair. Some investors love them. They're not for me.

I like single family properties. They can be attached or semi-attached. But I avoid two-person properties with upstairs people and downstairs people. The person upstairs is noisy, the person downstairs smokes, and both will call you at three in the morning and order you to do something about it. Aaargh!

The great thing about singles is the exit strategy. It's quick and easy. Commercial, office complexes, 50-unit properties— those can take forever to sell. If you're selling a building, your only buyer is another investor who buys entire buildings. There may not be lot of those in the market for your building, and you could be waiting quite a while. Same with commercial. If your restaurant tenant fails, you may have to wait a long time to find another restauranteur. Your pool of buyers is limited.

But everyone needs a place to stay, and people are always looking for a good single unit. If you're selling a townhouse, a condo, or a single home, though, you can always find a buyer, and you can find that buyer fast. (So long as it's a single unit you're selling, that is, and not a portfolio of four in a package.)

I also like mixed-use with a residential component—a first-floor business below, and an apartment or apartments above. The reason is the same. There are some very attractive aspects to commercial property, but if they go vacant, they can be vacant for what seems like forever. Add a residential component and you have a hedge that covers that possibility. It ensures cashflow —enough to pay down the debt, which, as I say, is one of my key goals in buying properties. Long vacancies are rare when it comes to residential, whether they're on top of a barber shop or insurance office or not.

The decision to buy that sort of investment property really comes down to simple math: if the residential income pays down the debt, it's a go, whether the commercial unit is filled or not.

I also like storage units. Recently, housing seems to be getting smaller and smaller. Where are people going to put their stuff? There's a seasonal angle to storage as well—where do you leave your skis in the summer, or your patio furniture in the winter? The nice thing about storage units, too, is that you don't get many late-night calls from live-in tenants. There aren't any! The more the population grows, and the smaller apartments become, the more I think storage is going to be huge.

I don't say there isn't money to be made in alternative real estate investments, but I tend to stay away from those sorts of things. There are other, more esoteric investments that pay off too (if you do them right): notes, liens, and whatnot. Those are specialist areas, and the area of specialization I know best is my own: my core business is still residential sales, and commissions remain my main source of pure income. What I'm doing now works. It works really well. Why would I go out of my way to invest in areas I don't know as well?

In the end, the simple, familiar systems are best: the ones that have worked thousands of times and don't have any surprises: a good residential property in a decent neighbourhood where

This photograph depicts a proud moment in Faisal Susiwala's career when he completed his first neighbourhood plaza and townhomes complex. It was here that he had to sleep for three nights, to protect the deal from collapsing, in a sleeping bag in an unfinished unit over Christmas in 2007.

prices are quietly rising. Save up some money, shop around, do the math, arrange for a mortgage, find a tenant, have them pay off the mortgage, rinse and repeat.

Does it all sound too simple? "20 to 20"? "Singles, semi-detached, townhouses?"

Well, it is simple.

So what are you waiting for? Go for it!

Chapter 14

BECOME A REALTOR

You don't have to be a real estate agent to be an investor. Some investors are not realtors. Some Realtors—a good many, really—are not investors. Incredible, but true. I'm fine with that. We make our own life and career choices, and I wish everyone well with theirs.

But if your goal is to be a successful real estate investor, there are so many advantages to getting a real estate licence and becoming a real estate agent and/or broker that I strongly advise any serious real estate investor who can get an agent's licence to do so.

It isn't just the obvious things, such as education and training, for example. Again, this is a no-brainer: you're going to have to crack some books anyway if you want to invest knowledgeably. Why not get a licence for it? Professional certification is something you can leverage, even if you're only trying to get someone to partner with you. Are fellow investors more likely to partner with a licensed professional or an amateur?

Then there's the benefit of concentrated study. True, learning to buy and sell houses isn't like going to medical school, but you still need to know the terms, the relevant laws, the legal conditions, the contracts, the taxes, all sorts of details, traps and opportunities. You can hire people to handle much of that, but you can't hire people to think and to decide. In the end, you're the one who's got to make the decision. The more you know, the easier it becomes to avoid making a very expensive mistake, and the easier it is to spot a first-rate investment. Nothing will get you there better and quicker than getting an agent's licence.

Let's not forget about the network you join when you become an agent. That alone can be worth the price of the ticket. Join an agency and you'll be talking to people who know the neighbourhoods, know the price trends, and know the demographics. You'll connect with people who can pull up a wealth of information that only they can access concerning any property you're thinking of investing in. These people talk properties all day long. Open your ears and listen! And when you hear of one that fits your criteria, and you settle on a good investment property to buy, you won't have to hire a real estate agent to arrange it. You are one!

What college or university lets you generate lucrative income from commissions as you learn and hobnob? What other business lets even the beginner buy and sell such incredibly high-ticket items? Sell a set of encyclopedia door-to-door and you may barely cover the week's grocery bill. Sell a $500,000 house at a 5 per cent commission, and you've made $25,000. That's a down payment on a house all by itself. Heck, you often end up helping the seller buy their next home too, and earn a percentage of that as well.

Grocery stores, clothing stores, bookstores, retail outlets, nearly always require the business owner to buy the goods first, stock and shelf them, and then (if he or she can) to sell them. In real estate the inventory comes to you. The inventory is free: there are literally millions of dollars worth of homes—billions! —waiting for us to sell, yet we don't have to pay a penny for it. In real estate we have the amazing opportunity to have all this inventory available to us at no cost, and earn a percentage when we sell it. When people want to buy a house, they call a Realtor. All you need to do is build your brand and make sure your name is in their mind, or on a billboard or a Google ad, when they start looking.

What environment could possibly be better for an investor? If you're an agent, you're spending all day with buyers, sellers and properties. Great deals pass in front of your eyes all the time. Look at them yourself: look at the actual properties you're selling and remember that you can buy and sell properties too. When you sit down and consider a deal, remember that you're not only representing your buyers and sellers: you also represent yourself.

Don't just serve the buyer. Be the buyer. Look at each deal as a potential buyer. If you see a good deal, and if, for whatever reason, that property isn't selling, buy it. Buy it yourself. Create a way to buy it. If you don't have your own money, partner with others. Joint venture with others.

I've said there are Realtors who don't own property. There are also quite a few who do. When you become part of the industry, you won't just find friends and colleagues and peers—you'll also find a vast pool of fellow investors and potential investment partners. I didn't always have enough money personally to invest in property, but I was always able to find an investment partner. Trust me: if you're a good, active agent, you'll find partners aplenty. If the numbers work, if you're licensed and credible, investors will come.

Join a brokerage that supports you and provides opportunities and access. Your broker has the ability to back you on projects, introduce you to the right resources. In some cases, a broker may partner with you or fund you themselves.

For instance, back in 2000, when I was getting married, I was going away for five weeks after just buying a house. I had commissions of around $50,000 coming to me over the next four or five months, but they weren't in yet, and there were things I needed to pay for—the wedding, the honeymoon, a down payment on the house, and so on. I went to my broker and asked him for a $30,000 loan.

It was the only time I asked for that kind of loan, but of course he gave it to me—why wouldn't he? I had $50,000 coming in. A strong brokerage may have over a million dollars advanced to agents at any given time. Around here they generate 12 per cent interest as they revolve it. So they've got funds to loan, and a good reason to loan them. (Brokers invest too. I've had brokers approach me asking to be dealt into investment opportunities I've identified).

This is something to consider when you're looking for a brokerage. You want to find one where the broker has your back, where you have access, where the broker has the wherewithal to support you—even partner with you. If so, and everything else lines up, don't worry. They'll gladly cover a mortgage on a house if you need one.

In the end, what really makes becoming an agent the thing to do if you're interested in investing in properties is no one thing: it's the combined power of all the above. If I had to put it into a single word, that word would be 'access.' You can have your business structure in place, you can have a solid investment plan, but if you don't have access—access to money, access to opportunity, access to information, access to intelligence, access to investors, access to the people that can help you fulfill those goals—it doesn't mean a thing. You want to be part of a network of people who are like-minded, people who will help you build what you're trying to build.

In the real estate business, we have a unique opportunity to buy what we sell. Even to have all our bills and needs and even the purchase itself paid for, eventually, by what we buy. We develop the ability to analyze deals that other people never have access to, deals they never even know exist.

Becoming a real estate agent is opportunity in its purest form. A door to opportunity that's always open.

82 VOLUME 1 • EDITION 2   CHOOSE WISELY. CHOOSE RE/MAX TWIN CITY.   WWW.REMAXTWINCITY.COM

RE/MAX TWIN CITY REALTY INC.
INDEPENDENTLY OWNED AND OPERATED BROKERAGE

Spotlight on... Faisal Susiwala
Broker

By Clyde Warrington

What to do for an encore when you've reached what is normally considered the pinnacle of your career and you're still just 40?

"I guess you hope they come up with a different award," responds a chuckling Faisal Susiwala, realtor extraordinaire, who last summer became the first realtor in the Golden Triangle to join Re/Max International's "Circle of Legends," a select group of agents with at least $400 million in career sales with the company.

The Circle of Legends can be likened to the Oscar for Lifetime Achievement, a fond tribute to a starstudded career typically verging on retirement.

"It felt surreal being up on the stage surrounded by all these 60 and 70 year olds," Faisal recalls.

It was a crowning moment, achieving at 40 what less than one per cent of realtors manage in a lifetime.

Faisal has been turning heads in the real estate world since the age of 18.

He was still in high school when he walked into the late Reid C. Menary's real estate office on Main Street in Cambridge and told him he wanted a job. Faisal had met with a real estate company earlier in the day, showed his newly acquired real estate licence. Instead of hiring or even encouraging him he was told, "Son, you're too young. Go back to school and come back later."

Between Grades 12 and 13 at Galt Collegiate that summer, Faisal had enrolled in Conestoga College's six-week real estate course. He received his realty licence in October, shaking his parents when he declared his intention to pursue real estate sales and not attend university.

"They were typical immigrant parents, blue collar, working class, who put great stock in the value of an education. To put it mildly they were very disappointed."

Reid Menary, who was thinking of retiring, found young Faisal so engaging he hired him on. He would postpone his retirement for over a year, mentoring Faisal in all aspects of the business.

"I was off and running," Faisal happily relates. "I had over two million in sales in the first two months of starting."

Faisal would join Realty World in 1990, then moved to Re/Max Twin City in 1994. His parents, retired and living in K-W, have proudly witnessed their son's meteoric climb to the inner circle of success. He has been a fixture among Re/Max's Top 10 agents in Atlantic Canada, placing fourth in Canada in sales in 2006, and has ranked as high as 23rd in the world. The Re/Max world is vast, encompassing more than 120,000 agents in 67 countries.

He was No. 36 in the world in 2010 and will find out next month in Las Vegas if he cracked the world's Top 10 last year, when Re/Max awards its top 100 agents at the annual convention.

He has managed all this on his own, eschewing the team approach that is so much in vogue.

"The team concept, it's not for me. I don't like it at all. When people call my office it's me they deal with, as it should be."

He loves all aspects of selling and developing property. He currently is spearheading the $100-million redevelopment of the Kress Hotel property off King Street in Preston. The project involves resurrecting a facsimile of the historic hotel which was razed in the late 1980s, possibly as a five-storey, 120-unit seniors' complex with a retail and commercial mix occupying the main floor and, later, town homes and a condominium highrise. The project stalled once when the economy forced a group of investors from Dubai to pull out. He has since assembled a syndicate of Chinese investors. A site plan may soon be submitted to the city.

A natural salesman all his life, he credits a driving ambition and a willingness to work hard at all hours for his success.

"I do everything that I am supposed to do each day. That consistency is important. I have never said to myself, 'well, it's November and things are slowing down so maybe I can take it easy for a while.'"

For Faisal, the passion to succeed continues to glow brightly.

You can reach Faisal at his office at Re/Max Twin City Realty Inc., at 519-740-3690. Be sure to visit his website at www.homeshack.com

Chapter 15

WHY BUILD WEALTH?

Silly question, isn't it? Why live in comfort and security, and not poverty and stress? Why give back to your family and community, and not fail them and give them nothing in return for all they've given you? Why make yourself able to help others, when you can't even help yourself? Why be rich when you could be destitute?

You know why you want material prosperity. If you didn't, you wouldn't be reading this book.

However, there's a special reason why I think we need to give our attention to investing wisely at this point in our history, and by 'we,' I mean, my generation—people in their late thirties to early fifties. Our generation has a unique window of opportunity. One our children won't have.

When many of our parents came to this country, their goal was simple: basic survival. They established a foundation for us. They even managed to build on that foundation. They weren't in a position to erect skyscrapers on it, but they did manage to provide us with a home, security, and a decent education. We, in turn, will be forever grateful to them because of all they did. Our fundamental needs were fulfilled as a result of their courage, kindness, hard work and sacrifice.

The next generation, my generation, had the opportunity to grow from that base. Many of us did. Many did what I'm suggesting here—we didn't throw away our earnings on credit card debt and a high-flying lifestyle. We worked hard and invested and kept investing.

We did it because we knew the threat of poverty. We saw how hard our parents struggled. We saw how hard it was to stay afloat, and how easy it was to drown. Our parents and family needed our help, and it was a privilege to help them as best we could.

But the next generation that follows us, the millennials, are different. They're a spending generation. We've given them prosperity. They haven't had to work to achieve it.

But let's look at history for a moment. The Great Depression generation of the 1930's hit my parents, and Mr. Menary, for example. They struggled to rebuild a strong foundation and rise above adversity. The baby boomers followed, and they were able to build on that foundation, and rise even higher, and create genuine wealth. Then came along Generation X. They didn't have to build wealth—all they had to do was enjoy it, and their parents let them, because we as parents and grandparents know how much struggle and discipline and sacrifice is needed to reach the point where you can be that generous to your children. We wanted them to enjoy the fruits of our labours, and not have to pay the price we paid for it.

The result is that millennials today—and I'm generalizing here—are barely able to pay their rent, let alone recognize, and buy, an asset. They know how to spend wealth; they don't know how to create it.

That doesn't mean this millennial generation isn't as smart, enthusiastic, creative or as ambitious as we were. It's not laziness. Some have just as much determination as we have. Rather, it has more to do with opportunity.

The problem is, they no longer have the same opportunities to create that kind of wealth. Take a look at the ratio of income to house prices and see how it has changed over the years. In 1980 when average household income was roughly $30,000 in my hometown, the average price of a home was $50,000 to $60,000—twice a household's annual income, or a ratio of 1:2.

Today, with the average household income in Canada about $80,000, the average price of a home in the same market is over half a million dollars—$550,000.

That's a ratio of almost 1:7—nearly seven times the spread.

As an investor, that's music to my ears. It's the perfect illustration of what I said—over time, real estate values keep rising higher and higher.

As a father, though, I find myself asking another question: what are our children going to do? They can't pay that home off as easily as we could. They may never manage to pay it off at all.

We need to give them the tools and the knowledge to be able to prosper under these very different, very challenging conditions.

If they, and we, want them to continue to live in security and comfort, we need to set a foundation today that will preserve them tomorrow. If we don't do it at this point, they're simply going to live off our assets till they're spent; and then they'll have nothing. It's so important for people of our generation to invest intelligently now. Because when we retire, our children may not have enough disposable income to pay for our nursing home or medical care. It's going to be the other way around: we'll need to help them.

You can already see it happening. People who are now retiring are giving down-payment money for a home, sometimes even rent money, to their kids. They're buying a home for their children, going to Florida for six months, then coming back to live in the basement.

We don't want to create an environment where the only way our children are going to have any sort of financial freedom is when we die. We don't want to die knowing that they'll take our legacy and sell that asset for cash, living high for a short time until, inevitably, it's all spent and the bitter cycle of struggling up from the bottom has to begin all over again, because for them, and their children, their resources have collapse to zero.

Again, it has nothing to do with laziness, or being spoiled, or lack of challenge. It's not how things are going to turn out for all of them, either; but it'll happen to many. Too many. It's not a matter of rising prices alone, either. People get illnesses, or struggle through divorces and bankruptcies. They make bad career moves and poor investments as well as good ones. There are a lot of factors involved in economic success. Sometimes bad things happen to good people. That's just how it is.

But you can guard against that kind of outcome. You can make plans to avoid it, strategically putting safeguards into place, and take the few simple steps needed to make the difference. Such as? Save or partner till you have a small pool of funds which you can then invest. Buy one property, and then leverage it to buy another, and then another, and then another. If you do just that, you can still come out on top.

Though I didn't learn these lessons in school, that's precisely where they should be taught, so that, unlike me, future generations won't have to learn them the hard way, through life experience.

I learned these things by seeing what my father and mother were going through in the worst of times. When I witnessed the loss of our family home at the age of eight, that was a lesson I would never forget.

I never, ever, want to be in a position where my children have to see that; where I, and the people I love, live with the fear of poverty, and are reduced to starting over again with nothing.

When something like that happens to you, your mindset shifts forever. You say to yourself, "What do I have to do to keep this from this ever happening again? What steps can I take?"

Everyone is always telling me what a great success I've become, but the truth is, when I wake up in the morning, I still have that fear; I still live every day with those memories of poverty.

I've come to be grateful for that feeling. I use it to drive myself to give my career and my investing my very best efforts, to put myself into a frame of mind that ensures I'll work hard, smart, empathetically and passionately to do my best, and then do even better.

That's not the mindset of poverty. That's the mindset of an entrepreneur.

R30   The Record - Cambridge REMAX Homes   Thursday, September 23, 2010

Joins Circle of Legends

Faisal Susiwala becomes 1st Re/Max agent in tri-county area to reach $400 million in sales

Faisal Susiwala, with Re/Max Twin City Realty Inc., Brokerage, has been presented with the Re/Max Circle of Legends Award, which honours highly successful agents who have sold more than $400 million of real estate and have completed 10 years of service with the company.

The Circle of Legends Award, created in 2001, has been achieved by less than one per cent of all sales associates in the Re/Max network. Faisal is the first recipient of this award in all of Waterloo, Wellington & Brant counties.

Faisal has been working in the real estate industry for more than 22 years and has extensive experience in residential sales. Among Faisal's achievements are the Hall of Fame Award, the Lifetime Achievement Award and he has consistently been ranked within the Top 1% in the World as well as the Top 50 Re/Max agents in Canada.

"Faisal has been an integral member of our team and is more than deserving of this very prestigious award," said Bob Stephens, manager/broker of Re/Max Twin City Realty Inc., Brokerage. "Winning this award is a tremendous accomplishment. Faisal continues to raise the bar in real estate, making us, and this community proud."

In addition, Faisal actively supports local community groups, sports & shelters.

Re/Max has nearly 100,000 agents in more than 70 countries who continue to out-produce the competition, averaging more sales than other real estate agents. With one of the most recognized brands in the world and one of the most trafficked web sites, www.remax.com. Re/Max leads the industry with experienced, professional agents – agents trained and educated through the award-winning Re/Max University.

Re/Max was founded in 1973 by Dave and Gail Liniger. From a single office in Denver, Colorado, it has grown into a global network of nearly 100,000 Sales Associates in more than 70 countries, an international presence greater than any of its competitors.

Re/Max International is proud of its Premier Community Citizenship, which has raised over $100 million for deserving organizations like Susan G. Komen for the Cure®, Children's Miracle Network and The Sentinels of Freedom Foundation.

Faisal Susiwala: Consistently within top 1% in world.

Chapter 16

THE OLDER INVESTOR

We need to think deeply—and take steps now—to ensure a decent economic future for our children, and for young people. But I don't want anyone to think that what I've written here applies only to young people. Far from it. The same rules apply to everyone, regardless of age: if you can put 20 per cent down to buy a house at age sixty and have it paid off by seventy, you'll have the same cash flowing asset as a thirty-year old.

The situation is different for an older investor. That doesn't mean it's easier or harder—just different. Time matters in real estate investments, and an eighty-year-old doesn't have as much time to play as a twenty-year-old. On the other hand, an eighty-year-old has life experience a twenty-year-old doesn't, and may have savings, connections, and a community and credibility twenty-year-olds can only dream of. Older investors, like young ones, have to play to their strengths and guard against their weaknesses. There's no reason an investor can't do that well whatever his or her age.

Would I recommend any *particular* properties for an older investor? I would. If you're an older person starting out investing, there's no question about it: buy a couple of townhomes in the same complex or area. Live in one, rent the other. Once paid off, this gives you a steady rental income for the rest of your life, if you want, and an appreciating asset that any real estate investor knows will be a desirable cash-generating, easy-to-sell property.

Don't *just* collect rent. You can, and should, take the equity out to buy other properties; but even if you don't, you can go a long way to securing yourself a modest but comfortable retirement with one townhouse alone.

But do you really want to retire? I can't imagine any point in my life where I would give up real estate. Why stop playing the most fun game in the world? It would be like giving up chess, or Monopoly. You never get too old for Monopoly. If you're a real estate agent, all that getting older means is that you have higher levels of skill and experience and credibility and can play an even better game.

Seriously. Age isn't a handicap in the real estate game. Not even in the real estate *agency* game. If you're an older real estate agent, you're at an advantage. I still remember the looks people gave me when I tried to get them to let me sell their homes as a teenager. "Shouldn't you be in school, kid?" What I wouldn't have given then for a couple of wrinkles and a few white hairs! Buyers might let me show them a house, but it took ten long years of aging before I even *started* getting sellers.

The truth is, buyers, sellers, bankers and investors all take age as a mark of experience and good judgment, even wisdom. Sure, that's a little silly, but isn't it true? Whether you're a doctor, lawyer, or real estate professional, people listen to the advice of an older person a lot more closely than they do to the opinion of a young person.

In the financial and investment world, the wealthier the buyer or seller you deal with, the more likely you are to be talking to an older person. If you're older too, you'll click with them better. After all, older people have lived through the same history and speak the same language. They share things in common, and when you're someone who has a good deal in common with the person you're trying to connect with, that connection is already half-made.

I know one 76-year-old investor who is still buying properties. Is it out of a pure love of the game? No, it's out of his love for his children. He knows they're likely to have it tough over the course of the next few years. He wants the properties he passes on to be his legacy.

Another fellow I know, now seventy-five years old, is a good friend of my father's. He's an immigrant who started investing at age 50 as a cleaning person—cleaning airplanes. That was all he did his entire career.

He came to me 25 years ago and told me he wanted to invest. I told him pretty much what I'm telling you now, and slowly, very gradually, he saved 20 per cent of his income and came to me to help him find a good investment rental property. I did. He examined it and bought that property. Just that one. At first.

Today? He gets around $20,000 a month every month from his portfolio of rental properties.

His children, meanwhile, have no assets. We met recently at a gathering and he pulled me aside and said, "Faisal, when I pass away, I want you to talk to my children. Please, I want you to convince them, whatever happens, not to sell those properties. They have jobs, but they're not making $20,000 a month at them, and I know how young people these days are—they'll want to sell and go on a spending spree. In the end they'll lose everything. I still have sisters living in those homes and apartments. My wife, too. When the property is out of family hands, who knows what could happen? Don't let them sell, Faisal! Promise me!"

I promised I'd talk to them. I also promise, here and now, that one day I will put copies of this book into their hands. I hope they read it and listen, and remember how much their father loves them. I hope anyone reading this book, anyone with as generous and loving a parent as this fine man, is listening too.

(By the way. When I left him at that recent gathering, he asked me if I knew of any new properties that looked like good investments. Now that's an investor. The next time I see him, he'll be making $30,000 a month, I'm sure).

Sure, the earlier you start, the better you'll do. But the lesson you need to learn is not to give up even if you've started late. The lesson is to start now. What, you think you're going to be younger ten years from now if you mull things over for another decade? Every five years in real estate, I find myself looking back and slapping my forehead and thinking, "Oh no, I should have gotten that property. Why, oh why, didn't I take part in that deal?"

I'm absolutely serious. There's never been one single period in my career, not one, where I haven't looked back five years and not ached with regret because I didn't make more real estate investments than I did. Appreciation is that strong. I have no doubt I'll say it again five years from now, and five years again after that. Just as I have no doubt that if you invest now— intelligently, and with due diligence—you'll look back in five years with satisfaction and relief, and say, "I did the right thing."

Of course you'll have done the right thing! In five years, your debt will have been paid down. In five years the property will have appreciated in value. In five years you'll be able to take more equity out to invest. In five years you'll have created an asset.

Don't wait. Young or old, start today. Start this minute.

Decision

"Start this minute." With those three little words, we've arrived at the most important element of them all when it comes to building a portfolio—to building real lifelong wealth. More important than '20 to 20.' More important than capital appreciation. More important than the whole Susiwala System. We come back to the very first lesson I shared.

Dare.

Make the decision to act.

Do it.

Now.

Nothing I teach, none of the things I'm sharing with you, will make the least bit of difference if you don't make the decision, right now, this moment, to act. To make it happen.

You shape your financial future every moment with each choice you make. If you choose to spend your time partying or watching TV or tweeting about nonsense, that's up to you. You'll bear the consequences. If you determine that your future will be a future of wealth and abundance, of support for those you love, of security and comfort, then you and all those you care for will experience different consequences. Brighter, happier, wonderful consequences.

When I was a young boy I made that choice, that determination, and I can assure you—the consequences of making the right choice, of choosing to build wealth instead of squandering away your precious time and income, are wonderful, soul-satisfying and extraordinary. I'm so glad I ventured down the road I did. I want to share my experience with everyone. I'm writing this book in order to do just that.

What I've put in this book contains all the tools you'll need to transform your life and your future into something rich, admirable and joyous.

It's as simple as digging deep inside yourself and seriously making the decision; taking that first step to lift your life to something better.

I say this from the bottom of my heart as a friend who wishes only the best for you.

Please take it.

Lessons

I've been investing in real estate for nearly thirty years now and have made millions at it. I've done deals that have been incredibly complicated in their details and stuffed with fine print.

And yet the funny thing is, when I try to distill what I've learned about real estate investing into just a few pages of advice and summary, what amazes me most is how little there is to say about it—how incredibly simple it all is.

Most of what I've made in property investment I've made through simple appreciation. Like compound interest, all you really need to do is put some money into a safe place and wait. You don't need genius. You don't even need luck. You do need common sense, and patience. It's true that common sense isn't very common, and that patience is even less common than that. Most of us want immediate gratification. We want to get rich quick and spend it even quicker. Yet it's so easy for immediate gratification to lead to lasting, long-term misery. Thinking in the long-term, putting something aside today because you know it's going to be more valuable tomorrow—that's the whole trick right there.

I know that that principle alone doesn't give you concrete advice on whether to buy this piece of property as opposed to that one. If I had to give one single bit of really rock-solid practical advice on that score, advice that would help you distinguish a good property from a poor one, one life-changing recommendation to help put you on the road to real estate success like no other, it would be simple—get a Realtor's licence.

Seriously. The cost in many cases is a few thousand dollars or less. The time needed to pass the exam can take a few months— in some countries and places, a few weeks. Yet it opens the door to an entire world of fellow professionals and colleagues, buyers, sellers, deals, commission income and conferences, all of which are invaluable.

I don't have to look for good investment properties and ready investment partners. They come to me! I don't have to ask myself if a property is a worthwhile investment. I've been trained to spot good properties and reliable investments. I'm constantly associating with people to discuss every aspect of real estate—prices, the trends, what's hot, what's coming around the corner.

The investment of time needed to become a licensed Realtor is so small, and the potential returns are so large, that I can't think of a single thing you can do that will set your feet more surely on the road to real estate investment success. You can listen to tips and podcasts, read books, watch videos—but nothing, *nothing*, matches actively immersing yourself in the world of professional real estate alongside real estate professionals as a working agent.

If there's a basic principle behind intelligent investing, it's "Invest in what you know." That's what I do. Sure, I dabble a bit in this and that, but when it comes to serious investing, I invest in real estate. It's what I know! It's what *you'll* know when you become licensed.

It's true that a licence alone won't give you the immediate depth of experience you'll get working at an office, or for a major brand, but you need a licence to get in the door, and once you are, experience (and friends and associates who'll share *their* experience) will follow.

So will the stream of income it provides—income that can allow you to live comfortably and responsibly while it gives you the regular funds you'll need to make investments and purchase properties. Yes, it may take a little time. But that's how smart investors think: in the longer term.

Becoming a real estate agent doesn't guarantee you'll become a successful investor, of course. All it does is give you the tools, the knowledge and the network.

But there's no better place to start.

Beyond that? It's as simple as the '20 to 20' formula I gave you. Find a decent property. Let the tenant pay off the mortgage and build up your equity. Then leverage that equity to buy more such properties and fill them with more such tenants. Rinse and repeat. That's all it takes.

Sure, you can branch out eventually (and carefully) into land or storage units or other forms of real estate investing. But there's really no need. Simple common sense, an informed analysis of property value and trends based on the education and skills your licence can give you, and patience—these will lift you higher and higher and provide you with ever-growing net worth, with a more than adequate passive income, and with a legacy you can pass on to your children and loved ones.

From there, you'll have the skills, the base and the resources to go in whatever direction you want.

Chapter 17

EVOLVING

Not long ago I was at a real estate conference giving a talk. One of the agents, a young millennial woman, introduced herself to me afterwards.

"Mr. Susiwala. I'm your biggest fan!" she said.

I was about to thank her, when she added:

"But Mr. Susiwala! You're as old as my parents! How can you possibly be getting more Instagram followers than me?"

Some people might argue that I would have been within my rights to run her over with my wheelchair and watch the incident go viral.

But real estate agents know how to keep their cool. Instead I suavely said, "It's because I like to notice what works; and social media works."

I gave her a core Susiwala System principle: Model Excellence Creatively. If I'm getting more Instagram followers than you—or calls, or listings, or commission income--then watch what I do, and do what I do; but remember to customize and adapt it. Each of us has our own personal goals and situations. See what works, and see how you can fit it into your daily routine and get the best results out of it.

In fact, that's what I did say. I suggested she follow me on Instagram and watch what I was doing that she wasn't. I hope it helped.

But the more I thought about it, the more I wish I had emphasized that she should go beyond that.

Finding a great benchmark and meeting that benchmark, even tweaking it to make it a little better, isn't enough. One little step isn't enough. You need to take a lot of little steps, and now and then a *big* step.

You have to learn to do more. To *evolve*.

Customers have evolved. Have you?

I remember starting out. If something was cutting-edge, I wanted it! Cell phones, scanners, electronic signatures, you name it. These new technological marvels always had one thing in common. They were aimed at reaching the customer faster, understanding them better, serving them better. I didn't pick up tech for tech's sake. I explored these new tools because I paid close attention to the people I was trying to serve. The savvy customers were the ones online, on Facebook, on Instagram, on YouTube. They were the ones using Zillow and Google Earth and iBuyer.

If that's where buyers and sellers were placing their attention, that was where I wanted the face and phone number and services of Faisal Susiwala to pop up.

I embraced technology and integrated it into my system not for its own sake but because people were embracing it. I turned away from some things, like print ads, because

Susiwala has always been eager to share his success strategies with other agents.

people were turning away. They were evolving, and I was evolving with them.

I wasn't *merely* following along, however. I was surfing the wave, but also trying to anticipate its flow, its direction—to get there just a little ahead of the market, and the competition.

If we really want to be at the top of our game, we need to think about the future. To think ahead, we need to ask ourselves where the game is going, where our market is going, and then be there to meet them.

So where is the market going? Where is real estate heading?

As I see it, there are three big challenges facing real estate agents today. Three new disruptors. (I'm tempted to add a fourth —For Sale By Owner—but that's not new. That's been a disruptor ever since the Flintstones decided to sell their first cave).

These new disruptors are causing a good deal of disruption already, but the good news is that they're not just challenges— they're opportunities, if you look at them the right way.

The first is a word that right now is causing more fear and trembling in the real estate world than any other—iBuyer.

What is iBuyer? It's a company that makes a near-instant cash offer on your house. You can go online, and ask for a valuation, and (if you accept their terms), they'll buy your house on the spot. Bang. End of story. You don't have to show your house for weeks or months. You don't have to pay an agent a commission or do any negotiating. You don't have to do any marketing. They make the purchase directly. The seller pockets the money and goes his or her merry way.

No doubt you're thinking, "If iBuyer lets you sell your house immediately, no fuss, no muss, why isn't everyone selling to iBuyer? What's the catch?"

Good question!

The catch is not small, and it's not new. You see, iBuyer is our old friend, wholesaling. You know what that is. You've seen those bandit signs sitting on the street corner and nailed to telephone poles. "We Buy Houses—Fast!" "We Buy Houses— Cash!"

Indeed they do. Only they buy them at a price cut that makes your jaw drop and your blood boil. Oh, they pay fast cash, yes indeed—provided you sell at 10 per cent to 20 per cent or more, often much more, below market value.

Give iBuyer credit. They've taken this cheap-looking, price-gouging, off-putting approach and spared no expense to make it look cutting-edge, cool and sexy. Instead of some gruff guy on the phone offering half of what your property is worth, you can plug your address into their sleek website, and the little 'wait' circle starts turning as it calculates the appalling price to come, and flashy algorithms and bullet-list popups appear telling you

R16   The Record · Cambridge REMAX Homes   Thursday, November 3, 2016

Time to Join the Party!

Realtor Faisal Susiwala says homes have long been undervalued here

By CAROL WARRINGTON

"This is NOT a bubble," writes realtor extraordinaire Faisal Susiwala in a recent blog he posted on his website (www.homeshack.com).

As the recent real estate numbers show, Cambridge and Waterloo Region are now following Toronto's footsteps with rapidly escalating resale homes prices. Estimates are that MLS® sales through the Cambridge and KW real estate boards this year will reflect a 16 to 20 per cent or higher price gain compared with last year.

Moreover, what has been the norm in Toronto for the past three to four years, that of multiple bids per property, has become entrenched here in the past year. A low inventory of properties, coupled with a huge demand from buyers, has led many local realtors to hold off accepting offers to purchase for 10 days or two weeks of a new MLS® posting.

"I think it's a very fair system," says Faisal. "It gives everyone who's interested a chance to bid on the home they want. We had been hearing so many complaints from buyers that they just missed out on this or that home – homes were selling almost as fast as they were being posted."

Much of the pressure on housing prices has come from the GTA, where the price of an average detached home has risen to about $1 million.

Home prices in Cambridge have languished in comparison with Toronto prices but not any longer, Faisal says.

"It's about time! We've been grossly underpriced in comparison to the Miltons, Burlingtons and Guelphs and I say that's because we've been guilty of underselling ourselves. Here you have Cambridge, right on the 401. You take the 401 home and you're in your driveway minutes after you get off the highway. All these other places (Milton, Guelph, etc.) they are at least 20 minutes off the 401. They may look close on a map but practically speaking Cambridge may offer the best location of all."

"We should have been out beating drums and selling the GTA what a treasure Cambridge represents an hour's drive or less west along the 401, he said.

"I've become somewhat of an ambassador for this region," he continues. "My marketing teaches Oakville, Milton, Mississauga, Guelph – Cambridge is now what Milton and Mississauga used to be to the GTA. Politicians and the Chamber of Commerce really haven't done the things that needed to be done to sell our community outside our region. But now we're selling the message that, a), we're open to business, and, b), that we have a community that's second to none in amenities and, most importantly, we have everyone here in quality of life."

"Our home prices, suppressed by lackadaisical marketing in the past, present a huge growth potential to potential investors or home owners, he said.

"The regions east of us have been partying for years. Only now are we joining the party," Faisal said brightly. He expects home prices to continue to grow robustly.

"I expect to see 30 per cent growth over the next three to five years. This is the new reality."

Homes prices have been suppressed in Cambridge and area by a reluctance to market our close proximity to the 401 to those commuting to jobs in the GTA, says realtor Faisal Susiwala. Cambridge is on the map now and the rapid rise in resale prices this year is the result.

Buying in the Waterloo Region

This is what I often hear today, and if I'm gauging this market correctly, all indicators point to another 16% to 12% increase for 2017. What does this mean to you as a buyer?.....BUY NOW and say "I'm glad I bought last year."

Just look at what has happened, and continues to happen, just east of us. The lesson learned is that the population is moving west along the 401 into the region of Waterloo.

We are thriving economically, socially, and in quality of life with great new infrastructure. We have better roads, transportation including LRT and GO services, and this will continue to make this region very

desirable.

There is still a significant gap in valuation between the region of Waterloo and other regions east of us. We are now on their radar and buyers are coming literally by the busloads to purchase in new home sites and compete in multiple offer situations on resale homes. At Home Shack, we continue to have the best inventory in the prime spots of this region. Reach out to me and I will personally ensure that you don't miss out.

This is not a bubble. Welcome to the prosperous reality of Waterloo Region.

Faisal, 519.624.5355, faisal@homeshack.com

---

how great it is to work with iBuyer. We are so hip, so cool, they seem to say. Look, look: we've put a small "i" in front of Buyer! It's like having Steve Jobs as your real estate broker!

I'm not saying this to put iBuyer down. Some people do need cash fast, for a variety of reasons. If they're OK with taking a severe loss in exchange for selling instantly, it's their decision. Very often it's a poor decision that they'll regret. Very often a knowledgeable, seasoned real estate agent could have offered them much, much better options, and saved them a fortune. But we have no right to judge. And whether it's iBuyer or a shark behind a bandit sign, there'll always be someone around to buy cheap from someone desperate to sell.

But this is nothing for Realtors to be afraid of. On the contrary. Once brokers and agents see iBuyer for what it is—an updated, modernized, beautifully packaged and marketed version of something that's been around forever and has never really cut into standard real estate much—all the competitive worry fades away.

I mean, let's face it: the vast majority of people aren't going to sell their house at a grotesque discount just to save a little time. They may plug their address into iBuyer to see what kind of offer they may get. When they see the number that comes up, they'll call a reputable brand name or branded Realtor. In the end, people want to get top dollar.

They also want reassurance. They want someone to 'lead the journey' and take them from their current home to a newer one where they have not just money in the bank, but also a sense that they've made the right decision, not an expensive mistake that they'll regret. They want the emotional connection and security, the trust, the informed consultation that you get from a licensed and seasoned professional—from a *person*.

iBuyer isn't a threat—not to an agent who can make the case that getting more money is better than selling your home for pennies on the dollar. That's really not a hard case to make.

Smart agents and smart agencies will go farther, though. These sharp people will realize that iBuyer and the iBuyer model is something that can boost their businesses, not threaten it.

How so? Simple. iBuyer generates leads. They're doing what I do when I price a house low to attract bidders. I do that to get attention from multiple buyers. It works!

iBuyer offers a fast cash purchase to attract seller attention. They get that attention. But once they see iBuyer's actual offer, a lot of sellers won't give them a second look, much less end up using iBuyer's services.

So what happens to the names of those people? The ones who have a house to sell but want to get a higher offer, not a lowball one? iBuyer doesn't throw their names and contact info into a wastebasket. Not nowadays. It all goes into a database. If the people behind iBuyer have half a brain—and they do—they'll eventually realize that those leads are something they can sell.

Desperate, stressed-out sellers approach real estate agents too. Those agents don't have a good time working with people near the end of their rope. They don't like making a lowball, low-price, low-commission sale. iBuyer can not only take those sorts of sellers off agents' hands, they can sell agents the names of those other sellers. Sellers who aren't willing to settle for less.

Sellers in their area who fit the agents' preferred criteria. Sellers who want the top price possible for their home.

Time to introduce sellers like that to the Susiwala System, don't you think? When those kinds of sellers see the offers they get that way as compared to the pennies-on-the-dollar-style offers iBuyer makes, they'll be even happier than usual.

So in the end, despite the hype, iBuyer isn't going to transform the way things presently operate. I predict that eventually iBuyer will become more of a lead generation service that serves the real estate industry than a competitor taking business away from it.

But why wait? Clever, active real estate agents can incorporate the iBuyer model into their existing services right now. I have.

When sellers come to me, I let them know that 'iBuy' houses too: I have a 90-day guarantee program in place to ensure that a qualified seller sells, and sells fast—but at a decent price. One that's acceptable to them. Why take a guaranteed lowball offer from iBuyer when they can take a guaranteed offer from me for way more—for the price they want? I'll take out my cheque book and offer to write the seller a cheque on the spot for $5,000 more than any iBuyer offer. No one has ever taken me up on that because they know I'll get them more money than iBuyer+ $5,000 if I'm allowed to sell their property the Susiwala way.

Why do I guarantee that better price? Why should you do the same? Because a smart agent never tries to make money at a client's expense. He or she wants that seller to make a profit. Their profit is your profit. Every last seller you deal with could become a lifelong client. She could become a future buyer. He could refer all his friends to you. When their children get out of college and start looking for their first home, who's going to help them get it? If you've treated their parents decently and fairly, it's probably going to be you.

Every real estate business should have an iBuyer option available. They just have to give it a more human—and humane —touch.

Another challenge—and opportunity—is social media. I know, I know: there are Realtors who hate social media. For them, social media means giving up time to show houses and do presentations, and replacing it with poking your finger at your iPhone and sharing what you had for lunch with Twitter,

Facebook, Instagram, LinkedIn, and fifty other places. How does that sell houses? It means having an unfair and nasty review sit there on Google till the end of time, or having to appear on YouTube every day with a blank expression trying to find something to say, or having geeks with PowerPoint, whose only language is technobabble, fail to explain search engine optimization to you as you write them an astronomically hefty check.

Oh, that internet marketing invoice…

It costs *what* to get to Number One on Google?

It costs *how many* hundreds of dollars when people click my ad on LinkedIn?

None of this bothers me one bit. Because I remember the days of print—the days when I paid hundreds, then thousands, then hundreds of thousands of dollars for newspaper inserts and yellow pages and full-page magazine ads. I don't do print at all now. Why bother? My social media team can focus in on exactly the kinds of people I know will be excited by my latest listing. They can put that listing right in front of their face, and do it faster and more affordably than I was ever able to do with print. Spending money on print advertising made me more money than it cost. Spending money on social media advertising does too— with much more bang at much less cost.

Social media is not a problem unless you're silly enough to do it yourself. *Professionally* done, it's the best way possible to put you, your brand, your services, and your listing *directly* in front of *exactly* the people you want to attract. It does so better than any marketing service ever has before.

The problem is to get real estate agents to realize it.

I sympathize. I had the same 'DIY' problem myself for many years. It's a mindset problem. You want to do it all yourself. No, you don't want to spend money on an assistant. No, you don't need a marketing guy to design your ad or tell you where to place it. You can do it all—you think. Your business is yours, and there's no need to throw money around on others who don't know your business as well as you.

I'm sorry. It just doesn't work that way. When I was young I worked morning to night, seven days a week, and I did everything myself. When I got old enough to know better, I hired an assistant. My income doubled the first year—and I was finally able to spend more time with my family.

The next assistant I hired doubled my income again.

Why? Because I was able to devote my time to the important things I do well, instead of to filing paperwork, licking stamps, and designing box ads. Don't get me wrong: filing paperwork is important, mail needs to go out, and ads draw in the customers who bring in the revenues. My assistants and associates do all that, and much much more. They're worth their weight in gold!

But it's like they say: 20 per cent of your efforts generate 80 per cent of your returns. You need to focus on that 20 per cent.

Someone else needs to take the other 80 per cent off your shoulders.

This applies 100 per cent to social media. The agents I see who get overwhelmed by social media are the ones trying to do it all themselves. They spend all day staring at pixels, friending people on Facebook, answering emails, trolling and tweeting and web surfing. It's the 21st century equivalent of standing around the coffee machine shooting the breeze and getting nothing done.

What they need to do is to get together with some solid social media specialists and work with them to isolate the ideal target audience, an audience that gets the agent the maximum measurable result.

Once your strategy is in place, social media people can put your message and your brand and your listings in front of your ideal target audience every time they log on, and your office staff and virtual assistants

Achieving more by doing less has long been one of Faisal Susiwala's maxims, but as he admits in this RE/MAX magazine, it took him a long time to figure this out.
- *The RE/MAX Magazine*

can help. You won't be sitting at the keyboard then: you'll be making one presentation after another.

Yes, you'll have to pay your social media experts a little money to make that happen.

Do it. You'll make back much, much more.

There's one thing more about social media that people miss, and that I want you to really understand. Yes, today's number one opportunity for real estate agents is social media. Instagram alone will get you more leads for less cost than just about anything else out there.

But just as important is becoming more social—period. Forget the 'media' part.

If you want to tap into any market, you don't need to 'friend' that market on Facebook or spam away the entire day with Tweets. Just go out and meet people. Attend events where they're going to be. Offline. Yes, you got that right—go up to them in person.

Some of you millennials may be shocked. What, actually meet people? In real life? Yes. Walk up to them. Smile. Say hello. Shake their hands, fist pump, elbow bump, do whatever's socially acceptable post-Covid-19. Look them in the eye. Listen to what they say. Engage with people!

What, you think they won't want to talk to you? They certainly won't if you immediately start twisting their arms to buy or sell. (Remember: Never Be Closing.) But never fail to mention that you're a real estate agent, either. Because believe me: everyone wants to talk about real estate. The value of their house, and whether that value is going up or down, is something every homeowner cares about. The state of the economy is something that concerns everyone.

When you simply share what you know with other people in casual conversation, you are engaging in social cultivation. You're cultivating your sphere of influence.

What do I mean by social cultivation? Let me give you an example. Recently I was at a charity dinner. I wasn't there to get business, I was there to support a good cause.

"So what do you do?" someone said, as they always do.

"Real estate," I answered.

I didn't sell myself. I didn't push. People immediately started asking me questions. I answered. I talked about price trends and home values. About the market, about demographic trends, about investment returns, about new legal and technological developments.

Then, at the end of the conversation, I got up to leave.

Several people jumped right up. "Can I please have your business card?"

I never once offered my card. I never tried to 'close.' I had a genuine honest conversation. I'd listen to what they were saying and I contributed to the conversation. That was enough.

That's half the battle when it comes to social cultivation. Just show up.

Here's another example.

If you've acted on what I've been saying, you now have a database. That database includes people you've sold a home to. You've talked to them, you've established a relationship with them, you know their means, you know their goals, and you can work out reasonably well the financial opportunities that are open to them.

Well, *follow* up with them. Talk to them. Engage with that person. Show them how they can use that house to invest in other homes.

"Hey, Mr/Mrs/Miss Potential Customer. You're 65 years old and you're living alone in a 5,000 square foot home. What can you do to maximize the amount of money you can still make? Did you know a lot of people in your situation sell their big, costly, hard-to-maintain home, buy a place that's smaller and comfier, a home they can live in happily right through retirement? Did you know they use the extra money to buy an investment that brings in multiple streams of income as it pays for itself?"

No, don't make it this blunt. You aren't selling. Never Be Closing, remember? Cultivation is just having conversations with people. Ask them, politely and easily, "How are things going? What's happening next? So where do you see the next phase of your life heading? Really! Can I help you to get there? What can I do for you to facilitate that? What can we do now, while you are of sound mind and you can make your own decisions? As opposed to you being forced to do something that you don't want to do because you didn't make the decisions when the opportunities were there? Because nobody took the initiative to tell you that such-and-such an action is a good thing?"

Yes, you're taking initiative as an agent, but as a human being and friend first. Using all your knowledge and experience, ask yourself what's best for them. What opportunities do they need to know about that could benefit them?

This is what cultivation is all about. These are your people. Your circle. Don't sell them a home and forget about them. Stay involved. Not in a spammy way, not in an annoying way, but be of use to them; be of genuine use to them. Reach out to them because you actually give a damn about that person.

Our business is full of people who are a flash in the pan. Once upon a time they sold a lot of homes, they bought their jacuzzi and their Cadillac, and they cashed out. Their customers? The hell with them. That was yesterday.

Don't be that person. Don't sell people a home and forget to provide your skills, your insight, your capacity to advise. Don't sell them a home and forget to show your value. If the house you've sold had no impact on their life, they'll forget you. And they should, because you haven't done your job. All you've done is made a buck. You can make much more than that. You can make a difference to peoples' lives. You can help change people's lives for the better.

Be that kind of agent, and you'll be getting business for the rest of your life.

The third big challenge — and opportunity?

No question about it. Artificial intelligence (AI).

Now when I say 'Artificial Intelligence,' I don't mean science fiction. Real estate agents don't need to be worrying about robots like data from Star Trek taking their jobs yet. I expect most people reading this don't really know what I mean when I say AI. And who can blame them? Everything in the world of technology is changing so dramatically, and at warp speed. A friend of mine thinks blockchain and cryptocurrency will turn the real estate industry upside down. Maybe he's right, but how many of us even know what blockchain is?

Well, you need to find out. Because you don't want to be blindsided by changes that are sure to come.

Even those changes are not as important as AI, though, because the changes that really matter aren't changes concerning 'stuff.' They're changes in how we think and behave. Changes not in the things we have but in the options and possibilities we have. Those are the things artificial intelligence is changing.

When I was starting out, I had the blessing of working with a wise, honourable man who, in my opinion, knew it all — Reid Menary. If I had a question, I went to him. Now if there's something a young agent needs to know, they don't go to a wise and respected mentor. They just open their laptop. Hey, there's Robert Kiyosaki! There are the reality real estate shows (so fake), there's Warren Buffett talking about just the right stock pick for you. There's every real estate guru in the universe, selling their system or product on YouTube.

This sounds like a blessing, but it isn't. It's a problem. The problem is that the sheer amount of information we now have at our fingertips is too much to absorb. There's so much that it's too much.

What's happening is that, because there's too much, there are now programs that go through all those reams of information and custom-tailor it to you. Artificial intelligence isn't a laptop bringing up a whole list of homes. It's a set of algorithms that measure and evaluate your behaviour online, that watch your searches and your browsing habits, accesses all available data about you, and serves up just those properties (or books, cars, restaurants, properties, even possible romantic partners) that it thinks you want to see. A lot of the time, and increasingly more often than not — it's right!

One of the things AI is doing now is estimating home values. Once, when I talked to people about comparable prices and home estimates, I had to introduce entirely new ideas to people who had never heard of them so I could make them understand what their home was actually worth. Now I talk to people who tell me what Zillow and Trulia and Redfin (and iBuyer) say their property is worth. End of story! These people have zoomed into a property from space and toured the neighbourhood using Google Earth. They play games online against people from around the world, and even against machines. They buy and sell virtual property on Second Life, and have their sim walk up a virtual staircase and inspect the virtual roof of a house that doesn't exist! These people have so much easily available knowledge at their fingertips that they think they know as much as you, the agent.

They don't. They don't have the training or the experience. But they may well know a few things you don't — along with a tremendous amount of misinformation.

Some information is more important than other information. Who decides which is which? Nowadays AI systems are looking at tons of data, plus all the information about you that's available online, and in millions of databases, and it's putting information it thinks you want to know in front of you, and not putting other information there. When I ask Google a question these days, it doesn't just give me an answer. It gives me the answers it thinks I most want to see. It serves up ads it thinks I am most likely to click on. It suggests websites and articles it thinks would interest me. Sometimes it's right. It's right a lot of the time.

But increasingly I feel like it wants to do some of my thinking for me. And for you, too.

I don't want to make this sound creepier than it is. Is personalized information a bad thing? Maybe not. But more and more programs are blurring the line between giving you better information on which to base your decision, and making that decision for you. Instead of searching for information, we may find ourselves with satisfactory information first time, every time. But 'satisfactory' may not be your best option.

There may be a bright side. A lot of my business is based on referrals. Someone happy with the good job I did for them will tell a friend looking to buy or sell a house, "Go to Faisal. He'll treat you right." I can see a time coming when someone types, "I want to buy a house" into Google, and Google will go through all my positive reviews and all my awards and tell them directly, "Forget Zillow. Just go to Faisal. He'll treat you right."

That's a big change. Bigger than buying a cell phone before it was trendy. Soon it'll require a lot more from you as an agent than just buying a smartphone. The Chinese call it a 'social credit' system, and it involves you doing a good enough job and building a strong enough brand to get those positive reviews and win those company awards consistently, and have a state-of-the-art social media team on your side to make sure all those things line up right—all so that Google will smile upon you.

That's a challenge, but it's also an opportunity in one special way in particular.

Tech is becoming more and more a part of our personal lives, and our professional lives. It doesn't worry me professionally, though, because I believe that the more machines involve themselves in decision-making, the more the human element will matter.

I'm not just talking about the limitations of technology. For sure, those are real. Sometimes they're even funny. I can't think of all the times I've looked at houses using Google Earth and seen walkthroughs in the form of YouTube video tours. Wow, nice-looking place! Then, when I arrived at the door and the door opened, the smell knocked me into next week.

Guess what? YouTube doesn't have a nose! And that beautiful exterior shot courtesy of Google Earth? It won't show you the mould under the five-foot pile of magazines in the basement. It'll show you the neighbours' nicely cut lawn, but it won't play you the latest Death Metal albums they blast out at 3 a.m.

The Internet can tell you a lot, but it will never tell you as much as reality.

Artificial Intelligence does not take away touch and feel. More importantly, it doesn't take away emotion. For that, Realtors will always remain relevant. Sites like Expedia.com or Hotels.com can replace travel agents because you know the hotel and you know the airplane.

But you need to know more than price and location when you buy a home. You need more than information. You need advice. You need an informed opinion. Buyers ask me, "What do you think of that water stain there on the ceiling? Is that mould? What do you think of that smell? Tell me, is this going to be re-saleable? How do you think prices are trending?" People want to talk before they buy. Like it or not, AI is turning real estate agents into consultants—in some cases, almost therapists.

(In fact, smart agents now *use* AI for just that—reassurance! AI allows me to double-check and let me know I'm in the right ballpark. It also helps buyers and sellers know that the Realtor is on top of things. Better than on top: Zillow may tell a seller that all the houses in this one neighbourhood are worth $400,000 on average when the truth is, Zillow is inaccurate. I know I can sell those properties any day of the week for $550,000, no ifs, ands or buts. So I get the listing and then I get that top price. When I do, I remind the sellers of Zillow, and say, "See? I just made you $150,000." Now *that's* therapeutic).

Not every such ending is happy. AI will burn 'For Sale By Owner' sellers more often than I can tell you. Your house *could* sell for $500,000, but if Trulia says it's only worth $440,000, the FSBO seller sighs and lets it go for $440,000. Not an amount to sneeze at, but a human being would have made that seller sixty thousand dollars more.

There is an important point to make here—something I touch on when I call on real estate presenters to 'Lead The Journey.'

Buying a house isn't just a matter of numbers. It's an emotional decision. It's choosing a home for yourself and your family. A community where you feel comfortable. Feelings are involved. They're involved even when you're buying purely for investment purposes. What investor is never nervous? What investor doesn't feel a struggle between hope and fear? Between the thrill of a gamble, and the anticipation of making a killing?

When I call on real estate agents to think of themselves not as salespeople, but as advisors and consultants, I mean that they have a responsibility to bring their empathy, their intuition and their humanity to a deal. People want and need to trust, and to work with others who are trustworthy. They'll never feel that kind of personal connection to a laptop screen, or a sheet of computer-generated numbers.

Yes, numbers matter. They matter a lot! But in the end people want to do business with a human being, not a machine.

My message to real estate agents is 'Embrace Technology.' It can make your job so much easier, faster, and more profitable that I don't know where to begin. But I have a deeper message, too. That larger message is: 'Embrace Humanity.' The humanity of the people you serve, and your own humanity.

The more complex tech becomes, the larger the opportunity it opens up for people in the real estate industry. Because in the end, people want to deal with another person. The more interfaces and popups they have to wade through, the more they appreciate hearing a wise, kind, friendly human voice.

Technology and innovation will lift more and more of the number-crunching responsibilities of a real estate agent from our shoulders. It'll never lift the need for insight, for imagination, or for intuition in a transaction. Only a human being can see the excitement, the uncertainty and the calculation in a buyer's eyes when they're bidding on a house. Only a person can see the joy on the faces of a young newlywed couple the first time they see their dream home, and think, "That's it! This is our home." Only a seasoned professional can draw a living picture of where the buyer and his whole family are likely to be in ten or twenty years if they invest and re-invest their equity.

Machines don't dream. People do. Helping people realize their dreams is something no machine will ever do better than you.

There's one more thing that I need to address. It's happening right now, as I write this, and many real estate people think it's going to change how we do real estate forever.

I don't agree. It isn't a new, updated version of something that's always been with us, like iBuyer giving a new online sheen to wholesaling, or Zillow and Craigslist providing venues for 'For Sale By Owner' sellers. It isn't a major, evolutionary change either, like social media or AI.

But it's hitting the real estate world and the economy like an earthquake, and it may be a while till things get fully back to normal.

I'm talking, of course, about the coronavirus.

Chapter 18

"PAN(dem)IC" SELLING IS NOT A THING!

As I'm writing this, the nation of Canada, much of the United States, and many nations around the world, are under varying stages of lockdown owing to the coronavirus. Hundreds of thousands of people have died. It seems shallow to talk about the impact of this crisis on real estate in light of so much human suffering. But should the economy collapse, that suffering will be even greater. A broken real estate market in 2008 sent millions into foreclosure and had the entire global economy reeling. Another such shock from the coronavirus will lead to additional personal tragedy across the world, as well as the careers of Realtors who fail to cope with the crisis. Some people are calling it a game changer. The way we live, they say, and the way we do real estate, will never be the same.

Is that true? It sure looks like it. As I write, Zillow searches have fallen by more than half. The number of mortgages being written is down more than a third. Home sales are plunging all over the world. Showings have almost come to a dead halt. In many places real estate has been deemed 'non-essential' and agents told to stay home and shut their offices down.

Will the coronavirus irreversibly change the business? Will it re-shape the direction in which the industry is evolving? What will that new direction be? How can we deal with it? We can only pray for the very best outcome for people who are infected. But at the same time we have to keep doing everything we can to protect and provide the best outcome possible for our families, our employees, our clients and fellow investors and our businesses.

So should we hustle even more? Cold call even harder? Just the opposite. Someone asked me the other day, "What are you doing to get business?" What I said caught her off guard. It even caught me off guard. I said, "Nothing. I'm not doing anything to get business. I'm not even trying to."

She just looked at me.

"Look," I said, "in times like these, you need to go from mindset to heartset, to soulset. In times like these, you don't scheme about how you personally are going to squeeze some last tiny bit of financial advantage out of all these tragedies. You do what you have to do, what you can do to help your people and your community pull together. We need to think about what we can give, not what we can get." (Doing some public good, along the lines of President Kennedy's famous challenge: "Ask not what your country can do for you—ask what you can do for your country.")

"And you think we can help by not buying or selling homes anymore?"

"I'm not buying or selling. I'm offering. I'm offering assistance. I'm offering advice. I'm offering whatever solutions, alternatives, options, I can. People are looking to me for help, so that they don't panic and make bad decisions—so they don't become impatient, or act on impulse, or out of fear. We can't let them go down a path that could really hurt them in days to come."

She didn't get it.

"When you come to people from a place of care, when you put your heart into your advice, the message you're giving to people is that you're thinking about what's best for *them*. That's the message we should always be sending. When they see that, it resonates with people. They need calm and reasonable advice, not someone panicking them into making a bad decision in order to get a quick commission."

"But people are in a panic," she said. "They're coming to me and saying, 'The economy's falling apart. We need to sell our house fast, now, at any price.' What should I say to them?"

"Here's what I say to them. I say, 'Has your business shut down?'"

"They say, 'No.' "

"Have you lost your job?"

"No."

"Can you still meet your bills?"

"Yes."

"Do you think you can still hold on to this house for three to six months?"

"Yes."

"Then why would you want to sell?"

"If I said that to them," she said, "They'd say to me, 'Because prices are going into free fall! What if the value of our home crashes to next to nothing?' "

"Calm them down. Explain to them that they'll only lose if they sell low now. Two, three, six months from now the value may be right back to where it was before. Two, three, six years from now it's almost certain to be more. It could be twice what it is today."

"But—"

"I tell people that if the price drops on their home, the price of the next home they get will probably have dropped too. So all they're really doing, basically, is moving sideways. They're not going up, they're not moving ahead. If they can sell at a high price today, and go to another, similar home that costs less, OK, they've saved some money. But a pandemic is not the time to expose themselves, their loved ones, their family, their home, to a general population walking through their house morning through night.

"Last night I showed a house. I had to put on gloves, a mask, boots—it was like doing a showing in a hazmat suit. Why put yourself and your family at risk to sell your home at a reduced price—at a loss?

"My advice," I say, "to most people coming to me at this point in the crisis is: let's press the pause button, just for today. When you do that, you take out the desperation and help them see the fundamentals clearly. *Oh my God, they say, no one's coming to view our house, no one's even looking anymore, we'll never be able to sell it.* Well, of course no one's looking. The government's ordering everyone to stay home! They're not looking, *for the moment*, because of fear. But that doesn't change the fundamentals—the condition of your property, the location, the access to nearby schools and roads and shopping. Lockdowns go away. The fundamentals remain.

"Look at the reality. Inventory is still at an all-time low. Demand is at an all-time high. Immigration is still at an all-time high. More people need shelter than ever before, and there aren't enough developments going up to handle them all. So why would prices drop? There's no reason for prices to drop."

"But they are dropping."

"Out of fear. Out of emotion. Over time, infections will drop and emotions cool down. The fundamentals will come back in force.

"Besides, where are you going to go? You sell cheap, and then you buy another house that's selling cheap. You're not saving money. All you're doing is playing musical chairs. Let it play out. Press the pause button, let the storm pass. Then press the resume button. Most likely you'll be at the same place financially, without all the upset, without all the bother, without all the costs and moving fees and expensive legal red tape, and without the unnecessary health risk."

"What if they already sold their house before the crisis hit?" she said. "What then?"

"That's different. If you've already sold your house, you have to find a new one. You have to buy. If you've already bought one, and you have to sell your old one to be able to move in, then you need to sell. You've got no choice. That's OK. If the deal is already in the pipeline, I tell people to let those transactions proceed. If you have a reason to buy or sell, do it. But if you're buying or selling because of the present-day, hopefully once-in-a-lifetime circumstances, think twice. This will pass."

She shook her head. I totally understood. What I was telling her was so much against the grain! Like so many agents, she was taught to chase commissions, and nail down as many as possible. If someone wants to sell, *sign them right away*! Say or do anything. Twist his or her arm. Take the money and run.

We don't need to do that, and in the long run we hurt ourselves if we do.

In Canada we're lucky. The government regards us (rightly) as an essential service. We're open for business. One reason for that is that there are deals in the pipeline that need to close. People sold their homes, and then the coronavirus hit. They need to buy. They need a place to stay. In those kinds of situations, in this kind of an unprecedented, volatile market, a good Realtor is a necessity.

Some Realtors, though, see this only as a personal opportunity to squeeze the desperate. "Oh, people are scared, so scared that they're hot to sell. Let me start hitting them with cold calls and scare them even more! Then I'll be able to list all these new homes on the market."

That's the wrong thing to do. Morally, and professionally. There's an agent I know of—no names—who just got annihilated in the media for sending out flyers in her area saying, "Due to Covid, this is the best time to sell. Do it now, before your home values drop 20 per cent."

This is what taints and cheapens our profession. It reminds me of 2008-2009. Here in Canada there was a glitch for about six months when prices dropped and interest rates shot up. Some people panicked and sold. Those people lost out. Some didn't sell. One gentleman called and told me he'd lost his job at Toyota. He needed to sell his house immediately.

I could have said, "Great, I'll come over, and we'll have your house listed right away." Quick commission, and goodbye.

What I did was to sit down and talk to him. "Look," I said, "Your home is worth about $500,000. Once you sell, it's going to cost you around $25,000-$30,000 in commissions, fees, legal costs and transfers. What then? You've got to stay somewhere. You're going to have to buy a home, or move into an apartment. What's your mortgage going to cost? $1,600 a month? What's your rent going to cost for an apartment? $1,800 month? What's your mortgage payment now?"

"'$1,600,' he said."

"So you're going to take a $30,000 hit just so you can pay an extra $200 a month more for a smaller place to rent? That's ridiculous. Let's look at some options. What can we do? Do you have equity in your home?

"Yes."

"Terrific. That means you can probably defer your mortgage."

"What's that mean?"

"It means you can talk to the bank and say, 'I can't make my next three payments. Can we add that amount to my principal?' Nearly always you can. You can't do it forever, but you don't need to—all you need is something to get you through your rough patch. In fact, if you have equity in your home, you can borrow on it. Say you borrow $10,000 to tide you over till you get back on your feet. You're an able-bodied person. You'll get another job. This will keep you going. Just don't panic sell."

That's the message. Whether it's a pandemic or a recession, you nearly always have space to maneuver. Things are negotiable. There's no need whatsoever to put your home on the market in these times unless special extenuating circumstances make it necessary. If that's not the case, and you don't absolutely have to sell—don't sell!

I put out a video before the government of Ontario called for a general shutdown. I wasn't waiting. I announced that I was shutting down my offices right away. I certainly didn't let my employees go. But I shut my sales operation down. I put a tagline on my Facebook and Instagram videos for other Realtors to see: "Stop Showing Homes."

Believe me, I took some heat for it from my peers. People want to sell? Come on, vultures, let's swoop in!

Well, maybe the vultures didn't like it, but every home buyer and every seller who saw that tagline became my fan. A lifetime fan. They thought, "Here's a guy who sells 400 homes a year. This is his bread and butter. But he's putting that on hold because he cares more about his employees, and about us. He's coming to us from a place of concern."

Trust is what gives an agent professional credibility, and nothing builds more trust than when people see you caring more about them than about making a quick dollar. Like so many things in real estate, it's about seeing things in the long term and not just the short.

Seriously. Would I allow groups of strangers to walk though my parents' home in the middle of a pandemic? Through my children's rooms? Of course not. So why would you allow them to walk through yours? We're not doing our part to stop this contagion from spreading if all we do every day is stream crowds of people through the same confined rooms. We don't live in a jungle, and we don't live by the survival of the fittest. We work together through cooperation, and if sometimes that means losing a little business today, and waiting for more tomorrow, that's OK.

The fundamentals haven't changed. This is a glitch, and glitches pass. The market is going to come back, and come back stronger than ever. We need to exercise patience till then, and not be led by greed. It's the right thing to do, and in the end, the right thing to do is the most profitable thing to do. Because the market remembers. People don't do business with people who nakedly take profit at their expense.

Of course, greed doesn't go just one way. The other day I turned down a listing. A person approached me and said, "I want to sell my house." I began to talk to him about all the reasons why this really wasn't the best time to do that, but he brushed it all aside. "I don't want to sell just to sell. I want to take that money and go bargain-hunting. People are panic-selling now. I want to take advantage of it!"

"Now is not the time," I said. I'm putting myself at risk, I'm putting you at risk, I'm exposing other people and families. You *think* you're going to sell your house for top dollar and buy all these properties cheap. But people will see you trying to sell during a pandemic and think *you're* the one who's desperate to sell. You won't get top dollar in times like that. All you'll get are lowball offers. Sure, you can take the money that you do get and start buying. But you won't be able to buy much."

This isn't the time to gouge. Not if you're an agent, not if you're an investor. It's time to wait out the storm. Let's be problem solvers. Let's be solution providers. Let's advise, not profiteer. This is a time to give back, not to take.

Every sign, every billboard I have out there has a new message. It says, "Thank you to our frontline workers, and thank you to our health care providers." It's not a message of 'Most Homes Sold." It's a message of gratitude. It's not a mindset of hustling and profit. It's a heartset of compassion for the community.

Yes, it's also the best possible marketing and promotion that an agent can possibly do. But that's the beauty of what I call heartset, of reciprocity. Once you really get it, you see that doing good for others doesn't mean hurting yourself. Doing good for others and doing good for yourself is the same thing. In the long run, taking advantage of others only hurts yourself. Put others first, lift them up, and in time, they'll lift you up, and lift you up higher than you ever imagined.

Give, and ye shall receive. Try it!

What agents need to do in crises like these is to hold people's hands — virtually speaking. Let them know that you're there to help them through these times. Calm their nerves. Don't let them make decisions out of fear that will only hurt them. The government of Ontario is right: we *are* an essential service. We're not a sales force — what we do *involves* selling, but more than that it involves helping people see how to live better lives through wiser property investment. We're a consultative service, and pushing people into making a bad decision because we can make a quick short-term profit is a disservice to our communities. It will only lead to long-term community rejection — especially now, when every dissatisfied customer can log on with a review and leave a permanent negative black mark on your brand.

But how is a Realtor supposed to live if he or she isn't buying or selling? Sure, some of us are well off — or at least well enough off that we can put our business on pause for a few months and survive. But some of us aren't. Realtors just starting out could be making as little as $20,000 a year or less. They have kids and parents too. They have people who may need their help as well. I've been there. I know how that feels.

No one wants to starve, but let me tell you: you don't need to act unethically to survive. There will always be people who legitimately need to buy or sell. In the midst of the lockdown, with rare exceptions, I'm not handling them anymore. But others who are more in need of income can, and will. That's OK. Agents who *must* stay in the game *will* stay in the game. People who must have professional help *will* find agents to help them. Whatever the circumstances, those agents have an obligation to help those clients honestly,   ethically and safely, and that's exactly the way they should play it. Smart agents will see this as an opportunity: not just for moral growth — and certainly not for a quick sale—, but in knowing that if they can handle a sale or a purchase honourably, to the best of their ability, fully informing their customer about the risks and dangers of these unusual market conditions, they can walk away with a lifetime fan and an evangelist as well as a client. You do your best within the limits of the possible. That's all any of us can do.

There's a lot of Realtor-shaming going on right now. For instance, I posted a listing the other day. I got a text almost at once. "How can you sell a house in the middle of this nightmare?" The person texting didn't know the whole story. A person called to tell me they'd already bought a new house, and the deal to sell the old one had fallen through. Without the sale, they couldn't pay for the new property. The time to cut a cheque was barely days away, and if they couldn't come up with the funds, they were going to be sued. (The people on the other end of the deal had bought a home too, and if they didn't get the money, they faced the same kind of meltdown).

Well, you need to be sensitive to these kinds of situations—to understand that there are always exceptions to the rule. Right now, in these special circumstances, there's no need to put a new property on the market if there's no pressing legal requirement. People who have to sell their home have to sell their home. People who only *want* to sell their home should give themselves a little more time. Better to sell a month or two later than to possibly infect dozens of people with a potentially lethal virus— yourself included.

This is my 'heart advice' to my buyers, sellers and fellow agents. This is what I suggest they do for the next immediate month or so, and, generally speaking, it's how I suggest they deal with sudden market downturns in general.

But where, in the longer term, do I see this evolving? That's a good question.

I would not be surprised if, in thirty, sixty, ninety days, the government of Ontario shut down everything—if the entire real estate industry were stopped flat, and only deals already in the pipeline were allowed to finish up and close. I would also not be surprised if in thirty, sixty, or ninety days, the government of Ontario opened up everything, and ended the existing lockdowns. I think a lot of it will depend on what happens to our neighbour, the United States. Some States are already opening up, while others are clamping down even tighter than before.

The government is probably going to be watching those areas closely, and taking their cue from the results. My feeling is that we're probably going to start easing out of the shutdown soon, albeit slowly.

However, I don't see lasting social changes. We're not going to be social distancing for the next 100 years. People like to interact. They'll keep on doing so. People also like to actually visit, see, touch, smell and walk around a house they're going to spend upwards of $500,000 to buy. It's only natural.

There's sure to be more of the virtual, from home tours to online bidding. I've said all throughout this book that Realtors need to watch for, and catch, the next technological wave. But in the end people live, physically, in a house. Doctors, lawyers, real estate brokers work, physically, in offices. You'll never erase that part of the equation as long as we have bodies. No matter how high-tech we get, people will always want to physically enter a house before they buy it. They'll always want to physically meet a Realtor before they sign a contract. That won't change. But there may be a little less of it, and more use of digital tools along the way goes without saying.

Virtual open houses, interactive floor plans, electronic signings—all of these tools have long been available. Those who've already adopted them are thriving right now. Those who thought they could get by without them are scrambling to learn. They need to hustle: there's only a short window of opportunity left to do it. Six months from now, agencies and brokerages that aren't up to snuff will be out of business. No question.

Let's remember, too, that just having new tools isn't enough: smart agents will be working hard to find new ways of doing business with them. Better ways. Let's say I'm the buyer's agent. I send you links to virtual tours of twenty homes that roughly fit your criteria—links to the floor plans, links to room-by-room descriptions, links to Google Earth videos of their neighbourhoods. I ask you to browse through them and pick the top three that appeal to you for an in-house tour.

What's happened? You're no longer a taxi service, wandering through house after house with them. You've stripped out the properties they're not likely to buy beforehand. You've saved their time and yours. These new tools are creating efficiencies. I can show three houses in an hour. No more wasted days sitting in traffic, driving around evenings, or in rush hours, only to arrive at a house where the buyer takes one look at the neighbourhood and says, "No way!"

Think about the savings, not just in time, but money. We're no longer spending as much time on client parties, on restaurants, on bars, on schmoozing, on gas, on clothing, on office supplies, even (especially!) on marketing. Mailing out to thousands of people regularly once cost tens of thousands of dollars. Nowadays emailing them regularly can cost zero!

It's sad, in a way, that so many people have been forced to interact more and more through Zoom and Skype instead of face to face, but, as opinion makers say, it's becoming the 'New Normal.' We, as real estate agents, have to see and exploit the potential benefits of these platforms to better serve our clients. For instance, I recently gave a talk on Zoom and over 200 people looked in. What's to stop me from giving a live tour of a home to two hundred prospective buyers—or two thousand?

I'm not suggesting that Realtors go 100 per cent digital. The exact opposite! The coronavirus panic has led thousands of Realtors to pull their postcards and flyers and stop what I call 'face advertising': simply putting your face, name and service in front of the public till all three become an automatic association in their minds. That's opened up spots for other Realtors (including me) to advertise. It's also lowered the prices as advertisers cut rates to attract a shrinking pool of prospects. I'm jumping right in.

"But Faisal, why advertise? You're not buying or selling."

I am *always* buying and selling goodwill. I am *always* buying and selling public attention. I am *always* trying to get people in my target market to associate me in their minds with real estate. Marketing means playing the long game, not only shooting for an instant turnaround.

When no one is advertising, and the only real estate face people see is yours—and when the message associated with that face is not "Buy, Buy, Buy" but "Stay home. Be safe. Be well. *I care,*" people remember. When the crisis passes, they'll still remember.

How many Realtors out there do nothing with social media except put out stupid memes? I put out a video the other day of personal reflections about this crisis. I was saying pretty much what I'm saying now. It was genuinely thought and felt, an honest talk about how people could best get through this crisis,

Put the Customer First

...It's more than a catchy phrase or slogan.

It's the foundation upon which my career has been built.

about why they shouldn't panic and possibly make terrible financial mistakes. The message wasn't "Sell with Faisal," the message was "Don't sell, don't put your home on the market now, not unless you absolutely have to."

I didn't just leave it at that. "Now that you're stuck at home," I said, "maybe it's a good time to spruce up your home and make it look its best for when you do decide to sell. Are you working from home now? Why not reconfigure a room to be a proper office space? There's overhead savings there. Sometimes a lot. Are you and your folks, or your children, paying more living apart? If you have enough space, why not live comfortably together?"

People don't read advertising. They read things that interest them, even if those things show up in advertising. When you provide quality content, advice that's genuinely valuable, and you also present a picture of yourself as knowledgeable, professional, sincere, as someone worth listening to, as someone people can trust, they listen. When you present yourself as a consultant who's there to provide answers to their questions and solutions to their problems, you'll naturally attract clients and customers. You'll automatically build a fan base. Ultimately, you are the product; and when they buy you, it's because you've demonstrated in every way that you are the best product.

If I could reduce my advice to real estate professionals in this time of crisis—in any time of crisis—to one sentence, it would be this: put the customer first. Make it plain that you're doing your best by your customers, and they will stay with you throughout that crisis. When the crisis passes, as it always does, they will reward you handsomely with their trust and their respect and their business. Rightly so. You will have earned it.

The same general advice applies to real estate investors, but with a few tweaks. Put your partners first. Be absolutely honest and transparent. Yes, prices and values will fluctuate. Yes, profits may temporarily decline, and what looked like small risks may suddenly look like large dangers. Don't try to paper it over. Don't hide it. Handle partners the same way you handle customers: search for answers and solutions, seek out and present the best available options. They're nearly always there, if you think clearly and creatively.

Panic headlines may abound, but, in Canada at least, the government and regulators have fairly level heads. Things are rarely as bad as they seem, and never as bad as our fears and the media can make them. Real estate is the opposite of gravity: what goes down eventually comes up. If there's one thing about real estate that I've learned throughout a lifetime of investing, it's that property values rise. Even if you wipe out completely— I have—you can come back stronger than ever, and come back fast.

The only thing that is almost impossible to recover is your integrity and your reputation—your brand. Anyone can recover from an honest mistake. A dishonest mistake will haunt you forever. Whatever happens financially, keep your brand spotless and you'll be all right.

Most seasoned investors will weather even the worst-case scenarios. They don't even look at such situations that way. They see crises for what they are: opportunities. Yes, there will be panic sales, there will be bankruptcies. That means there will also be bargains. It's a sad reality, and I personally do what I can to dissuade people from selling in a market like this one. Still, some people have no other options, and some are determined to sell whatever your advice. Properties, residential and commercial, will be put on the market for a song, waiting for investors to pick them up. If you don't, others will. You aren't helping the sellers by hurting yourself. Who knows? If you're the buyer, and you act with honesty and integrity, maybe you can make the sellers' landings softer, and, when things improve, help them back up.

There are some larger changes to consider. The coronavirus, and viruses in general, seem related to population density. That means people concerned with health safety—and who isn't, nowadays?—will likely want to leave dense urban areas for less dense suburban ones; towns just outside the suburbs that are smaller and somehow safer. After all, you can work remotely anywhere, and you don't need to pay top dollar in slightly more distant locations.

For that reason I'm sure there'll be more business coming to my region—Cambridge, Kitchener and Waterloo. There's more sheer space in our region, and at far less cost, than in cramped and crowded Toronto. There are more than enough amenities too, and access, as well as ample space to social distance in smaller communities. The crowded elevators, subways, and five-hundred-unit projects in the big cities can't compare, and those who absolutely must have a dose of big city life now and again can simply drive over. A half-hour drive through hills and forests can be a joy all by itself. Working from home will not only lower overheads for businesses as they relinquish excess leased space, it will provide a cost savings to the employee. Put those funds toward upgrading into a larger home with a yard and more space. From unhealthy, noisy, expensive, crowded big city life to clean, quiet, open, affordable, spacious life rich in natural beauty just outside your doors. Welcome to Cambridge, friend!

Compared to the big city, there's no question that the rate of infection (as well as crime, crowding and stress) decreases with a lower rate of population density. So the more crowded the cities become, the more I see waves of families, retirees and remote workers moving into properties and areas like the one I serve. From an investor's point of view, it's not only existing homes that are more likely to sell. Land that I thought might not have been developed for twenty years is more likely to start being developed in ten, or five, or even two years. It's a good time look at those areas.

Economic decline is never total. The stock market has taken terrible hits—but has made equally incredible daily gains. As I write, many stocks are failing, but Amazon is at a 52-week high! Yes, restaurants are closed. But grocery stores are doing business at levels never before seen. It isn't hard for a thoughtful investor to see where things are going in the next month, the next few months, or the next year. For some industries, and areas, and people, it may be bumpy. But recovery is inevitable.

I know, I know. These are weird times. Who ever thought that Canada would close its border to the USA? But seriously: do you really expect the borders to stay closed? For years?

The coronavirus is pushing the real estate industry into rapid evolution. But it's not a change in fundamentals, only in terms of speed. Sure, we're going to be doing more virtual showings; yes, we're going to be talking to buyers and sellers more and more on Zoom; yes, people will be moving into lower-density areas as the high-density areas become less attractive. The coronavirus made it all happen faster. It was going to happen anyway.

Some things about real estate don't change. People searching for homes will continue to look for safety, security, comfort, and affordability. They'll always prefer nice neighbours to nasty, noisy ones. People who seek to invest will always want the value of their investments to rise. Both groups like agents who look and act professional, and who give them information that's genuinely helpful.

It all goes back to what Mr. Menary told me at the start: "Do a good job. Do the right thing."

I could condense that even further, into two words.

Act honourably.

We may evolve new ways of doing things. We may evolve new ways of interacting with each other online and off. It pays to think about how those things are evolving, and how to make the best use of them that we can.

But the basic principles behind them—integrity, honesty and service? Those will never change.

In summary, here is a 90-day plan during a pandemic—this one, second waves (God forbid), and crises in general.

Days 1 to 30

Your message must be of support and gratitude. Change all ads to reflect that message. Tone-deaf marketing and self-promotion is not what people want to see during these times.

The message is simple: "I'm here to help provide solutions, provide opinions and to support you. It's OK to do nothing. Don't panic! PAN(dem)IC Selling is not a thing!"

Don't cover up bad news. Face it, explain it, and provide your honest opinion on how to best deal with it.

Encourage and empower those around you; your associates, staff, family, friends and clients. Don't bring them down—lift them up.

Empathize. Let them know that we're all in it together. "We may not be in the same boat, but we are in the same storm."

Provide market updates. Point out trends, and help people see positive developments and opportunities.

Provide tips and tricks on what clients can do while they're at home with their kids. (Take the advice yourself if you're at home with yours.)

Set up a home office space. Search the net for helpful techniques and strategies on working from home.

Advise clients to prepare their home now for when the market opens up again. Do things now yourself to prepare yourself and your business for when that time comes. Because it will.

Day 30 to 60

Abraham Lincoln said, "Give me six hours to chop down a tree and I will spend four hours sharpening the axe."

This is the time to prepare and sharpen your skills. Learn technology, put systems in place, hit the books. In particular, improve your Internet and social media skills. From Zoom to social media, people are interacting online now as never before. Use this time to elevate your presence.

Educate. Show people why a surge in the market is inevitable.

Show them that the fundamentals of real estate remain unchanged.

Provide examples from the past, and compare it to what's happening now. Learn from that comparison. For instance, explain the recession of 1990, when there were high interest rates, high inventory, high supply speculation buyers and sellers. When agents quit their jobs and were just depending on flipping.

This isn't the case now—we have low supply, low interest rates and high demand from buyers.

A lesson should also be taken from 2008. We had a quick recovery in 2008. Why? Because most homeowners decided to do nothing. There was little to no panic selling.

Day 60 to 90

Get ready to hit the ground running. Change your ads back to self-promotion. Let the public know that you're opening up again, and doing it safely—that you're ready, and following government protocols.

Have clients get their homes ready to list, and get your own listings in ready order to launch.

Provide market data, show pre-pandemic sales, show sales during the shutdown and post-pandemic values, show comparisons from last year. Use recent market performance as a benchmark. When we recover from the new normal, it's probably going to look a lot like the old normal, and the old normal looks pretty darned good.

Remind people that despite the pandemic, sales and prices have not fallen. On the contrary! In my market, at the time of this writing, after 60 days of shut down we were *up* seven per cent in average price at resuming business.

Yes, we may have missed the "spring market," but that market really only extended into summer. It didn't disappear, it just arrived a little late. Buyers and sellers aren't likely to go away on holidays at the moment, so we'll still have eager buyers on hand wanting to buy homes.

I don't have a crystal ball. But I honestly believe that in 90 days, the worst of this crisis will be over, and even if it takes a few days more, it will be over sooner than you think. So, again, don't panic. Instead, prepare. Every market downturn I've ever seen, sooner or later, has been followed by a roaring recovery.

When times are great, always hedge your bets and get ready for a downturn. Because they'll always come. And when times are not great, like now? Prepare to take that rocket to the moon. Because good times always follow. You can make them into great times—if you prepare now.

So. iBuyer, social media, AI, global pandemics! Things to think deeply about when you consider selling real estate in the future. Wild times for the real estate industry, for sure. Big changes, and no doubt more to come.

"But what about you personally, Faisal?" you may ask. "What lies ahead for Faisal Susiwala?"

Well, I intend to keep selling real estate. I mean—I love it!

Seriously. real estate is cool. You meet new people all the time. You have millions in property inventory to sell. You can make amazing money. The awards ceremonies make you feel bigger than Elvis. You can make a visible, lasting, tremendously positive difference to people's lives. You can develop homes and neighbourhoods, shape communities, rub elbows with movers and shakers, network with the rich, help the sick, shelter the poor and support the people you love. If you're a Donald Trump, you can even become a billionaire president of the United States. Say what you will about The Donald, it's real estate that gave him his base.

What a profession! What's not to like? If I live to be 100, I'll still be buying and selling real estate.

I have to admit, though: I've reached a point in my career where I find myself thinking about new directions. I'm evolving too. No, I'm never going to stop going over the MLS, or give up presenting to sellers. It's too much fun! But I can do things now that I couldn't do before. Things that matter to me.

For instance? Development. Buying and selling a house is great, but actually seeing houses rise up on empty land, watching entire rows and neighbourhoods rise up—wow. Talk about community building!

I didn't have the network or the experience before. But I've worked with enough builders, planners and city officials now to know what I'm doing. I know the trends and the demographics and I've gone through the financing process. Once you've done it successfully a few times, it's almost impossible to keep from doing more.

Yes, it's profitable, but more than pure profit is involved. It's like you're building a part of the nation—making Canada itself larger and greater. I feel like I'm giving back to Canada itself, the Canada that's given so much to me.

Then there's education.

Nowadays I give talks to students. Not students of real estate especially—just regular high school students. They're up on the latest apps, they know Reddit and 4chan in and out, they can tell you the name of every rapper who ever lived, and every Japanese anime ever screened—and they know nothing about finances. Nothing about saving or investing.

I can see the suffering they're setting themselves up for, and it eats me up.

There should be a compulsory class in every high school across Canada that talks about saving, investing, compound interest, building a portfolio, financial goal setting—every practical thing that all young people should know about their coming financial life. A class in every high school teaching financial literacy, so that when a young person comes out of that school, they're not coming out saying, "Oh, I've got to go buy the fastest car I can find! I'm going to go work in a factory so I can take two vacations a year." Every young student in the country should know all about investing, compound interest, building a portfolio, budgeting, financial goal-setting—all the fundamentally simple things anyone can do to get their financial life in order, and put themselves on the path to self-sufficiency and wealth.

It's so important, and so neglected, that it drives me crazy!

Achieving more while doing less has allowed Faisal Susiwala to spend more time with his family.

Chapter 19

WE NEED FINANCIAL LITERACY FOR OUR YOUTH!

(Ahem. Sorry for getting so excited. This subject really matters to me.)

Seriously. Every young person should walk out of school saying, "OK. I have a roadmap. I'm going to get an education. I'm going to go get a job and save 20 per cent of my income. Once that starts to accumulate, I'm going to put it into some asset that's an appreciating asset, be it land, a cottage, a personal residence, or a rental property, whatever. I'm going to be disciplined, and learn how to pay that property off, and I'm going to pay it off."

That young man or woman should be thinking, "I'm going to learn how to use that property to generate income. I'm going set things up over time so that I can retire when I want to retire, knowing that I won't lose one dollar of income. I'll arrange things so that I have the support of a stream of passive income and cash flow all my days. Not just for me. Enough to help my parents, my brothers and sisters, and my spouse and children, too."

That doesn't usually happen, though. Upon graduation the first thing on their minds is, "Oh, I'm going to get the fastest car I can find," or "I'm going to get a high-paying job so I can blow it all partying on weekends." It shouldn't be. That kind of thinking sets you up for lifelong debt and hard financial struggle.

That young student should come out of school saying, "OK, now I'm going to college or will get a job, but either way, I'll have to generate some income, and I'm going to save 20 per cent of that income and put it into an appreciating asset, be it land, a cottage, rental property, whatever. I'm going to pay that asset off, and then invest in more assets. I'm going to work out exactly how long it's going to take for me to build enough assets to guarantee that, when I retire, I'll have enough in the way of assets and cashflow for me and my loved ones to live in security and comfort."

Money matters. Property matters. I learned that lesson the hard way—it was taught to me by life, not in a classroom. It was taught to me by seeing what my parents went through when they lost their home. I never want to be in a position where my children have to see that. I never want to be in a position where I have to pack my belongings and go rent a place and start again from zero. I never want to see it happen to any one of the boys and girls I talk to. Never.

The image I see reflected in the mirror each morning of that poor young boy is one that continually drives me to hustle and succeed. That's the mindset—the heartset—of an entrepreneur. It's a mindset of someone who's suffered loss; the heartset of someone who lives in fear of losing what they worked so hard to build.

I know now that there's a silver lining to that cloud that hovered over us when I was a boy. You learn to not accept poverty. You learn to struggle. To fight. To think. You say to yourself, "What am I going to do? How can I safeguard myself against that ever happening to me again? How can I create a life where that can never happen to me? What steps can I take?"

Most young people today don't have that intensity. I don't just mean that they lack the financial knowledge, though they do lack it. They lack the heart knowledge that sets an entrepreneur on fire.

So, all too many of them find themselves in a situation which, year after passing year, threatens to lock them out of financial independence forever.

The numbers don't lie. Let me reiterate here that in 1980, the price of a home was $50,000 to $60,000—two times the average annual household income. Today, the average price of a home in the same market is $550,000—but the average income is only $80,000.

That puts an entire generation of young people at risk. If they want to set aside 20 per cent of the $550,000 needed for a down payment, they'll have to work harder, and save far longer than my generation ever did. And prices just keep going up. How are they going to manage when—not if— home prices shoot up even farther?

240

This is why building a real estate portfolio is important not just for them, but also important for adults, especially older adults. Because when we retire, our kids are not going to have the disposable income to pay for our medical care or our nursing home. The need is going to be the other way around.

You see it now: parents who should be retiring are instead giving their kids down payment money to help them buy a home. The parents are going to Florida every year for six months, then coming back and living in the basement of the home they bought, so that their children can live upstairs. Even so, that home doesn't belong to the kids. They're tenants. They may never be anything more.

We've created an environment where the only way our children are ever going to have a semblance of financial freedom is when we die. Only by then are they going to have any sort of asset. Tell me this isn't sad.

The coming generation will barely be able to pay their rent, much less buy an asset. So we have to take responsibility, and take it now. We have to take steps to set the foundation today for what's going to happen tomorrow, to give them a decent shot at life in days to come, and the opportunity to build further on that.

Because if we don't do it at this point, if we don't give them the knowledge to know where their poor financial habits are taking them, they're going to inherit our homes, sell them for quick cash to pay their debts, then spend what's left over and eventually be left with nothing.

It's not their fault. It's ours. For not arming them with basic financial skills.

The most important thing you can do for your children financially isn't just to give them money or pass along property. You need to give them knowledge: to give them a financial education. Teach them about money and property and investing.

But how can you pass along something you don't have yourself? Not all adults have basic financial skills either. Many adults, perhaps most, were never taught those skills. As a result, many went on to have a tough go of it. Some have gone bankrupt. Some have gone through divorces, or had illness or a death in the family, that cause deep financial hurt as well. We all go through many things in the course of our lifetimes.

But even people in difficult circumstances can learn to save slowly, put strategic safeguards in place, and create small but growing levels of wealth. Buying one investment property, leveraging it to buy another, and then another, and so on isn't done overnight, or even over the course of a year. It takes time. But it doesn't take all your time. It doesn't even take very much.

If you invest with a clear goal in mind, if you say to yourself that, "At age 65, I want to retire with enough assets to give me the same amount of revenue as I earn at work, even to support me"—you can do it. Your lifestyle won't need to change as you do it. All that will change is your future—and it'll change for the better.

What I want to do with my future is dedicate a part of it to showing young people how they can take a path that's been so very rewarding to me. It's not too late for them—or for you—to build a good, bright future like that. You only need someone to point the way.

"So, Faisal. Now that you're the top-selling real estate agent in Canada, you plan to chuck it all and become a school teacher?"

Well—I plan to do *some* teaching at a few high schools, yes. But that's the thing about evolving: the more you evolve, the more new horizons open up. Take this book, for instance. I can't sit down with every student throughout Canada, but every student across Canada can sit down with this book. I sincerely hope they do. And I hope it inspires them the way a great many people inspired me! (Check out the acknowledgements section at the end of this book. It's a long list!).

I'd like to give adult classes too. Building wealth is not just something for young people. Time and appreciation matter in real estate, but smarts, and hustle, and the right attitude matter more. It's never too late. If you're sixty years old—if you're *seventy* years old—you can still say, "I'm going to come up with enough to purchase a townhome, this will provide me with income and an appreciating asset which I can leave behind for my loved ones without the fear or dependency."

I also plan to give talks to my peers in real estate. Once you learn a few things about a game, you want to pass them along to new young players. It's what our ancestors did when they gathered around the fire—the older hunters passing their tips and stories along to the young.

Development, investing, teaching, speaking. Did I miss anything? Setting up a foundation? Writing this book?

There's an incredible number of things I could do in the future. You too.

But will I ever leave Real Estate? Never.

Chapter 20

THE TOP

RE/MAX International sends out monthly and annual stats that rank agents and brokerages. There's a wide number of categories—which agent sold the most residential houses, which agent earned the most commission, what brokerage does the most business, and so on. Needless to say, I follow all that closely. It's a RE/MAX thing: once you go from Executive Club up the ladder to Diamond and beyond, you just get that competitive edge. You want to see your name on that chart. You want to rank. Heck, you want to be number one.

For the month of June 2019, I was number one in terms of commissions earned. That was great. Still, I had never been number one for the year. I'd been in the top ten for the year. I'd been number three, number four, number seven for the year. Never number one.

The people that put out the rankings like to keep that annual outcome a mystery. They want to build suspense and anticipation. So what they do is that they stop listing the monthly rankings after October. November, December, maybe you're doing great, maybe you're bombing. Maybe you'll turn out to be the winner, and maybe not. You'll only find

Real estate's ordinary superstar

Despite extraordinary success Twin's Faisal Susiwala remains humble and grateful for all the support

out at Las Vegas, where they hold a huge Awards Ceremony called the "R4."

The R4! That's like nothing you've ever seen. It's like the Academy Awards for Realtors, only more flamboyant. I'm serious. They host it at the MGM Grand Hotel and Casino, and talk about *glitz*! It's red carpets, big bands and movie spotlights, the whole shebang all the way. Six or seven thousand agents from around the world go each year and all of them seem to end up crowded into a massive stadium, applauding for the top winning agents who appear one after the other on stage. Everyone who is anyone in the business shows up, everyone is dressed to the hilt, bands play, champagne flows. You have to see it to believe it.

Needless to say, I went too. Maybe—I wasn't *certain*, but *just maybe*—I might be getting an award myself. I had sure worked hard all year to try and earn it, and the monthly stats looked promising. (Till they stopped.)

So I flew to Vegas and booked a hotel and went to the RE/MAX desk to register. When I did, I was given three little cards. Each one said, "You, Faisal Susiwala, are up for a Special Award."

Three awards? Wow, I'd never been up for three Special Awards the same year. Cool! Unfortunately the cards didn't say which Special Awards. They never do. They want it to be a surprise.

Three awards caught me off guard. What I was hoping to get was top seller in Canada for the number of homes sold. That was *the* award, as far as I was concerned. I'd gotten it before, and I didn't want to lose it, and slip down in the ranking.

I was also hoping that *maybe* I could get into the top three for sales volume, which is commissions earned. I didn't really think any agent working from Cambridge, Ontario, could get Number One, though. The average price of a home in Toronto or Vancouver was well over a million. Cambridge was nowhere near that. The top three? Maybe I could reach that. But number one? I might dream about getting it, but actually getting it wasn't something I had any good reason to expect.

I had no idea what that third award might be. Most Money Spent On Bus Advertising?

The cards also told me that I'd be recognized at an Awards Ceremony attended by my fellow brokers and my peers and

As a kid, Faisal dreamed of exotic cars and a beautiful home. Real Estate has allowed him to realize those boyhood dreams, and much more.

other award winners. So could I please be there at such-and-such a time to appear on stage and receive my awards?

Me, on stage at the MGM Grand in front of a cheering crowd of thousands? Sure I could appear! When the time came, I walked in dressed to the hilt and as proud as I could be. I presented my cards, and the awards people took me aside and led me to a waiting room behind the stage. Other winning agents were there too, and they and I were expected to sit there till the award announcement would be made. Out front, the winner of that award would be named. At that point, if the winner happened to be me, a host assigned to me would escort me from behind the stage curtain and I would go onstage and pick up my award. I'd smile and wave, the crowd would applaud, cameras would flash, and the RE/MAX people would roll out the whole Academy Awards ceremony with all the bells and whistles you could think of.

I'd won awards before, and I'd seen many top performers receive awards many times. I'd applauded with all the respect and admiration I could muster. Why wouldn't I? The people I was clapping for were the industry's best. I was up for three awards this year. Would I be one of them? Did I really have a chance to be Number One in any of them this year?

It didn't look like it. The awards were for the top ten in the industry, and in that waiting area there were ten chairs. I was seated at chair number eight. *Number eight!* I almost groaned. I'd hustled my brains out all year, and now it looked like I was going to be the eighth person called. Of course I might be the *second* person called, but still, number three isn't number one. I'd gotten the award for most homes sold in Canada the year before, and the year before that. That year, 2018, I hadn't expected to get it at all, and I was ecstatic. I'd even placed at Number Four for commissions earned that year.

But I'd never beaten Number Four in Canada in that category in my entire career. This year, just maybe, I thought I had a chance to get both. I wanted to get both so badly. To have both was to be at the top of my profession.

But I had doubts based on where they had seated me backstage. No, it looked like this year I wasn't going to get either. Number eight. I'd given it my best, but it looked like I'd been out-hustled. I shook my head.

I felt deflated. I was really disappointed. I hadn't cut it this time around. I wasn't performing—I wasn't keeping up to my own mark.

I'll just have to work harder next year, I thought.

There was some introductory talk in front of the curtain, and then the announcement came.

"Number One in transactions in all of Canada for Most Homes Sold. The award goes to—."

I sighed, smiled and raised my hands to clap. Whoever it was surely deserved it.

"—Faisal Susiwala!"

My jaw dropped. Someone patted me on the back, and the host beckoned me to go on stage. I passed through the curtain and into the lights. The crowd exploded with applause. I got my award and held it up. The crowd went nuts. I didn't know exactly what had happened, but I was too happy to think about it.

Normally after that I'd go down into the audience, but the host whispered me aside. I needed to go back. There were more awards to come.

"Why am I Number One? I thought I was Number Eight."

"What? Oh, that. We seat people randomly."

Behind the curtain I sat down again on Chair Number Eight. For some reason it felt a lot more comfy.

Other announcements came and went. I waited for the big one.

Was this the year? *Was I finally going to break Number Four?*

The announcement rang out.

"The Number One Agent in all of Canada for Commissions Earned—Faisal Susiwala!"

Yes!

I was up and on that stage in less than microsecond, and my smile stretched cheek to cheek. I looked like the Cheshire Cat. I can't even describe the emotions I was feeling. I was still holding the first trophy in one hand, and then the announcer put a second trophy in the other. The crowd that had gone nuts before went doubly nuts this time.

As people began to stand up and the applause washed over me, I felt—I can't describe how I felt. I thought back to Tom Vu and his yacht and this young kid still in school watching a late-night infomercial, thinking *Wow! That's what I want to be. I want to be the best! I want to sell more houses than anyone in the nation!*

My dreams had come true.

I thought of my parents, of Natalie and I putting post cards in all those mailboxes, of Mr. Menary for giving me that first break, of so many friends and colleagues and partners and all the people I'd helped find homes. This was everything I'd worked for for so many years. I was where I had always dreamed of being. Above all I felt this incredible sense of gratitude for every person who believed in me and trusted me.

I was overcome. I needed to get off-stage and sit down.

But the host at my elbow whispered at me again. *No, there's more coming.*

More? What more is there? I had everything!

But I guess not. Because I was led back behind the curtain (and it wasn't easy getting through with those two mini-towers in my arms), and I sat down again.

I wasn't the only one getting an award, of course. Other names were called, and I clapped away for every last one. I knew how they were feeling! After a while, though, I asked one of the awards people passing by, a lady, what award, exactly, was I still waiting for. I knew they couldn't tell me which ranking I had won. Could she at least say what the category was? I was genuinely puzzled. Besides, the awards I was holding were getting heavy!

"The Top Ten Producers in the world," she said, and walked off

I was one of the Top Ten Producers in the world? I didn't know that I was even being considered for it—there were no monthly rankings for that category. Had I somehow actually made it to the number ten spot? Unbelievable!

The Number Ten Spot was announced.

It wasn't me.

The Number Nine spot.

Not me either.

Number Eight, Seven, Six.

Nope.

"And now! The Number Five Top Producer in the World—from Cambridge, Ontario—Faisal Susiwala!"

So there I was. Onstage again, now holding three trophies in my arms, as thousands of people stood applauding like there was no tomorrow. I was as proud and as happy as it is possible to be.

Again, my entire life from the very beginning to this moment seemed to pass in front of me, and—what can I say? I had done something that I had hoped for, dreamed and fantasized about, but that never in my wildest imaginings did I really think I would do.

How could I? I was still just a guy from Cambridge, Ontario —a wonderful, wonderful place to live, but also a place where the population was too small, the price points were too low, where there wasn't a lot of inventory but there sure were plenty of agents always competing against you. I had arrived as an immigrant, and started out from a childhood of foreclosure and bankruptcy. All the odds were against me.

It didn't matter. I beat the odds. I won.

It was a beautiful moment. It was made even more beautiful by reactions of the people there. They were in awe. All of them, from the most famous and respected names in the business, to people just starting out, all of them took the time to come up and congratulate me and truly celebrate that moment with me. One

especially touching moment took place when a group of six or seven South Asian agents came up and asked if they could have their picture taken with me.

"We've never met," one of them said, "but you don't know what a proud moment it is for us to see someone from our culture and our background come to this country and reach this level of success." As he said it, all their eyes shone. They thanked me. Soon all of us soon began thanking Canada. What other nation could have been this welcoming, this open to giving us all a chance to excel? It was an emotional moment for us all—pride in our parents for giving us the history and culture that had shaped us; pride in our nation, the nation of Canada, for giving us a culture that allowed us to flourish and become all that we could be, the best that we could be.

As a real estate agent, that's exactly what I had done. I had become the nation's best. It was 2020, and I had reached the pinnacle of my profession. I had reached the top.

Alhamdulillah. I thanked God from the bottom of my heart that I only reached Number Five in the world.

Now I had something to shoot for, next year!

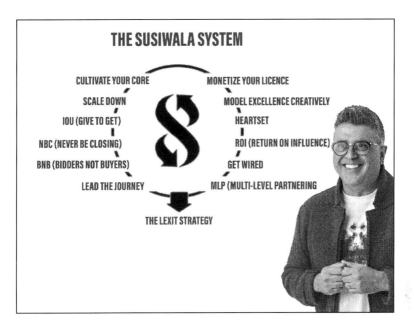

Chapter 21

THE SUSIWALA SYSTEM

Throughout this book I've talked about the Susiwala System. It's how I do real estate. My system made me the number one agent in Canada in terms of commissions earned and houses sold. It brought me to where I am today: at the top of my profession and at the top of my game.

In this chapter I'm summarizing and reinforcing what I've outlined throughout the book. Some things are worth repeating. Reiterating these Principles here is important, because it will allow you to easily take, and then apply, these 12 Principles of my System, as a reference or quick guide, rather than having to go through each chapter to find specific Principles.

Some principles of the System may seem counter-intuitive at first. That's why I wanted to tell you my story and show you how I got there. I wanted you to see my learning process. I'm going to explain those principles now, but the best way to really understand them isn't to think about them: it's to apply them. Once you apply them, and start seeing the results, that's when you really get it.

A lot of what I say goes against conventional wisdom. Because of that, you may be a little skeptical. After all, there are plenty of books, and gurus, and people out there ready to give you advice about real estate, especially when you're just starting out. What they tell you may not agree with what I'm about to say. They don't even agree with each other.

But ask yourself this. Are the people giving you that advice getting actual sales results, or are they just all talk? My system has made me millions, and made me one of the acknowledged top producers in the world. It works. Yet I know there are people who will go into real estate and crash and burn because they're still taking that bad advice, and doing things that don't work.

You'll hear that same stale advice repeated day after day:

Make 50 cold calls a day!
Yeah, right. Prepare to get rejected 50 times a day almost every day. There's no better formula for quickly hating your job.

Knock on doors!
Most of those doors will be slammed in your face—then you'll *really* start hating your job.

Always be closing!
That's right. Twist people's arms out of their sockets to get them to sign at all costs. Pressure them. Aggravate them. Promise them things you know you can't deliver. Push them so hard that you push them away, and they never want to see you again.

Cut your commission!
Oh, is that why you got into real estate? To make less money?

Price high sell low!

That's a classic. Promise the seller you'll push to get some impossibly high price to get them to sign, then disappoint them by always getting less.

Then there's my favourite:

Fake it till you make it.

In other words, do a bad job and lie about it. Who knows? Maybe one day you'll be actually able to do a good one.

These are the clichés of the business. The conventional wisdom. They just don't work. They're a formula for failure.

I wanted to succeed, not fail, and so all through my real estate career I kept looking for what worked in my line of business, honourably and ethically. I kept trying to spot, and avoid, the things that didn't.

So, gradually, I worked out the principles and practices that I'm going to share with you below.

If I had known these principles when I was starting out, I would have become a lot more successful much faster. They're quick and condensed, the pith essence; and, like I say, you'll learn them best if you apply them in practice. All I ask is that you try them.

Applying them in practice has brought me wealth and success, and a life well lived. I believe they can do the same for you.

Principle #1:

CULTIVATE YOUR CORE

Your 'core'? What's that?

Simple: if you want to have any realistic chance at succeeding in real estate, you need to start with certain basics. Don't listen to these people who say you can keep your day job and make a fortune in your spare time flipping slum properties with no money down. Yes, on rare occasions that can happen, but your odds of arriving at genuine lasting wealth by playing the real estate game that way are about the same as your chances of winning at Lotto.

To win the real estate game, or any financial game, you have to address certain core basics. For instance, if you want to invest in real estate, you need money to invest. That means you need income, and a steady income at that. You need to have access to funds.

You need knowledge. You need to be able to analyze a good deal, and know when you're looking at a bad one. You need to know what's legal and what isn't.

You need to have and cultivate a network of people: you need to be able to connect with buyers, sellers, fellow investors, banks, contractors, accountants and attorneys. These need to be people on whom you can trust and depend.

You need to be competent in a wide variety of areas. You need to understand market and demographic trends. You need to be able to understand marketing and branding and promotion — and you need to apply all that, because your goal is to become a personal brand; and to become that, you need to be known.

How can you get all that?

You can study, and struggle, on your own. But in my opinion, there is one path that's better than all the rest. Become a Realtor. Take the classes. Get your licence.

Yes, it involves a few months of training, and exams. Yes, you'll have to pay a few thousand dollars, and really hit the books.

But once you've gone through the process, you can get a position at a brokerage and start building commission income immediately.

You'll have become part of the real estate community.

You'll connect with investors.

You'll have the guidance of experienced brokers.

You'll get referrals, and you'll give them—you'll be building your own network.

You'll see a constant stream of properties pass before your eyes every day, properties that can lead to commission income or that you could end up buying yourself, or buy with partners as an investment.

If you sign up with a brand name agency, you'll share the sparkle of that top brand and it will give you instant credibility with the public; it can also give you an office, marketing material, and legal and professional oversight right out of the box.

Training and getting a licence give you a core, and by a core I mean not just book knowledge, valuable though it is. It opens the door to a consistent, structured source of income. A network. These things support you when times are booming, and they give you something you can fall back on when times are not; and yes, you *will* face those harder times. There are down years in real estate, deals that go sour, time lags between purchase and receipt of commission, long waits between gaining ownership and profiting from appreciation.

Maintaining an income-generating core is the best possible way to get you through the storms we all sometimes encounter. Maintaining it in the very field in which you intend to excel is the ideal way to do it.

Real estate is a very profitable, player-friendly game. But, good times or bad, unless you have a regular and significant source of income—without real life boots on the ground knowledge and experience of real estate and its rules, laws, dangers and opportunities—there is just no way you can make it to the top in that game. You need to have a base. Something that provides you with enough funds to allow you to put skin into the game, and something that can back you up and pay your bills while you're building your brand and/or your portfolio.

You must maintain that core. That's Priority Number One.

But, more than that, you need to cultivate that core. The more income you generate, the more you can invest. The more people who know about your interest in real estate, the more potential investment partners you can attract. The more books you read, the more courses you take, the more deals you do, the more friends you make in the business, the more knowledge and experience you acquire.

The more you cultivate your core, the stronger you become. And the stronger you become, the more you succeed.

Take my word for it. If you want to make a fortune in real estate, there is no better way to start, and no better way imaginable to build core knowledge and experience, than to become a real estate agent.

I've done very well in real estate. I could retire tomorrow, and live handsomely on the cashflow from my investment properties alone. Even so, I would never give up my licence. I still buy and sell houses for clients, I still work happily each day, and I still use the income stream from those things to pay my bills, cover my expenses, feed my family and fund more investments. That core secures my funding, my family, my ability to play the game of real estate at maximum profit and maximum effectiveness, and I take very good care of it.

Find your core. Maintain it. Cultivate it.

Principle #2:

MONETIZE YOUR LICENCE

.

One of the worst myths about real estate is the notion that being a real estate agent is a snap. Anyone can do it—or so they say. Put a sign on a lawn and enter a listing on the MLS, give people who call up a tour around a house, and you're done. The money will just roll in.

Nothing could be further from the truth. I've seen beginning agents without a clue do nothing more than sit around the coffee table at the agency, expecting in vain that calls to the company will just stream in. When cold reality sets in and they realize they have to actively get business, they start making cold calls. That's literally all they do. These would-be agents burn out fast.

Experienced and intelligent agents put a good part of their commission money into marketing, and use that to attract more buyers and sellers, and build more commission income. Good for them!

But even these sharper, more active go-getters aren't squeezing the full measure of value they could be getting out of their profession. To do that, they would need to do all they can to elevate their profession in the eyes of the public—and themselves. They need to monetize their licence.

Ask yourself seriously—as a legally licensed and trained professional, in an industry that involves client investments often in the hundreds of thousands of dollars, sometimes *millions* of dollars—is putting out a lawn sign with your picture on it really all you can do to impress a public *thirsting* for competence, trust and reassurance? Is presenting yourself as a quick-turnover salesman, instead of a trained, qualified, thoughtful investment professional, the best way to attract business? To generate income? To maximize your profitability?

Steve Jobs famously said: "Think Different." That's where monetizing your licence starts. It begins with seeing yourself differently. Too many agents think of themselves simply as salespeople. They sell a house the way a used car salesman sells a car. They walk the buyer to the car, let them kick the tires, and then cut the asking price a bit. Sold!

What agents need to do is to start thinking of themselves as professionals on par with other professionals—as government-licensed, provincially-certified individuals with unique access to knowledge that can have a significant impact on their clients' futures, an impact that can be as lasting and important as the impact of a doctor or lawyer. Why not? It's true!

A home buyer doesn't just buy a home. He or she buys an appreciating financial asset—a form of equity that can be used to secure their retirement. One that can pay for their children's educations and can provide a base for further investment.

With proper professional advice, that initial home purchase can lead to genuine wealth for the buyer and his family. Over time it can provide enough equity to buy several properties. It can serve as collateral to start a business. It can be the basis for a happy and satisfying retirement. As a seasoned and experienced advisor who can present and explain all these possibilities, the agent may be cultivating future investment partners, and developing client evangelists whose appreciative reviews and referrals bring in ongoing lifelong commission income.

It doesn't even stop at commissions. If you're seen as a knowledgeable professional, you can generate new, entirely separate, multiple streams of income. You can become a speaker, a paid guest blogger, a teacher, a coach, a paid mentor, an author of articles and books, a paid consultant. By informing clients of the equity and investment possibilities of their homes, you're acting as a trusted financial advisor. All these other streams of income are potentially yours, right alongside higher commissions, *if* you present yourself as *what you are*: a trained expert in a field *critical* to people's finances and their futures.

Why aren't you generating profit from all these possible extra streams of income right now? I'll bet anything that the only reason is that you haven't thought about it. Well, think about it! How can your real estate licence, your certified expertise, bring in additional money? There are a dozen ways you can monetize that licence of yours, from the start of your career to the end.

And when retirement comes? Possibly the very best way to monetize your licence is to sell all those streams. Define your business processes, pull everything together into one business-in-a-bundle, and then include your brand and sell it.

If you've built a real estate practice that makes even a modest $500,000 a year, do you really imagine that someone out there isn't willing to buy an income-generating operation like that? People buy businesses all the time. They'll buy yours if you can spell out every step of the process by which you generate your profits, and show that keeping those operations running will keep that income stream coming in.

If you include your branding, your database of clients, contacts and investors, if you lay out all the things you do that make your system work, do you really think that people who buy businesses—not to say agents and Realtors who want to really hit the ground running, or to expand—won't pay good money for that operation?

(There's even a better way to leverage your licence along these lines, but I'll save it for the section at the end of this chapter, on my LEXIT Strategy).

Your real estate licence isn't just a piece of paper that lets you buy and sell houses the way a pawn shop clerk buys and sells whatnots. It's a document that confers professional status and financial expertise. It allows you to creatively generate streams of income for your clients, partners and investors. It allows you to creatively generate ongoing multiple streams of income for you, all the way to retirement and beyond.

Don't regard yourself as anything less than that kind of expert professional. Stop thinking of yourself as just a salesperson. You're more. Much more.

And if you don't think that's so, then *lift yourself up* to that level. *Become more.*

Principle #3:

SCALE DOWN

What do I mean by "Scale Down"? Simply that you need to focus.

You can't do it all, and you can't do everything. You can't target every market in the world, or win every battle. So what can you do? You can concentrate your skills and services on those areas that interest you most. You can farm those areas where you do best. You can learn to fight the battles you can win, and win big and often. Don't scatter your efforts. Pick the battles where victory is most assured.

When you do that, you not only build your base—the core that makes building real wealth possible, but you turn your weaknesses into strengths.

Take me, for example. When I started out, I had every strike against me. I was a minority—in fact, the *majority* of what I was, was minorities: I belonged to a minority religion, a minority ethnic group, and a minority population (immigrants). Even my age put me at a stiff disadvantage. I was too young, my skin was too dark, my experience was zero. Education? I didn't even have a high school diploma when I started. I didn't have a car! I had a monopoly on being a minority in almost every sense of the word.

But these weren't weaknesses, because I didn't take them as weaknesses. I asked myself, "Where are the strengths, the opportunities, in these things?" I recognized that belonging to different minorities made me a part of different groups—and that different groups tend to like and trust people who also belong to those groups. Why wouldn't they? When an immigrant needed a house, they preferred a Realtor who understood their situation and shared their immigrant experiences. That was me. It gave me special qualifications. If a person who spoke only Arabic needed a place, he or she wanted a Realtor who spoke Arabic. That was me. Hindu immigrants who were new to English needed an agent who knew Hindi. That was me. The things I had in common with those clients didn't guarantee me those clients, but they sure helped.

Nowadays it's getting trendy to call such groups 'tribes.' I don't really like that word. It sounds too ethnic, and that's not really what I'm talking about. Of course there's nothing wrong with being part of an ethnic group, or thinking of it as a tribe, if that's what you want to do. We all have some background or another. In fact, we all belong to several groups, to different overlapping communities—that's just part of being a person. So long as we don't disrespect or devalue people in other groups, belonging to a community can be a very positive thing.

We all have such communities. I think of them as 'circles'— networks of people who know you, like you, trust you, and feel like they share something in common with you, even if it's only something like cheering on the same hockey team.

There's something you should remember about each such circle. Everyone who's a member needs a place to stay. Small communities like that offer a real estate agent target markets that he or she is uniquely fitted to serve, markets that can become a lifelong stream of income and support.

What exactly is your circle? That's the amazing thing; it's anything you share in common with another person; and you share something in common with almost every other person. You just have to find it.

You belong to several groups already. It can be your extended social network—your friends and family. If you're a student, your classmates and professors are your circle: they know you, like you, and accept you—and some of them need housing. If you're a retiree, it's the same thing. Retirees looking for a house will see you as one of their own. Are you a fisherman or a golfer? Once a community learns that you're one of them, once you establish a kinship, business follows. That's your target market. That's the small community that can start you off and keep you going, in good times and bad.

I scaled down. When I started out I didn't try to sell to all of Canada or even all of Cambridge. I didn't go to the top firm in the country—then. I got my first job in real estate from an old friend of my family. I made my first big sales to some distant relatives I met at a family party. I soon found myself helping immigrants—like me—find their first homes.

I didn't really think of it as 'scaling down' or as 'marketing focus' at the time. It happened too naturally. But it should have been obvious. You sell more easily to the people that surround you, the people you hang around with, the people who know you and trust you and have access to you. Those people are what I call your 'circle.' In marketing terms: they're your niche.

A niche can be a lot of things. It can be geographic. I was raised in Cambridge and I'm still based there today. People ask me, "Faisal, how is it possible to sell nearly three billion dollars in property in an area where the average income is $80,000 and there are only 130,000 people there?"

It's possible because, after thirty years of doing real estate, I know Cambridge like the back of my hand. I know every street and every house, I've seen the directions in which every development has moved, I've met the bankers, talked to the real estate attorneys, put flyers on every door and postcards in every post box. I can get my clients the best price possible because I know this area in as much detail as it is possible for a broker to know.

This is where scaling down comes into it. I don't have to leave and drive one hour to Toronto to get business. All I have to do is place ads in Toronto saying, "Want to drive 60 minutes and pay $350,000 less to live in the exact same kind of house?" When the caller calls, I can find that caller the exact sort of house they're looking for, because I know my niche. I know it because I scaled down: I concentrated on this one location.

If you want to be successful in real estate, scale down: find one location—one postal route, one suburb, one group of neighbourhoods, one region. Grow from there. Get deep and thorough knowledge about every street and neighbourhood you handle. That's mandatory. You can't sell and should never buy what you don't know.

But when you *do* master your chosen area, when you've become *the* subject matter expert on that area—or any area, real estate or not—people will come to you, and you will flourish.

This principle applies to investment too. I invest in real estate —Cambridge real estate. I don't invest in silver, gold mines, or tax liens. I don't invest on other continents. I don't know those places, and I can't master twenty different areas of investment with complete expertise. Cambridge real estate I know. I know the value of a property here, the value of land here, what rates of appreciation I can expect here. I know how much rental income I can expect to get here from a home in one neighbourhood here, and how much I can get from another neighbourhood over there.

If I need investment partners, I don't seek them out globally. I've bought and sold homes right here to prosperous doctors, lawyers, professionals and people in my circle. I let them know that I invest and that I invest with partners. Once they see the price I get them for their home, or the way their home has appreciated in value, they call me. They ask me if they can partner with me.

After all, we've already partnered on the home they live in and they've seen it go up in value. They've made money. Why not make some more?

I don't have to beat the bushes for venture capitalists. I've *scaled down*: I've served the small community I know as best as I can, a community that's near at hand and knows me, knows my record, and trusts me. Why should I be chasing after investors in places I don't know, trying to establish myself with people who don't know me? I've completely mastered the areas of property and areas of investment in which I deal because I picked ones that were small enough and close enough *to* master.

Scaling down real estate *techniques* is another great application of this principle. I wanted to be able to get the maximum bang for my marketing dollar. Did I run around studying and copying everyone everywhere? That's silly. I simply looked around and asked myself who around here marketed themselves really well? Answer: RE/MAX! I joined, and almost automatically the power of their marketing and branding passed down to me like a priceless inheritance.

Who else marketed themselves really well? Coke! When someone wants a soft drink, they don't ask for a cola. They ask for a Coke. In Coke's case the brand completely replaced the product or the service. How did they do that? How could I apply that effect to me? How could I get people to instantly and automatically think of 'Faisal Susiwala' when they thought 'real estate agent'?

I looked at what Coke was doing, and what they were doing was simply being everywhere. Wherever you turned, there was a Coke ad, a Coke commercial, a Coke sponsorship. Did they cold-call you to buy a bottle? No way. They never pressured anyone to buy a Coke. They were just there, all the time. You saw their advertising everywhere you looked, every single day.

I couldn't do that. That kind of global advertising costs Coke billions!

But I *could* do it if I scaled down. Maybe I couldn't be everywhere in the world, but I *could* be everywhere in Cambridge. It still cost a lot, but on a small scale. It was small enough to be possible, and manageable; and the more I put into it, the more I made.

In that one area, the one area in which I concentrated, the one area I knew perfectly, I became like Coke—seen and known by everyone who needed real estate services. I'd taken a lesson from one of the biggest companies in the world, and adapted it to suit my own needs. In Coke's case, they covered a global market. I *scaled it down* and applied it to the local market, and to my local company.

It worked.

Word of warning: there is one serious danger when it comes to scaling down. It's that scaling down can work so well that you never break out into the larger market. That isn't necessarily a disaster. If you only serve your circles, you'll never starve. Scaling down focuses you—on your market, your skills, on those techniques and approaches that time and experiment show you work the best.

But you shouldn't develop tunnel vision, and look the other way when opportunities outside your niche turn up—especially opportunities to learn. I happily still serve the immigrant market. But if the *only* market I let myself serve was that one, I'd be making a lot less. Your circles are a wonderful place to start, but a terrible place to remain. You should return to them, but you shouldn't let yourself be restricted by them. We all belong to many circles, including the biggest one of all—humanity. That's a community we should never forget.

The principles in my system have what's called 'synergy': they work well with each other, and together they add up to more than the sum of the parts. Scaling Down is a principle that harmonizes beautifully with another principle: Cultivate Your Core. Scaling Down helps you focus and concentrate on core: the target market and area, and the key techniques, that provide you the income you need to live, learn and invest.

Still, we live in a fast-changing, ever-evolving world, and new techniques, new options and new opportunities are opening up around every corner. And it's not just the world that's changing—we change too. Scaling down is an incredibly good way to start, and to thrive, but carefully expanding outward from that base is a natural part of business growth too.

Professionally—and personally—you need to be prepared to adapt, and to grow. To enter new circles. Maybe even to start whole new circles of your own.

That's where the next principle may help.

Principle #4:

MODEL EXCELLENCE CREATIVELY

This principle came from Tony Robbins. At least at first. Like so much else in my career, I practiced it even before I ever heard of Tony, without really knowing what I was doing. But Tony helped clarify it for me, and that helped me to do it better. That gave me the base from which I could develop this fourth principle.

Really, it's very simple. (Though I give it a little extra twist that makes all the difference.)

When you see someone doing something that works, copy it. 'Model excellence,' as Tony would say. Are you in an office where one or two Realtors are superstars, and a couple others can't seem to attract business at all? Just look at them, and ask yourself: what are the successful people doing right? What are the unsuccessful ones doing wrong? What are both these people doing that's different from each other, and from what you're doing?

You want to do what the winners are doing. It works.

You want to stop doing what the losers are doing. It doesn't.

Everything you see your colleagues doing, every result you see them getting, is a teaching lesson. Learn from it. Don't just learn from it intellectually, with only your head. Do it. Put it into practice. As Henry Ford said: "You can't build a reputation on what you're *going* to do."

Tony's approach is based on his NLP (neuro-linguistic programming) training, and sometimes he makes this simple approach a little technical. At those times it's often called 'modelling.' An NLP practitioner may have you imagine you're actually inside that successful agent's body, or have you try to copy that agent's tone of voice, gestures and posture. Talk the talk, they say, and sooner or later you'll be walking the walk.

Now, to me, that's a little too close to 'Fake It Till You Make It"—a principle I completely reject. You can wear Air Jordans, but that doesn't mean you can jump as high as Michael Jordan. They may make you feel like you can, but at the end of the day you sink the ball or you don't. If you don't, it's a bad principle.

If it helps you even a little, I don't wish to discourage it. Yes, a bit of external modelling can help. If those Air Jordans inspire you to jump so much as an inch higher, it could still help you sink a basket. If looking sharp makes you feel confident, look sharp!.

I'm talking about something different, though: the need to cultivate your skill and determination to spot excellence, to adopt and adapt the practices of excellence, and then develop your own excellence *further*—to take excellence to the next level, and go beyond it to reach new heights of your own. Don't just *copy* excellence: examine it, analyze it, and use all your creativity to make it more excellent than before.

Spotting excellence is not as simple as it looks. My first (and worst) year at RE/MAX was saved from complete disaster for one reason only—a fellow Realtor brushed off a walk-in customer who had the dusty look of someone who'd walked in off the farm. That Realtor was a superstar, the top-selling Realtor in the firm. If I'd been copying him, I'd have brushed the customer off too. Surprise: that wonderful dusty old gentleman bought a million-dollar property the same day. It not only covered my bills for that year, but got me my first RE/MAX award as a result.

I learned a lesson that day, all right: don't be a snob, or judge a book by its cover.

But also, don't copy *blindly*, without thinking. Use your head. Do better.

Mr. Reid Menary was the man who gave me my first break, the man who opened up the world of real estate to me. A kinder, nicer, more knowledgeable, more ethical gentleman never walked the streets of Cambridge. I was a raw beginner at the start of my career, and he taught me lessons I remember to this day.

But I have to be honest: there were things about his agency that needed improving. I had to struggle to get him to invest in a cell phone. Give the man credit! He heard me out, listened to my arguments, and got me one. They weren't cheap in those days, either.

But a personal computer? No way!

The next agency I worked for was co-led by a fellow who was insistent on every last part of a real estate deal being meticulously and legally correct. He was absolutely right, and I still keep to the high standards he set.

Yet every time I left his office, the other co-owner would say, "Yeah, yeah, keep it legal and above-board, that goes without saying. But that's not what real estate is all about. It's *also* about charm! Salesmanship! Making connections! Shmoozing!" He was right too.

One side didn't contradict the another, not really. You needed to get the paperwork right. You needed to be honest and ethical, and to the letter; you also needed to get on with people, and to network.

What an aspiring real estate agent needs to do is cherry-pick the best lessons from the agents, investors, books and gurus they encounter, and combine them. They also need to adapt those lessons so they fit his or her personal style, and meet the challenge of their personal environment—their evolving environment.

One of the people above was slow to adopt new technology. Another agent snubbed people on account of their looks. One broker was always telling me, "Meet people. Hang out. Shmooze." They were each successful Realtors with a good deal to teach.

But I went with new technology anyway, and I make a point of treating people nicely regardless of how they look, and when I schmooze nowadays it's more likely to be on Instagram and Twitter and Zoom. Bars? They're not for me.

Each had good lessons to teach. But I used the lessons, or the parts of the lessons, that worked out best for me. When the lessons were not so good or no longer applied, I pushed the envelope and developed a few new ones of my own.

In real estate, you're going to find plenty of people, lots of gurus, and a multitude of books, YouTube channels and podcasts, all of them giving you advice on what to do. Some of it contains good stuff. I hope you feel this book does too. If so, great. Take what works and apply it in practice. See how well it will work for you.

But do it *critically*. Do it *creatively*. Do it *ethically*. I once had a competitor who came close to doing nearly as well as I was doing. He did it by copying everything that I did to the letter. My system works, and because it works, it worked for him too. Then he slipped up in a way that led to his licence being taken away. He copied everything except the part that mattered most, and threw away his career.

That's not the way to approach real estate, or apply the Susiwala System. What you want to do is to take the best elements you find here, and elsewhere, then exercise all your intelligence and creativity, and do even better. Don't copy me. *Beat me!* Show me how to invest and do real estate in even better and more effective ways—so that maybe one day I can learn from you, too.

Principle #5:

HEARTSET

When I'm driving to a listing presentation there are certain rituals I follow. I listen to uplifting music, remember past successes, I daydream about the presentation going perfectly. I'll recall a conversation I've had with someone who makes me laugh or feel positive (Often my kids). I get my head straight! Sound strange? Try it, it works.

When I present, I bring along a book showing how much more than the original asking price I've made for my sellers. The book shows that I did a good job for other clients. It helps convince those people I can do a good job for them, too.

But I do it for another reason as well. It makes me feel good!

My office is filled with every award I've ever won. They're there to impress prospective clients, true. But every time I walk by them, I feel proud and happy. I'm lifted up. When I see all that I've accomplished, I'm grateful, and confident. I feel inspired to do even more.

These are all tricks. Mind tricks. *Good* mind tricks. They work. They put you in the right frame of thought: the mindset of a winner. Real estate people love these things. They go to motivational conferences, listen to motivational speakers, and play inspirational podcasts all the time. "Never take no for an answer! Be the best you can be! Go for the gold!" Rah rah rah!

I'm not making fun of these things. They really do help. They can help put you in a better, stronger frame of mind. I subscribe to these practices. I listen to Tony Robbins DVD sets constantly. Mindset, even on that level, is absolutely a part of the Susiwala System.

But I take mindset more seriously than that. I think you should too.

You see, the problem with mind tricks—fun and helpful as they are—is that they don't go very deep. You've seen this many times, I'm sure. A colleague goes to see a motivational speaker, and returns all charged up, so high and full of enthusiasm. They're ready to take on the world!

Then they sit down and start going through those fifty daily cold calls. They start out like a lion. After the tenth time someone hangs up on them, they're a lamb. By the fortieth, they're lamb stew. By fifty, they're road kill.

You can't live your life, or sustain your career, on an emotional high that never ends. And it always ends. You always come down. Fortunately, that's true of depression as well. You may feel down at the moment, but sooner or later you'll feel up again. Feelings pass; that's just how we are.

To do your best, though, to do it consistently, to really excel, what you need are not emotional peaks and valleys, but something deeper. Something that can sustain you, and centre you, and drive you forward through the highs and the lows.

For me, only one thing does that: giving sustained attention to my values. It's critical for me if I want to do my best. I believe it's just as important for you, too. Find and dwell on what matters to you the most. You need to get in touch with your deepest values to fire you enough to inspire you to your best performance.

I like, and practice, mindset. What I'm talking about is more than mindset, though. It's what I call heartset. It's about connecting what you do and who you are to something higher, deeper and bigger than yourself.

What got me started in real estate was seeing a real estate guy, Tom Vu, on a yacht. Man, I wanted a yacht too. Badly! But later on, when I went bankrupt at age twenty, it wasn't yearning for a yacht that kept me in real estate. I stayed because of my parents. I love my parents, and more than anything—more than a yacht, more than all the yachts in the world—I wanted to pay off their house so they would never, ever, have to face foreclosure again. Being in real estate made that possible, and I knew it. So I wasn't going to step off that road till they were safe and secure. Period.

When I got married, that kind of love, that caring, that responsibility, enwrapped itself around my wife too. It happened again when we had children. The reasons pushing me to do well and be successful grew stronger and truer. I know, I know—it sounds incredibly corny to say it, but it's the truth. What made me one of the most successful real estate agents in the business was love. All right, go ahead, laugh!

But that's what it was. What it still is.

Building a success-driven *heartset* involves digging down deeply into yourself. It isn't about walking around repeating affirmations or rubbing your lucky rabbit's foot before a presentation. Fine, do that too if it helps. But if you want to get *really* motivated, to reach a level of *total* commitment and absolute determination, you need to dig deep, concentrate, and connect with what matters most to you.

That includes your own integrity and self-respect. I've seen people get into real estate solely because they thought they could make a quick buck. I've seen such people go after money and success in ways that were selfish and ugly. Even illegal. Those people aren't around anymore. They approached the business the wrong way, and it wasn't a matter of their skill levels or what they played in the car on their way to a presentation. Their heart was in the wrong place.

Elsewhere in this book I talk about reciprocity. Maybe it will help some of you to think of it as Karma. 'Do good unto others, and good will return to you.' It works the other way, too. Hurt others and hurt will come back to you. I've seen this rule hold true over and over.

A keystone for having a good real estate heartset is knowing that you're doing good for others. When I present to a seller, when I speak to students, when I talk to a partner or an investor, I consciously focus on doing good for that person—doing the best I can for them, getting the best outcome for them I can get.

I trust it will work out for me too, and guess what—it does. That's the beauty of real estate: what's best for them works out best for you as well. Get people the best house possible for their dollar, sell it for the best price you can get, and not only do you earn commissions, you make customer evangelists who'll send you business all their lives long. It works! But it's not a mind trick. It's not a heart *trick* either. It's a willingness to explore your heart, and see to it that it's on the right path.

Try it. Go to your next presentation thinking of how you can do the best you can by that person. That decision, that feeling, that *heartset* communicates itself. Clients sense it. Really feel that way and you'll get the listing; because what you feel inside shows on the outside. They'll know.

In the end people want to work with people who care about them, not people who are out for themselves at others' expense. Henry Ford said "If you think you can, or you think you can't— you're right." In the same vein, if you care—and if you don't—it will show.

The payoffs are more than financial. You've helped someone. You've made someone's life better and happier. By improving their lives, you've given them a better future. When you remember that, when you think about it during your day, you'll just plain feel better about yourself and about what you do. You can't help but feeling good about yourself.

Will that make you do your job better, will it make you feel better, will it make you be better? You bet it will!

But how do you focus yourself to that degree? How do you connect with your highest values, and with that much intensity?

As someone with a South Asian background, you probably figure that I'm into meditation or yoga or that kind of spirituality, and that I'm recommending some esoteric practice like that. Not really. I think well of people who meditate, and all the studies I know about say that it helps people emotionally, physically, and mentally. Meditation gets you working systematically on your thoughts and feelings. It's worth doing, and if you want to do it, go right ahead.

To tell you the truth, though, what helps me most is prayer. Relax, relax—I'm not going to get all holier-than-thou. A good Muslim should pray five times a day, and I do my best, but I'd be lying if I said I never missed a prayer. I slip up sometimes too. But honestly: when it comes to heartset, there is nothing better than getting in touch with God.

Prayer is like capital appreciation. You don't do it for an immediate return; you don't do it to get something out it for yourself. Nevertheless, the benefits are endless, and come back to you many-fold over a lifetime. Sometimes I'll pray purely out of gratitude. God has been very kind to me. Why shouldn't I be thankful? Sometimes I'll ask God's blessing on a specific business project. Why not? If you're doing it in the right spirit, and with the goal of bettering not just yourself but everyone involved, why shouldn't you?

This is the big distinction between mindset the way most real estate gurus present it, and heartset the 'Susiwala System' way. Don't get me wrong: I'm Tony Robbins' biggest fan. My old friend Tony Puim and I used to consume motivational tapes by the truckload. I still listen to them, Golden Oldies and all.

The fact remains, most of those motivational talks are about generating enthusiasm, about getting you worked up emotionally. I'm talking about something different.

The strongest emotional driver isn't enthusiasm, it isn't even a craving for wealth: it's love of parents, love of family, love of friends, love for your community and your clients, love of everything that's ethical and right and good because it is ethical and right and good. If you act out of love and respect for others, out of love for God, everything falls into place. You'll do better because you are better.

When you approach your work in that state of mind, there's no question about doing a bad, or sloppy, or shoddy job. When your business practice is part of your spiritual life, you're not going to take a questionable profit at someone's else's expense. If you feel that a good and just God is there beside you, you'll do the right thing by everyone, yourself included, because what you're doing is *meaningful*. Sure, profit will follow, but it's no longer about what you *have*, but about what you *are*, and what you'll be able to say when the time comes to give an account.

There's no need to overdo it. Joining a brokerage isn't entering a monastery. (Some days it's more like a lunatic asylum). All the stuff I've been discussing goes on more in the background of your head than up front. When it's there, you know it. In terms of day-to-day experience, things are a lot simpler: you head out to a presentation making sure you've got the comparables right, that you've brushed your hair, that "We Are the Champions" is on the car's playlist. If, while all that is happening, you just sort of know that your heart is in the right place, and the universe is in good hands, then you're good too, in every sense of the word.

This doesn't begin to cover all there is to say about heartset. I'm only passing along a few of the main things that keep me motivated and on the straight and narrow. But a good agent has to cultivate those things. In fact, heartset is 'cultivating your core' at its very highest. It needs to be done because in the world of real estate, there are a good many ways to slack off and cut corners and make a profit by taking advantage of others. That is always the wrong path. What keeps you focused, motivated, active, and honest always helps. Fortunately there are a lot of things that do that.

But there are three things in particular I want to mention.

The first is something I do often: I imagine things working out right before I go and do it. Later on in the System, I talk about 'Leading The Journey'—describing things to the client in a way that helps take them from where they are to where they want to be. I do that for myself, too. I rehearse the presentation in my head as I'm driving over. I see myself explaining everything clearly, and answering all their questions perfectly. I see their faces light up when they see all the marketing that I'll be doing on their behalf, and how everything is geared to getting them the best results possible. I see that handshake happening, and the signature on the document naming me their agent. I never, never ever push them to sign. I just see it happening, naturally. And hey—most of the time it does!

Sometimes, too, as I head over, I'll think not only about the future, but about all my past successes. The many times that everything turned out just right for everyone. The presentations that went perfectly. The happy looks on the clients' faces when everything works out for the best and they see all you've done for them. You can replay your successes too, even if you're just starting out. Even if you've never sold a house!

No matter who you are, you've succeeded at something. At some point in your life, you've helped someone. Somewhere, somehow, for someone, you've made a difference. For the better.

Remember those moments. Trust in them. Build on them. And many, many more such moments will come.

Another key is perhaps the most important element in real estate: Time.

People who succeed in real estate and real estate investing are people who are able to think ahead in terms of time. People who can put off an immediate short-term rush for larger long-term gains. How many careers go nowhere because the minute the agent makes a sale, he or she books a vacation, buys a new TV or purchases that Gucci bag? How many blow it all on a wild weekend, or worse, on gambling? They could have put that money into marketing, skill development, or buying an investment property purchase all their own.

But no. They want instant gratification. To get it, they sell out their own future. They don't save, they don't invest. They consume; and after it's all gone, they've got nothing.

I honestly believe this has got something to do with the mental imagery they practice. I see myself winning a presentation. They see themselves winning at a casino. I visualize my phone ringing off the hook because I've reinvested my profits in marketing. They seem themselves driving down the street in a Jaguar they can't afford to a vacation spot where no one interrupts them with a call. Well, what we dream of, we get. I get calls, and they don't.

The long-term returns on real estate are incredibly richer and more satisfying than the short-term. But you have to train yourself to see things that way. You have to see deals — see yourself — in terms of that longer time frame.

Bodybuilders work out because they see themselves looking like Arnold Schwarzenegger one day if they do. They see the long-term fitness payoff naturally. Most of us have to make an effort. We have to train ourselves to take that long view, to see the pot of gold waiting at the end of several years, instead of the comparatively small but instant payoff at the end of a quick sale.

Well, the road to wealth isn't a road: it's a timeline, and the farther you can see that timeline extending, the more clearly you can see capital appreciation, land development patterns and long-term demographic trends.

The more clearly you see the long-term consequences of your actions, the wealthier you'll eventually be. If you see yourself sticking a sign on the lawn and enjoying the afternoon off, you can take that afternoon off — but it'll cost you the future that could have been yours. If, on the other hand, you can see yourself making Diamond in another year, becoming a Luminary of Distinction in five more, standing up on a conference stage getting well-earned applause from a roomful of your colleagues for being the rock star performer that you are in ten, you'll be that rock star. All it takes is mental focus, consistent effort, and time. (And if you want a dash of Eternity to that, add a little heartset).

Your business is literally a reflection of your mind and heart. Your mind is the chisel that gives your business shape and expression. Your heart is the marble. It's the inner strength and integrity that helps you build a business that reflects your values.

If you're lazy, if you don't pay attention to details, if you're willing to cut ethical corners, your real estate practice will reflect those qualities. If you're honest, but unimaginative and uncreative, if you're bored and just go through the motions, your real estate business practice will reflect those qualities. If you're creative and energetic and ambitious, your business will reflect those qualities too.

Yes, luck—good and bad—plays a part, but only a small part. In my experience there's an almost one-to-one relationship between your mental and spiritual integrity and creativity, and the business you build and the business results you get. Your business will tell you a lot about the person you are and your thinking, and the way your mind operates. Listen to it, and use what you learn to lift yourself up, professionally, financially and personally.

Principle #6:

IOU: GIVE TO GET

This is another core principle that you see working all around you every day. Give to get. I saw it work again and again with Mr. Menary, and no part of what I do has brought me more lasting success—or happiness.

We see it, we use it, and we experience it all the time. It's so obvious! It's so powerful, and so simple! Yet we easily overlook it.

Here it is: give someone something, good or bad, and you will get something in kind back from that person. Help someone, and they will return the favour. Perform an act of kindness, and the person receiving it will return that kindness to you. Do someone a favour, and they'll do you a favour back—sometimes tenfold.

How many times have I seen houses on the point of foreclosure? Or houses that were a complete mess? Or a place with one glaring issue that a few thousand dollars could resolve, yet the owner, for whatever reason, didn't have enough funds to do anything about it? Some Realtors will just walk away. In so doing, they not only let the homeowner down, but shoot themselves in the foot.

Not me. In cases like that, I've paid out of my own pocket to bring in cleaning services, or contractors, or whatever's needed to make the necessary fixes. I've offered to *make the mortgage payments* till the house got sold.

Guess what? I've gotten those listings! And when that newly gleaming house got top dollar, I not only got the commission that went along with it, but the clients paid me back what I loaned them (interest-free). They made more than they could ever have made without my help.

But I made out well too: the more their house sold for, the more commission I made. I made a few other things as well—I made a lifelong friend out of that client, a friend who'll come back to me every time they buy and sell a house in the future. I also made a client evangelist—someone who raves about me to their friends and family. "A house? Go to Faisal. He'll treat you right. Want to know what he did for me?"

When you do something nice for someone, they generally want to do something nice for you in return. How simple is that? How obvious. Doesn't that happen to you? Someone does you a favour, or puts in a little extra effort for you, or helps you out when you never expected it? How do you respond? You want to do something in return! We appreciate these things, and because we appreciate them, we give back. We're hard-wired that way.

This photo, taken early in Susiwala's career, shows a cheque presentation to the hospital with Cambridge Real Estate public relations committee colleague Louise Boudreau.

I saw this from the very start of my real estate career. Without it I might well never have had this wonderful career. When I was a boy and my father was injured, the real estate agent who found us our first home, Mr. Menary, visited my father in the hospital. I never forgot that kind gesture. When the time came for me to start out, and seek a broker, who came to mind? Mr. Menary.

I was amazed when I saw the way he **worked** with people. "Folks, I know you like this house, but it's expensive. Very expensive. It'll be hard to make the monthly payments. Now here's a house that's nearly as good, and costs a lot less."

A lot less? I couldn't believe I was seeing a broker take a cut in commission just to help others.

But then I saw those others tell the whole community that Mr. Menary was the best in the business—a friend, someone who had their interest in mind, not a shark. Those clients of Mr. Menary's became lifelong clients, and he didn't need to pay a penny in marketing to do it. The way those clients chatted up their friends did all the marketing for him. What else would you expect? He'd given them something first. Something important. They wanted to pay that I.O.U. back.

Later on a friend of mine with academic connections told me about a psychologist named Robert Cialdini. Cialdini studies the psychology of persuasion, and for several years now he's been examining the thing I nicknamed 'I.O.U.' He calls it 'reciprocity' and his summary of hundreds of studies and social experiments made it official: give something to someone and they will find a way to give back to you. It's a principle I've applied to my real estate business with massive success.

True, it can take a little insight and creativity. If people expect you to roll out the red carpet, they may not see an exceptional effort as being exceptional at all. You have to find out what they do expect, and then go beyond it, and give that little extra. You need to know their expectations before you exceed them.

But when they do see you giving them that something extra, when they see you going above and beyond for their sake, even just a little, it registers. They appreciate it. They remember, and sooner or later, they'll find a way to pay that I.O.U. back. Mr. Menary knew this, and Professor Cialdini proved it.

There's a catch to this principle, though, and before you apply it you may want to re-read the section called Heartset. Because whether you call it I.O.U. or reciprocity, it has to be sincere. You can fake a smile, but you can't fake an honourable spirit, or kindness of heart. People see through it. Yes, if you pay out of pocket to clean up a house so you can sell it for more, everyone benefits. They make more money and so do you.

But if that's the *only* reason you're doing it, it won't make you fans that send you lifelong referrals. You can't just look like you care. You have to actually care. If you don't care—well, maybe you need to go into some other line of work.

Luckily, most of us have this capacity instinctually. Caring isn't that hard to do. When you see how much your help is needed, when you see how happy and grateful people are after you've come through for them, when you see how much you've helped them and how much relief you've given them, you can't not share in that happiness.

At times like that, you won't believe the self-respect and personal satisfaction you'll feel. That's when real estate stops being just a job, and becomes the best job in the world. It becomes a pleasure. A high. You feel ten feet tall.

Put your clients first. Do good for yourself by first doing good for others. It's just that simple. And—like all the other principles—it works.

Principle #7:

NEVER BE CLOSING

Whenever I bring this one up during talks or at a conference, heads explode. It's outright blasphemy! "Never be closing? Never be closing? Faisal, what are you saying? It's *all about* the close! Close that deal *now*! Get that signature at all costs! Call them every day, bang on their doors, cut your commission, email, text, do whatever it takes, but close, close, close! ABC: Always Be Closing!"

Bull.

'Always Be Closing' is the silliest principle in real estate.

I never push for a close. Never. I don't make cold calls, I don't knock on doors and I won't cut my commission to get a signature. When people call me to do a presentation, I do it, and then I tell the sellers that since I don't like getting follow-up calls myself, I don't plan to make any to them. If they want to talk further, they have my number, and they can call me. Then I walk away.

When I say this to agents, their jaws drop. They lose their minds.

But it's so obvious. How do *you* feel when a robo-call interrupts you over dinner with your family? You've worked hard all day, you've finally arrived home, you've pulled off your shoes, you're lying down on that comfy sofa at last, and—*ding-dong!*—"Say, want to buy a complete set of encyclopedia?"

No!

I learned this principle as a very young boy when our school sent us out to raise money by selling chocolate bars door-to-door.

"Ma'am, would you like to buy some—." *Slam!*

"Sir, would you be interested in purchasing—." *Slam!*

The truth is, people hate to be sold. Sometimes, they like to buy. And if they want some information before they finalize the decision to buy, and you can give them that information quickly and clearly, without exaggeration or twisting their arm out of its socket, they *will* buy.

But they're in the driver's seat. And the last thing they want is for you to push them one seat over and take them in a direction they don't want to go. It never fails. Or rather, it always fails. Pressure people, and you kill the sale.

Let me say that again: pressure people, and you kill the sale. But let someone who is hungry to buy come to you, and you don't have to sell. All you have to do to satiate that hunger to buy is let it take its natural course, and not get in the way.

"So, what are you telling me, Faisal? I should just sit in my office and wait for clients to call or stroll in? Good luck with that!"

In fact, as the top-selling agent in all of Canada, consistently saturating my target market with my non-intrusive presence, I have had good luck with clients calling or strolling in.

But no, I don't wait. I do something else. Two things, actually.

The first thing came to me early on. I kept asking myself, "What makes people buy houses? In fact, what makes people buy anything, period?"

What I noticed was that when people wanted to satisfy some desire—food, shelter, whatever—they went to a place or person or brand they knew. If they wanted a computer, they'd go to an Apple store and buy a Mac. If they wanted a cup of coffee, they'd go to Starbucks and get a Hazelnut, or to Tim Hortons for a double-double.

Did they ever schedule an appointment with a Timmies or Starbucks coffee salesman and read competing brochures on the pros and cons of Kenyan decaf? Of course not. If they wanted a coffee, they went to a place that sold coffee. A place they knew. A place they didn't even think about.

They didn't have to. Because the association was already made in their head through repetition. Where people go depends on name recognition; and that name gets its recognition by being all over the place, all the time.

Now that takes marketing. And yes, marketing costs a lot. But the strange thing is, the more you do, the more money you make. It's like a machine that gives you two dollars for every one you put in. Yes, I was hesitant to feed my hard-earned income into that machine too. Initially. But after seeing marketing ramp up my income time and time and time again, I eventually ended up putting 25 per cent of my entire annual income into marketing. That sounds like a lot—until you see your income double, and double again and again, as a result.

Think of it as 'zero resistance selling.' Someone interrupts you over dinner? That's intrusive. It's pushy and disrespectful and invasive.

But if someone sends you a flyer or a postcard with a picture of their face and phone number and the words, "I Sell Real Estate"? That's not intrusive, and it's not pushy. It's just a piece of mail in between the other pieces.

It doesn't always sell, either—not immediately. (Well, sometimes it does). But persistent repetition eventually leaves its mark. A year may pass, or two years. Still, the day comes when that person needs to move. That's the day they think, "Gee, I need to sell this house. Who's that guy who's always sending me postcards? The one always popping up on my social media feeds? That guy on the back of the bus…. Fred, Frank? No, no—Faisal. Faisal something. Faisal Susiwala, that's it!"

Zero resistance selling: your face, your contact info, on a billboard, on the back of a bus, on a bench, on a soccer sponsorship banner at the big game. That's how all your marketing should be. Not aggressive. Not 'in-your-face.' Not asking for a sale, or twisting anyone's arm. Just a simple postcard or a flyer or bumper sticker with a picture of you and a few lines that say what you do and how someone can reach you.

It's like the background music in a shopping mall. You barely even notice it. It's soft and quiet and you pay no attention to it at all. And yet, when you're driving home, you find yourself humming that melody.

So it is with marketing. Push hard and loud and people push back. But just quietly be there, everywhere, all the time, and your face and name sink in. You become the first thing people think of when they need your service.

When you become the brand, you're on your way to a pipeline that never ends; to many sales. Lifelong sales, without pushing, without generating resistance, and without even having to be there! The business falls into your lap because your face and number are everywhere, and you're not doing anything aggressive or intrusive to push people away.

This kind of salesmanship, the kind that involves no selling at all, will get you more calls than you can handle.

There's another kind of 'closing without closing' that I do as well.

When the call turns into a presentation, I practice the same zero resistance approach. I don't push my prospect to sign; I don't twist their arm, or make self-destructive concessions. What I do is present a bullet-proof case that shows I can get them the best price possible. I'm not pressing for a close at any point: the case I'm making is doing the closing, and it's so tight that the prospect simply can't help but see they're going to lose money if they go elsewhere.

Making that case isn't hard to do. The vast majority of real estate agents don't do much more than put a seller's house on the MLS and stick a sign on the lawn. Job done. Sometimes that's enough. Sometimes it even results in a price the seller is happy with.

Still, it's almost never the best that can be done for the seller. When I sit down with a seller, I want them to know I'm giving them my best. I walk them through all the comparables and tell them honestly what they can expect. I show them how their house will be blasted all across the top social media, across multiple platforms, in town and in the outlying areas. I explain how I plan to bring in multiple bidders to push their returns to the very top dollar. I present a book detailing hundreds of cases of rapid turnaround, and sales reaching many tens of thousands of dollars over asking. I convey everything in a tone of authority and confidence, and that tone is compelling. It's compelling because I've worked in my region selling real estate for over thirty years, and I know every street, every house, every trend, everything I need to know to get them the best price possible for their home.

The icing on the cake? I typically guarantee the results I promise. Again, it's a simple matter of knowing your business to the point of professional certainty. Of authority. I know the house will bring in a certain price. Period. If, for whatever reason, it doesn't do so in the time frame promised (and in most cases I'm certain that it will), I have the resources to buy it outright and keep it on the market till it does. That's what I do.

When you push people to buy or sell, they push back. When you show them exactly what you're going to do to get them the best results possible, and why your strategy is going to work, when you present examples of it working hundreds of time for others, when you guarantee the results—what is there to 'close'? There it is. The plan is self-explanatory. The results are guaranteed. Take a journey that mandates success.

When you start walking away after a presentation like that, they'll grab you and drag you back!

You won't have to pressure them to sign a thing—*they'll* pressure you to be their agent.

Principle #8:

ROI: RETURN ON INFLUENCE

I have a special liking for this because it came out of earlier principles, and works beautifully in support of the other principles. That's a point I want to make strongly. This stuff works separately, but it works best together: the principles support each other. They're synergistic. You can give more emphasis to one element than another, depending on your needs and situation, but each works best when all the pieces are in play. And when they are, they not only work together, but grow together.

(That's right: the Susiwala System evolves. As time goes by, I'm sure the existing system will develop even further).

But although ROI (Return On Influence) and NBC (Never Be Closing) work together closely, there's a subtle and important difference that I want to emphasize. That's why I mentioned Never Be Closing in the context of a presentation. There's a difference being pushy and being quietly everywhere. NBC is about not being pushy, and you cannot be pushy in person or online or in your marketing. 'ROI' is about being all over the place. If you're all over the place and you're aggressive and obnoxious, you can actually push people away. The *wrong* kind of marketing can destroy your business. But if you're everywhere without that abrasive aggression, then you establish yourself as a presence, you build an association between yourself and your message.

I can put ROI into six words:

Be Everywhere and Become the Brand.

Why do you ask people to Xerox a document instead of copy it? Why do you need a new Mac and not a new personal computer? Why do you ask for a Kleenex, not a tissue? For a Coke, not a cola? For a Band-Aid, not an adhesive bandage?

You do this because these companies have so completely saturated your environment with their brand, that the brand has become completely identified with the product. In the mind of the public, that brand is the product.

That's what you want to achieve as a real estate agent. When people think, "I need to sell my house," or 'Realtor' or 'real estate agent,' you want them to instantly, and without reflection, think of you. You want to become the first, if not the only, name that immediately comes to mind. It's this principle that allows you to 'never be closing.' Why twist their arms to close? After all, in their mind, you're *the* agent, the only game in town.

This is not that hard to achieve — if you follow one of my first principles, and 'Scale Down.' If you can scale down and focus your real estate operations on one region, you can be as well-known and immediately recognized there as Coke is everywhere. You only need to achieve that goal in one single prime area to achieve a lifelong success and wealth in real estate.

The beauty of this approach is that it allows you to grow smoothly and easily, at a pace you can handle, step-by-step. The more you market yourself in this way, the more business you'll get, and the more your marketing you can do. It becomes a loop: yes, you spend more, but you also generate more and more every time you spend. It's the kind of spiral that can take you to the top — fast.

When I was making $100,000 annually, I saw what saturation marketing could do and I threw myself into it hard. I spent $25,000 and I admit it — it made me nervous. At the time, that was a lot.

But it got me so much business that soon my earnings reached $400,000 annually. I was stunned. I looked at those results and decided to put in 25 per cent of that: I spent $100,000. When *that* kicked me up to $1,000,000 in annual revenues, I spent *$250,000*, and this time I didn't hesitate or regret it for a minute. It made the $25,000 I had been so worried about pale by comparison. That kind of money spent on targeted saturation marketing simply left all competitors in my area completely in the dust. I became *the* go-to person for real estate.

Once that happens, there's no longer any boom-and-bust. It's all boom, all the time.

Newer agents look at the price tag and their eyes roll. "I can't spend hundreds of thousands of dollars on advertising! I need to feed my kids! I still have to pay off my car!"

Open your eyes!!! Scale down, and you scale *up*. Every dollar you spend gets you back several dollars! Would you give me a ten if I gave you a fifty back? Would you give me a hundred thousand if I gave you *four* hundred thousand back?

It's a no-brainer.

The trick is to target a small but desirable area and be everywhere: every billboard, every bench, and launch targeted social media campaigns in those areas. When people type 'realtor' or 'home sales' or 'sell my house' into Google, you want to pop up first every time. (Trust me, there are agencies now that are so search engine savvy that they can focus in on exactly the kinds of buyers and sellers you want. They can pop your face and contact number in front of your perfect target audience for next to nothing compared to the old full-page print ad rates).

Pick your area, settle on your agency, and start saturating it today. You'll start getting results—results that can fund even more lucrative marketing—almost instantly.

As soon as I understood this, and applied it, my returns as a real estate agent zoomed up like a rocket.

It didn't happen because I was following conventional wisdom. If I'd taken that path, I'd still be sitting around the coffee machine putting off making cold calls. Instead, I applied my principles:

I became the brand—by joining a successful brand and piggybacking on *their* brand. Suddenly I had brand recognition overnight!

I modelled excellence creatively: I saw what the big companies were doing, and I adapted it to a different industry and a smaller area.

I scaled down: I didn't try to market myself to the world, I concentrated on farming the one tightly focused area I could serve best. I put my face and name and number and professional information in front of specifically those people that I wanted to see it.

I gave to get: I wouldn't just send postcards, I'd sponsor local high school hockey teams, give to hospitals, send useful little presents in place of postcards.

I was never selling: I made sure my face and my number were always there, but not in a way that was aggressive, intrusive or offensive.

I monetized my licence: my ads emphasized that I was a skilled, trained professional—they weren't "Crazy Eddie's Used Car" advertising; they communicated certified expertise, qualifications and skills that allowed me to charge strong commissions.

I maintained my core: I outsourced my marketing effort to professional agencies. I didn't try to do it all myself, or do something at which I was not an expert. I didn't let marketing eat up all my time, or keep me from doing my job, or keep me from doing a *good* job—as good a job as I could possibly do.

Just like a new leaf sprouting on a healthy growing tree, all those principles came together and produced a new principle, what I call Return on Influence (not to be confused with Return on Investment, although the financial outcomes are equally positive). ROI involves marketing yourself in such a way that you seem to be everywhere but intrude nowhere. It's almost like a kind of subliminal advertising. You want to be universally known but not quite noticed, always there at the back of people's minds, like a friend they've known since forever and often think about, but haven't actually run into for the longest time.

Once again, after the fact, I found backup from the academic community. In Professor Robert Cialdini's latest book, *Pre-suasion*, I found study after study supporting what I'd learned through practice: that you could predispose people to want to do business with you, that you could even get them to seek you out to do business, without ever having to push for that sale. You've closed the sale before you ask for it because you've *already* convinced them that you're the best choice. The *only* choice. They want to sign. They ask you! As Cialdini puts it, these people have been 'pre-suaded'—favourably disposed to you the agent before any business has even been considered.

When you operate on this scale, you're doing way more than 'zero resistance selling.' You're becoming a community icon. You find yourself sponsoring local sports teams, helping local charities, giving talks on financial education to young people. You can become a positive social influence, and while there's certainly a rich financial return once you reach that status, there are new responsibilities too. Ethically, you need to be immaculate. You're in the spotlight. You no longer find yourself just following trends—you can make trends happen, shape the characters of neighbourhoods. When everyone knows you, politicians know you, journalists know you, high-level investors know you, other people of influence know you. They know you, and they come to you. That's good for you financially in ways you never imagined, because it opens doors and possibilities you may never have thought possible.

If your goal is to dominate your local real estate market, ROI —Return on Influence—is undoubtedly the way to go. The more sheer presence you have, the more influence you have, and the more influence you have, the more money you can make and the more good you can do.

But as you're making all that money, remember that famous line from Spiderman: "With great power comes great responsibility."

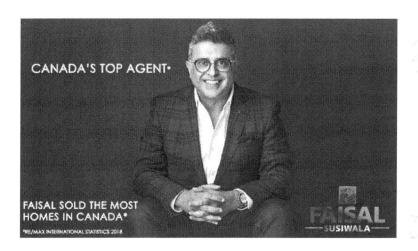

Principle #9:

GET WIRED

Do I even need to mention this one? Is there one single real estate agent anywhere in the world nowadays who doesn't have a laptop, who doesn't have an email address, who uses a landline instead of a smartphone? (Don't even get me *started* on the ways technology has changed the amount and kind of research you can do).

Get wired! Tech won't automatically make you rich, but if you're not using up-to-date tech, if you're not up on the latest cutting-edge technological innovations or the technological developments coming around the corner, you are dead meat. Seriously. You shouldn't be in real estate at all.

I've said that the Susiwala System is always evolving. There was an earlier version of this principle called "Get Online." Getting online is still a big part of it. Do that right now, right away. If you don't have accounts on Facebook, Twitter, Instagram, LinkedIn, YouTube, do it the moment you finish this book. Get familiar with Zillow, with iBuyer, with Google Earth, with Craigslist, with Kijiji. Trust me, the buyers and sellers you're going to be talking to are familiar with them already.

Technology develops so quickly nowadays that I don't want to give you too many specifics. What you need to do is be able to use the new tech as tools in association with more time-tested principles. For instance, thanks to Internet advertising, I don't do magazine print advertising at all anymore. It just doesn't get results. When people look for a house or an agent, they don't go to the newspaper classifieds. They go to Google. They ask a friend online, or see pop-up ads on social media. Seriously, who reads classifieds anymore, or goes to the Yellow Pages? Print no longer works, so I dropped it. Instagram? Instagram works. When I have a new home to sell, it goes on Instagram first thing.

Social media not only allows you to put any home you're selling in front of hundreds of thousands of more faces than a print listing or a lawn sign (and not random faces, but a specific target audience based on their search habits and history), it also helps to brand you. Is it any surprise why? Social media is social. Yes, I know that sounds silly, but when people see a video of Faisal Susiwala talking about current events, hanging out with his family and friends, donating uniforms to the local school hockey team, that reaches them in a way that a list of homes just out on the MLS doesn't.

It's 'pre-suasion': you make a positive impression. When people see your face and hear your voice and you're not selling, that positive impression slips under their radar, making it likely that you'll be remembered more (and more favourably) than any competing service Realtor; more likely that eventually a sale will happen.

You just can't do this in print. It's only online video that lets this happen. Mind you, it's not the *only* thing you want to put out there. My Instagram feed shows every new house I list. But if I can advise people to stay safe during a pandemic, and mention a local service that dispenses free face masks, I will. It's sandwich marketing: a slice of Faisal saying hello and giving a thumbs up to a new movie between two amazingly great home deals that just became available.

I don't wing it online. When it comes to online ads, I rely totally on 100 per cent professional Internet marketing services. They can zero in on exactly the target market you want with a precision that is scary. Yes, this kind of precision can get expensive, but the returns beat the investment by a very, very large margin. When it comes to building and maintaining my personal brand, I spare no expense.

The strange thing is, the online videos themselves aren't especially expensive. What does it cost to take a video of yourself with your smartphone and upload it? Or put the smartphone in front of your face and give a simple talk where you let people know how they can stop mould from attacking their house by doing one or two simple things? Can you believe that something like that can go viral and be seen by half a million people? It can! Total cost of production: nothing!

If you want a crystal-clear idea of what I'm talking about, put this book down after you're done reading it, open up your laptop or pick up your phone, and subscribe to my online accounts and channels. I have a list near the back of the book. They'll give you clear and perfect examples of what I'm talking about, and it is clear and it is simple: get online, open some accounts, let people know what you do (and just a little bit about who you are) and show them the houses that you're selling.

Give to get. Give them information that will help them make good decisions, good investments, find good houses. Soon you'll find yourself getting: getting a growing following that eventually will go from small to gargantuan. Ask them to subscribe. You'll get their email addresses and, voilà, there's another database you can monetize! You can even automate your posts, so that homes you're selling and ads showing your face and your services can appear while you sleep.

Yes, setting it up takes a little time. An assistant (real or virtual) will be a big help. And yes, there are potholes along the way. Sooner or later, for instance, you'll get a bad review or a snarky comment. Because of the nature of the Internet, that snarky comment will be there a long while. My answer to that: do the best, most ethical and most transparent job you can in the first place, so no one has cause to criticize you. If they criticize you anyway? If you do a good job, you'll have many more positive things being said about you than negative. The good will overwhelm the bad.

Do as good a job for as many people as you can, and make as many people happy as you can. Remember: the Internet never stays the same. A bad review on the top of page one today goes to the bottom of page seven and is forgotten tomorrow.

Remember, too, to always reply to each review, good or bad. Don't just ignore criticism. Respond honestly, professionally and respectfully (even when your blood is boiling). Many a critic doesn't know the full story; give them (and the public) that full story. People want and deserve to know.

How you respond to a negative review says a lot about your character and how you will treat the reader if the two of you have disagreements. Don't obsess, and don't give all your attention to a bad review. Instead, do all you can to get as many good reviews as possible coming in regularly.

As with all the other principles, getting wired works. Being a presence on social media is like being a physical presence on shopping mall walls or billboards. You just have to be there. (The digital you. The real beauty of Internet marketing (like billboard ads) is that they're effectively selling 24/7 while you can go have a coffee or analyze an investment or make a presentation.)

Yes, I still do billboards, and postcards, and flyers. Why wouldn't I? They still bring in business. But ads work so much better online than in real life that it's almost ridiculous. You might hope that an interested buyer will drive by your lawn sign, but targeted advertising will put the house you're selling and your contact info in front of the exact kind of person—your target audience—you know will buy; people with the right credit rating, the right income level, the right age and number of children to make that neighbourhood school nearby irresistible.

Riding the wire effectively—getting familiar with developing technology as it applies to real estate—is a bigger issue. Yes, you need to get familiar with the latest tech and where it's trending. It amazes me sometimes when I think about how real estate was done thirty years ago. I was there, and wow: those days were like life on an alien planet. Cell phones, personal computers, social media, smartphones and Google have changed everything. Artificial Intelligence is changing and disrupting the way we do business even further.

Understand it, get ahead of it, and above all don't fear it. Chase it and embrace it.

I remember agents back in the 80's sitting next to their landline and making jokes about cell phones being a fad that would soon blow over. Those agents are history. You don't want to be history: you want to ride that rising wave and make millions.

Getting tech-savvy and using it well is mandatory. Dabble fast and dabble early, and be sensitive to how quickly tech can transform things. Zoom, for instance, appeared almost overnight in the wake of the coronavirus, and now virtually everyone seems to be using it. How can we as agents make the best use of it? That's a work in progress. We're still learning.

In the meantime, apply the principles here, because they work with every sort of tech. In particular, apply principle #8 ("Be Everywhere And Be The Brand") to social media and major search engines just the same as you would with billboards and bus advertising. *Be everywhere.* When everyone everywhere knows who you are and what you do, you'll get more business than you can handle.

Principle #10:

LEAD THE JOURNEY

Leading the Journey is another principle that grew out of earlier ones—but mostly it grew out of direct experience doing presentations. What a real estate agent needs when making a presentation is a sense of authority—of being so sure that he or she can provide the best possible service and do the most good for a client that that *certainty* just naturally communicates itself

We see this in other people. The superstar athlete. The celebrated doctor. The leading contractor. Even the in-demand plumber. They know they can deliver what they promise. One look, and so do you. You see how they talk, you see the way they hold themselves, and you know. That feeling of authority resonates. It's a good example of the 'Never Be Closing' principle. It sells without selling.

How do they know they're that good? Usually it comes from years of experience, years of study, and a track record anyone would envy, but often because they know what they're doing so well that they can explain it. I know I can get such-and-such a price for a home, and if the seller I'm presenting to asks me why, I can show them the comparables, the number of people that will be seeing their house over social media, the hundreds of thousands in savings that people living a half-hour away will make by buying the property, and so on and so on. The numbers tell the story, and when I'm selling a home or proposing an investment, I sometimes feel that all I have to do is lay those numbers out, and the sale is a done deal.

But it isn't. Or, at least, very often it isn't. I don't fall into the trap of thinking that persuasion is a purely logical process, and neither should you.

The fact is, people don't buy solely because of reason and logic. You can give them all the data they need, to see what the best course of action will be, and a few people will act on that, but many won't. Most won't. They'll hesitate, because they need a 'gut' feel, an emotional sense that they're making the right decision, not just a rational one. They need reasons too, and good reasons, but that alone doesn't guarantee their signature.

Big decisions aren't always 'gut' decisions either, and they shouldn't be. Both reason and emotion need to be present for a sale.

Many agents don't realize that. Some err on the side of logic and fail to close, but most err on the other side. They'll see that pure logic isn't enough to close a deal, and so they go into their used car salesman act: "Oh, this deal is just so fabulous, amazing, incredible, once-in-a-lifetime. It's a house fit for kings," yada, yada. We've all seen too many embarrassing examples of that, and it's an approach that doesn't work, either.

So how do you bring them together? The approach I've refined over the years is called 'Leading the Journey.' When someone wants to talk to me about selling their home, I do my research, gather all the information I need, and plug that into the thorough and comprehensive marketing, pricing and buyer-bidding system that I've developed. It's all but guaranteed to sell the home. (In fact, it's so compelling, even to me, that I do guarantee to sell the home).

But as I present it and explain it to the sellers, I put *them* into the picture, and I lead *them*, mentally, through the series of steps that will get them exactly to the place they want to be. I tell a story, and they're the heroes of that story. In the story I have them imagine they've already hired me and then I lead them through the journey we're about to take together, a journey in which the entire process is concluded quickly and painlessly and in which they achieve complete success.

What this does is present a watertight, well-planned explanation of why my approach will work best for them, a rational approach that's already proven successful in other cases; *but* it also presents the process in the form of a narrative where they personally go through the process, and see how well it's working, and imagine how happy they are when it's all done and they have exactly what they want. The seller hires me because, in his or her mind, they've seen themselves having already hired me. The sellers sign because the house, imaginatively, has already been sold.

Putting them into the story this way activates and involves their imagination and their feelings. Bringing that story to a successful conclusion seals the deal. After all, no one objects to a suggestion when they've seen and felt themselves accepting it, and seeing that it's already worked out great.

Like Never Be Closing, this approach is non-aggressive and so low-key it's virtually unnoticeable. It's not, "I'm going to do an auction and bring in big bucks!" It's, "When we sit down at the auction together, we'll be speaking to the agents individually when they make their offer. They'll be looking for your reaction, but you'll be calm because you know that even if they offer a high price, the other agents will go higher once we give them a chance to better it. Then we'll ask the next agent in and--."

You put *them* into the picture. You put yourself into the picture as their trusted advisor. You tell additional stories: "I once sold a home much like yours for someone in the same area, and they thought that the Zillow value was as much as they could possibly get. Well, it turned out that once the bidding started—"

Like ROI, I eventually found that this principle also has academic support. A friend of mine with a background in psychology told me about a 1954 paper by a Dr. Milton Erickson called "Pseudo-orientation in Time as a Hypnotherapeutic Procedure." (Hang on, now! Don't fall asleep on me!). Dr. Erickson would hypnotize people with a problem and have them imagine themselves at a point in the future where the problem was resolved. Guess what? Those problems would either get completely resolved or show progress toward being resolved. Apparently, when people are able to imagine a problem being completely solved at some future point, somehow they tend to drift toward that solution.

The takeaway? When you see or imagine yourself succeeding, you're more likely to succeed. If you see yourself on the beach in Cuba having a great time, you're more likely to go. If you see yourself riding on a camel over the desert sands like Lawrence of Arabia, you're more likely to actually do it. (I did.) And if you can get others to see themselves doing things—like making you their agent and getting a great result, they will. Or at least, they're a lot more likely to.

I've seen the pure logic approach fail, and I've seen the emotional arm-twisting approach fail, but the 'Lead The Journey' approach lets you explain the full logic of your case at the same time that you get sellers personally excited and engaged by involving them in the story. You combine the best of both worlds, and you're *not selling*: you're just describing, as truthfully and accurately as you can. And when you describe *their* success, the profits *they're* going to make, *their* happy ending—you tend to get that listing. They know that hiring you will work out for them; because, in their minds, they've already hired you, and it already worked out.

There's a mindset bonus with this technique. One day as I was driving to a presentation, I thought to myself, "If getting the seller to walk through the process and arrive at a happy ending makes it more likely that they'll really achieve that happy ending, why can't I apply this principle to me?"

I did.

It worked!

Nowadays, as I'm preparing to do a presentation, I run through the coming events in my head. I see the sellers welcoming me in with an open mind, nodding with understanding as I make my points, getting on well with me personally, really engaging with me as I lead them on their journey, and seeing me become their agent once I'm done. I go through it in my head before it happens, and in my head, everything works out perfectly. Most always when I do that, it *does* work out perfectly—or, at the very least, a whole lot closer to perfect than if I were to run pictures through my head of me goofing up and the whole presentation falling apart.

It's the same with you, my friend. If you see yourself applying the Susiwala System smoothly, professionally, successfully, in real-life situations with actual people, chances are a lot better that that's what will happen than if you run pictures through your head of you blowing it. You'll just be shooting yourself in the foot if you approach things seeing yourself fail. You don't have to *believe* that it will work or *convince* yourself or *argue* yourself into thinking that it will work if you imagine yourself in a real-life situation where it is working. If you do that, it will *feel* right. And if it feels right, it's a lot more likely that it will work out well in real life. It's common sense. Imagine yourself giving a talk and seeing uplifted faces and fascinated expressions. Aren't you more likely to want to give that talk, and do it fluently? Imagine yourself winning the Diamond Award at an event as people cheer and applaud. Aren't you more likely to try to earn it?

We're rational creatures, but we also want a road map to follow—an emotional road map that takes us from where we are to where we want to be, and that does so in a compelling way. That's what Leading The Journey does. Without being nervous you will blow it.

You can 'lead a journey' for your associates, for your staff, for your partners and fellow investors, for young people and high school students listening to you talk about their financial future. "Twenty years from now, young lady, young man, if you invest a bit of your earnings every year, one day you'll be driving up to this school in a Ferrari and cutting the principal a cheque to build a new wing in your name!" (Ideally, devoted to financial literacy).

When you see those young eyes light up as they put themselves in the picture you've drawn, you just know that some of them are going to take that journey.

When they've arrived, they'll remember you. With thanks.

Principle #11:

BIDDERS NOT BUYERS

Here's what most real estate agents do. They find a seller and then tell them to price high, because everyone underbids. So they price a house that will never get more than $450,000, say, at $500,000. No one calls except a few people who call to laugh. Half a million for *that*? Ridiculous.

Inquiries are few and far between; time passes. More time passes. Then, even more time passes. Eventually someone offers $400,000. After all, if the agent can price it way too high, a possible buyer can place an offer that's way too low, right? It's not like actual home values are being addressed either way.

The seller, insulted and offended, turns this lowball offer down. Even more time passes.

This back and forth goes on for months. The price slides and slides, and eventually, before the listing expires, the agent gets an offer for $425,000. The seller isn't happy, but he or she is sick of the waiting, and the house showings, and sick of the whole process. They're so unhappy that they may go for it. The agent's not happy either. He or she has spent far more time than he or she wanted to spend selling the house; he or she has done many more time-consuming showings than they would have liked, and now they've ended up with a reduced commission, and an unhappy client who won't be sending in any referrals, but *will* be bad-mouthing the agent and otherwise harming his or her brand.

Is there a better way? Of course there is.

What I do is price low. If a house is worth $450,000 — and every Realtor and most every buyer can do a simple Internet search nowadays and find that number — I put it on the market right away for $400,000. Possibly even lower.

I can hear the howling already. "Are you nuts, Faisal? The seller isn't going to hire you if you list their property $50,000 lower than its estimated value. They'll throw you out the door!"

No, they won't. Because I explain to the seller that they're under no obligation to accept a low offer. I explain to them the reason I price it low is that I know that any number of agents and buyers will immediately see that it's a bargain compared to other similar homes, and move to send in an offer fast, hoping to beat the rush.

However! I make it clear that any buyers will need to wait one week to ten days to present their offer. (I do allow pre-emptive, or so-called 'bully' offers to be presented before that, provided the offers are well above asking price, have no conditions, and include a bank draft attached to the offer.)

Buyers don't wait when they see a possible bargain, and a deadline to secure it. This strategy brings in offers. Fast. Often several offers. (On occasion, dozens).

Once they arrive, what I do is bring the buyers and their agents together on the specified date to bid on the property in question. I call it my "Offer Party."

I create an auction situation. Guess what happens at an auction? That's right: offers rise. When buyers compete, bids get higher and higher. People just don't like to lose. The bidding doesn't start at $400,000, either. The buyers have seen a house they like, and their agent knows the house's market value is $450,000. When they come to the auction they know there are likely to be at least five or six people there. Maybe a dozen or more. They know a low bid of $400,000 is likely to be outbid. They still think they can get something of a bargain, though, even if it's not quite that low.

One buyer weighs all this and tells his agent to offer $420,000.

The agent presents the offer to me. But I have maybe half a dozen to a dozen offers now in front of me. One is for $425,000. The highest is as high as my client's target—$450,000. (This one we don't touch).

We review the offers. Then I tell the agents with the lower offers to go back and try again.

"Go back," I say, "talk to your buyer. We have a higher offer. Ask your buyer if they can do better."

That's what each agent does.

The buyers grumble. But they know it's a good house in a good neighbourhood, and they know that even at $430,000—

even at $450,000—it's still a good deal. The agents each come back with another round of offers.

What I'm looking for is for someone to beat the $450,000 we have on the table. Finally, after a round or two, we see a $460,000 offer.

We don't take it. In fairness, we go back to the original highest offer and (without disclosing any terms of the other offers) we ask them to improve their offer too.

Bingo! This time we get $475,000!

I continue going back to the second, third, fourth and all the other bidders, until they throw in the towel and walk away. (Warning: never send all the offers back. Always keep the best one in play. If I have an offer that's already acceptable to my seller, we've won! What we're playing for now is to get my seller the best price possible.)

Price alone isn't the only consideration. The terms of the offer matter too:

The closing date—will it inconvenience the seller? How badly?

The conditions—is financing required? Inspections? A solicitor's approval? (These and more could all be clauses a buyer uses to terminate the deal).

The deposit—did the buyer bring a deposit? Cash? Cheque? Is it certified? Is it a bank draft? (No money, no deal).

The highest price doesn't necessarily win the property. Provided the minimum target selling price has been achieved, an unconditional cash offer is always better than a higher offer with conditions. I've seen those conditional offers terminated often, and deliberately: the buyer comes back a week later and wants to renegotiate due to a leaky roof found during inspections. The roof may only cost $10,000 to fix, but now the offer is $50,000 less, because the other bidders have all gone home, and now it's take it or leave it.

These bidding wars are carefully arranged. You don't put everyone in the same room or outside where they could possibly collude. You don't want one bidder to guess what the opposing bidder is likely to do by reading their body language. You don't want your client to grin and nod at one offer if you feel the agent making it could come up with a still better one next round.

Also, the process must be *meticulously* honest and transparent. You can't say, "Another bidder offered more," if they didn't. That would be worse than stupid: it would be a crime. Every offer is carefully registered, and each one is available for review after the presentation by the licensing body. An agent should never lie, period; but in cases like these it's not enough for him or her just to be clean. They need to be so clean they squeak!

All too many real estate agents will take the first acceptable offer they get straight out of the box for one reason: instant commission. They're not thinking of their client's best interest. They're not even thinking of their own best interest. All they're thinking about is immediate gratification.

They're not making their clients as much as they should be making, and they're not making as much for themselves as they could be making. They're not doing a job that's likely to make their clients refer or recommend them. In short, they're hurting not just their pocketbook, but their brand. That's just foolish.

My system of underpricing attracts multiple buyers who, because they've already shown interest and commitment, are easily converted into bidders. They're mentally prepared to raise the amount they're willing to pay. That allows me to not only deliver the seller's desired price quickly, but to exceed it. Sometimes by many tens of thousands of dollars.

Put yourself in that scenario. Once you've delivered more than the asking price for your client, does it make it more likely that client will refer you or recommend you, or call you again when they want to sell in the future? What do you think?

What you're really doing when you use this kind of 'Price Low Sell High' strategy is lead generation. You're getting buyers —several buyers—each of whom is interested in a particular kind of home in a particular price range, to contact you. It goes without saying that their names should go straight into your contact database.

It also goes without saying that after the sale is made, you can approach those who were interested. Why send them away? Suggest a similar property. Share their names with your buyers' associates—your network. Offer those buyers homes that fit their criteria, start a dialogue, provide other options.

I like to sweeten the pot for clients with a few extras. For instance, the day I list, I guarantee a sale. If I can't sell their property, I'll buy it myself! After all, I've done my due diligence. I know the value of that property, and what I can make if I meet their price. If they want to take the money and go without bidding or listing at all, I'm OK with it. I'm more than confident I'll get my purchase price back, and then some.

I won't take a client on if they're unreasonable, or aren't interested in a realistic value. You must be fair to everyone concerned. If I see a home worth $550,000 and the seller tells me to sell at $650,000, I won't take the listing. If the buyer asks me how I arrived at that price, I can't look that person in the eye and tell him or her that that's the price the seller picked out of a hat! Yes, valuations are soft: the price of a home can vary a few thousand here and there, even a few tens of thousands here and there. Simple appreciation will eventually build the home's value to that point, and likely beyond.

But you can't name a price *wildly* out of range. That's just not right.

"But you *do* get buyers to spend more on your sellers' properties. Doesn't that make them angry? Doesn't it hurt your brand? You want people to rave about you, and become 'evangelists.' Surely the people who pay $30,000 over asking, or lose the bidding entirely, must be furious with you."

Nope. I don't force them to buy. If the price is too high for them, it's too high. If they feel they're receiving sufficient value, they buy. If they don't, they don't. They *may* feel that, thanks to me, they paid the seller more than they might have paid otherwise, and that may hurt a bit. But when the time comes for them to sell their house, you'll be the first person they think of. (Which is something I sometimes point out.)

Who do you want to sell your house—the agent you've seen deliver $20,000 to $50,000-plus over asking, or the agent who pressured you to take a lowball offer for a fast commission?

It's not only sellers and bidders who pass along word that I got my seller a price well above asking. Selling a house above the expected price makes you a hero to the people in the neighbourhood. When a house sells over value, all the houses in the neighbourhood rise in value. It's the Susiwala Effect: I sell a house in a neighbourhood, and neighbourhood values rise across the board. And when house values rise across the board, and everyone knows I sold their neighbour's home well over the asking price, I become the leading candidate for that neighbourhood. Not just in that neighbourhood, either: in every neighbourhood where I sell a house over asking.

Those neighbourhoods add up. Believe me, when those neighbours call, there's no problem whatsoever concerning my commission.

Residents of Waterloo Region have long grown accustomed to seeing Faisal Susiwala's familiar face on buses. It's been part of the reason why residents in his market think 'Faisal Susiwala' when they seek to buy or sell.

Principle #12:

MULTI-LEVEL PARTNERING

I love it when people come to me and say, "Faisal, you're so good at selling houses! When are you going to start your own real estate company and build a team to help you out?"

What they're really saying is: "Faisal, you're so good at selling houses! Why don't you stop doing what you're doing, and pay other people who aren't as good to do it badly?"

Why don't I stop doing what I do and instead hire employees? Why don't I form a team and become an office manager? Because it's *management*. It's not real estate.

What happens to a lot of real estate agents—especially ones who get a little name recognition once they market themselves properly—is that eventually they get more leads and more business than one person can handle. They don't want to lose those leads. That's bread and butter for a real estate salesperson! So they look around and what they see are agents building teams. The team leader gets the leads and feeds them to his team. The team hustles, doing the showings, and handling the buyers and sellers.

People imagine that the team leader running the operation relaxes and the team members run around doing the work. It's not like that. Team members are employees. When you have employees, you have to manage them, motivate them, help them through dry periods, and above all, consistently feed them leads. What if the market dips? Then all of them—and their families— look to you to keep them going even if the business itself may be threatened.

In short, you become The Boss: a business executive, someone more and more distant from the actual day-to-day business on the ground. You become a manager. You stop being a real estate agent.

Now, for some people, that works! Some brokers would much rather sit at a desk all day going over office reports than show houses. Just as some agents prefer working as a team member to making a success of themselves on their own.

Is that the best and most enjoyable way to do real estate? For some. Not for me. There's more revenue that way, sure — sometimes. But there's also more expense, more hassle and more risk.

Become the boss or stay a free agent? There are pluses and minuses on both sides. Fortunately there's a third option that most Realtors never consider. One that's got far more pluses and way less minuses than either.

You see, real estate is uniquely structured in such a way that it allows agents (and brokers, and even people not in the agency business at all, like investors) to work together in a *loose* way; an open, almost informal way that's much more productive, profitable and satisfying than the conventional team model.

I call it Multi-Level Partnering.

I call it that because, like multi-level marketing, it involves getting others to generate profits for their business by generating profits for yours. It can involve a little bit of training, too.

But let me explain the model to you in detail.

You see, on the agent-to-agent level, Multi-Level Partnering works because of the unique referral system used in the real estate industry.

In real estate, if you give an agent a lead that turns into a sale, the agent gives you, the person sending him that lead, a part of that sale. It's not a small part, either. Generally it's something between 25 per cent to 50 per cent of the gross commission.

Let me say that again so that it sinks in.

You blast some Instagram and Facebook ads, and you get a call to buy a house. You give the name to another agent. When he or she sells it, you get up to half the sale for doing nothing but the marketing! If you can get 200 successful leads and your cut for each sale referred averages out at $5,000, you've made one million dollars. Again, let that sink in. You've made *one million dollars* in real estate *without showing one single house!*

That's not something theoretical. I'm giving you real numbers, based on commission income generated by the system I'm using and describing.

Now of course it isn't quite as simple as all that. You do need to do your marketing, and pay for it, and do a good deal of it, and do it consistently and do it well. You need to build your brand, put your lead generation model in motion, and identify a reputable, competent and trustworthy network of agents to work with. (This is something you'd be doing anyway, even if you never referred a single lead to anyone.)

If you're me, you'll even instruct those agents in elements of the Susiwala System to ensure that they earn top dollar, so you do too.

Once all that's done, you can create a strong, rich, consistent stream of significant real estate income through referrals alone.

This is one of those breakthrough insights that simply fell in my lap one day but took years to sink completely into my thick head. I could kick myself for not having seen it earlier. I went on my honeymoon for five weeks and had another agent handle any work that came my way. It was the first time, as far back as I could remember, that I wasn't actively working! I came back terrified! I thought my time spent honeymooning would be a total fiscal loss. All those weeks not working, not making even a single penny! Next stop—the homeless shelter!

What actually happened? I came back to see commission checks all over my desk. I had continued generating income all that time. Not just income. *Significant* income. All while honeymooning, without showing a single house or taking a single call!

I'd split the income generated with the agent looking after my business 50/50. What I learned was that 50 per cent of a lot of money is *still* a lot of money.

You're thinking, "Yeah, but who wants to lose half their income?"

I could respond by saying, "Would you rather work morning, noon and night every day for a million dollars a year, or would you rather kick back, relax and have some balance in your life for half a million?"

But that would be the wrong way to look at it. You can get the best of both worlds. You can continue to work all day, every day, for that million, Ms./Mr. Workaholic, and let others kick in an extra half million too, from the leads you feed them! After all, once you generate more leads than you can handle, why toss them away? It's one more income stream. One more source of income for property investment.

Why don't more agents do this? I think it's because most agents learn early on to see other agents as competitors. There are only so many customers out there, so each agent begins to think that they have to aggressively elbow the other agent out of the way to get to that customer.

Also, we operate on commission, so when a sale comes in, we want 100 per cent of that commission. Business fluctuates, and we want to get all that we can whenever we can. Business may not be as good tomorrow.

That's simply the wrong attitude—the wrong *question*. What agents need to ask themselves is this: how can we generate the most mutual revenue as agents while retaining our independence?

The answer is simple: put more emphasis on marketing and lead generation, and show more willingness to make, and accept, referrals.

Last year (2019) I sold 415 homes. I tell people this and they can't wrap their heads around it. "Faisal, that's more sales per day than there are days in the entire year. How can you sell more than one house a day?"

Easy. I can't!

But I can send a lead I've generated to another agent, and she can sell it. And because we worked together to make it happen, it counts as a sale for each of us

The beauty of what I call 'multi-level partnering' is this kind of informal partnership between real estate agents allows each party to maintain and build their own business without stifling obligations and restrictions. One agent doesn't blur their brand under another agent's umbrella. One agent isn't dependent on the leads that another agent manages to feed him, and the other agent isn't saddled with having to constantly generate leads and send over a steady supply. Each can take the initiative and make their own brand and their own business as large and strong and as niche-specific as they please. They can have multiple agents feeding them leads, not just one. They can profit from the leads they feed to others.

Independence allows a realtor to customize this approach to fit his or her own preferences. For instance, I refer business out mainly to six agents that I know. I selected them partly because of their professional skills, but partly also because of their styles and focus. I personally prefer working with sellers more than buyers, for instance, so one of my select agents is a person who loves working with buyers.

By referring out business that, for one reason or another, is not my main interest or specialty, I get to focus on the business that bring me not just the most revenue but the most satisfaction. For me, that's listings. I never refer a listing to another agent. Listings are what I most like to do.

My marketing and my bidding approach generates buyer leads as well. What should I do with those leads? Toss them in the wastebasket? That's crazy! Thanks to my system, I can turn them over to my buyers' agents and get 25 to 50 per cent of a sale, in addition to the credit for making a sale, for doing nothing more than generating the lead.

This approach isn't radical or novel. Just about every agent eventually makes a referral or gets one. The key is doing it *systematically, regularly* and *consistently*. That's where most agents fall down. They know what works. They do what works. They just don't do it consciously, deliberately or consistently.

What happens when you do it consistently? Well, one of the six agents in my network, Stacey, made over $300,000 last year on my referrals alone, and over a $100,000 more on business she generated on her own. How does she feel about our partnership arrangement? She's happy. Me, I earned $300,000 as a result of generating $300,000 in leads for her. I'm happy too! We did it with no heavy-handed management, no additional overhead, no bossing and no babysitting. (Thank you, Stacey. You're the best!)

Even calling this arrangement a 'partnership' is a bit much. It isn't a formal business entity. Agents make referrals to other agents all the time. I know first-rate agents who can serve people who call me really well. When my hands are full, I send them the extra business. I think of them as my network. What's so complicated about this?

When I send them those referrals, I make sure they handle that extra business Susiwala-style, applying the proper strategies outlined in my system. After all, it isn't my winning smile that gets top dollar for houses, but my system. I make sure that anyone who calls me gets that system. That's really why they're coming to me — to get those results.

The agents in my network know me, they know how I get my results, they know my systems work, and they know those leads called me because they want that system applied. So they handle that referral 'the Susiwala Way.' But that doesn't require a complicated legal entity that takes all my time and ties everyone up with regulations and paperwork. All by itself, it's another one of the Susiwala System principles in operation: Scaling Down. It's a little network of friends and peers that share referrals. Everyone wins!

This loose confederation is something I've mapped over onto my investment practices as well. I make about as much investing in real estate privately as I do buying and selling real estate as an agent. People may think that that's because I belong to some mysterious consortium of wealthy fellow-investors — you know: those spooky guys in thriller movies who meet on the top floors of skyscrapers wearing hoods as they pull financial strings behind the scenes.

Good grief! My fellow investors are your doctor, dentist, insurance agent — the people who've bought houses from me!

A past client may be looking for a house for her family. I find her one, and I do my best to see that it's in an area that's likely to appreciate in value. A few years go by and she finds that she's been building up equity since the day she bought that property, and by now it's added up to a lot. She'd like to get another property that can build some equity for her family too — and maybe some monthly rental income along the way as well!

This very intelligent woman calls Faisal. She lets me know she's interested in investing. I work with developers regularly to develop just the sort of property she's interested in. So I invite her to a presentation that lays out all the details. She sits through it, talks to her family and attorney and the bank, and shows them the numbers. They all concur; she decides to buy. A few months later she's either getting steady rental income, or further building her equity, or both. A few years after that? The value of her property has risen once more. She and her family are on the road to wealth.

Again: everybody wins.

Is this some complicated financial investment cabal? No, it's just a loose network of people who want their money to grow, and look to real estate to help them achieve that. I've already achieved that for them, through the home I helped them purchase. Now they want to do more. Yes, we're partners. And yes, we're multi-level: we come from different strata of the community. One of my very best and oldest fellow investors (and friend) used to clean airplanes. One of my very earliest fellow investors was a British professor—my Uncle Rasheed. One investor could be a young agent in my referral network. Another lady may be a multi-millionaire banker.

I often take the lead in this informal collection of investors. After all, I've been doing real estate in Cambridge for thirty years now. I like to think my opinion on an investment property here carries a little weight.

All of us have the same thing in common, though—the desire for a safe, profitable investment to provide more wealth and security for ourselves and our families. It doesn't require a gigantic business entity with every possible corporate bell and whistle and a top-down hierarchical structure. All it needs is a network of intelligent people willing to come together and give some thought and time to an investment into which they may want to pool their funds.

I'll tell you a secret. Investing in properties profitably is not that hard. Not if you've applied a Susiwala principle I just mentioned: Scaling Down. If you live in a community all your life, the way I've lived in Cambridge, and if you're constantly following the demographics, price trends and movements in neighbourhoods, and if you hear about the places where new shops and roads are opening up, and if you know something about the areas that the City is discussing developing, you simply *know* that certain properties in certain areas are going to be rising in value in a few years and that they're going to be doing a lot better than other properties elsewhere. Call it professional insight or expertise if you like. It's just obvious.

True, nothing is ever 100 per cent certain. That's why it's good to operate as a loose network. When I'm discussing a possible investment opportunity, my partners, the developers, bankers, builders, officials and fellow investors don't hesitate for one minute to bring up questions, objections and new spins on the idea. Sometimes their funds are tied up, or they opt out. That's fine. It's a 'multi-level partnership,' not a top-down dictatorship. We pool our ideas the same way we pool our funds, and we work together because we're comfortable with each other and how we see the project going.

Some say that in the future there won't be bosses and employees any more; that we'll all be free agents selling our services as contractors to the highest bidder. I don't know about that. There will always be people who are more comfortable in highly structured, top-down sorts of organizations. Best of luck to them!

All I can say is that when it comes to real estate referrals and real estate investments, loose networks—informal partnerships —have given me a flexibility and a scope that have lifted my real estate practice and my real estate investment projects to the very top levels of profit. It's a core principle.

If you want to reach the top, you can't be just a cog in the machine, and you can't be a lone wolf either. You have to learn to work together with people. But not so closely together that you lose your independence and freedom of action and decision. I call this way of working 'Multi-Level Partnering.' Once you try it, I think you'll find that you've gotten the best of both worlds.

Bonus

So there you go. That's the Susiwala System. (For now. It's a system that continues to evolve. I'm always learning. Hmm, maybe 'Always Be Learning' should be another core principle. Check the Second Edition and see.)

For the time being, though, get those twelve principles under your belt, and prepare to see your returns accelerate to a degree you didn't think possible. This isn't something a guru dreamed up to sell you the same old stuff you've always heard, under a new label. Every principle is based on my direct experience in the marketplace, buying and selling real estate for over thirty years; they've made me wealthy and taken me to the acknowledged top of my profession. I'm giving you the concentrated essence here, and if you've skipped ahead to this chapter and want to know more about what experiences led me to work my approach out, read the earlier chapters. It's all there.

The point is, it's not theory. I've been successful, and I wanted to understand and describe what I was actually doing that led me to this point in my life—what really worked. That's what this book is all about.

Now some of it may strike you as a little strange. What, never be closing? *What?* Put *how* much of my money into marketing? Don't cold call? Don't knock on doors? Hand my leads to *other* agents? Price *under* market value? No, Faisal, no! That's not how things work!

That's not what conventional wisdom says works. Following conventional wisdom is why the average salary of a new real estate salesperson is around $37,000 annually.

Does my unconventional wisdom work? Well, let's just say that a few months ago (February 2020) I received an honour that I'll remember all my life. At a special awards ceremony at RE/MAX International in Las Vegas in 2019, I received an award for being the #1 Individual Agent (not team) for closing the most transactions in all of Canada for the entire year.

Then I got another award. This time for being #1 for commissions earned as an individual residential RE/MAX agent in all of Canada.

Lastly, I was recognized for being ranked #5 in the entire world for individual earnings in the RE/MAX network, a network consisting of 130,000 agents.

Most homes sold. Most money made. In the entire country. Number Five in individual earnings for the entire world.

Yes. My unconventional approach works. You bet my unconventional approach works.

A last word (for now) about the System. You've just gone through twelve tested Principles that will serve you well throughout your real estate career. You don't have to put them all into effect at once. If you want to start out with just one or two, that's fine. You also don't have to do them in the exact order I put them in. I tried to put them in the order that I actually did them, and I think that's a pretty good order if you're starting out, and if you want to go at things systematically.

But everyone's situation is different. If one principle appeals to you more than the others, or is a better fit, go for i*t*. Start there and above all, feel free to modify, experiment and adapt. As I like to say to bidders—"Do Better!" I didn't become Number One by mindlessly copying what people told me. I thought about it, played with it, tried what I thought would work better. You can too. Think you make any or all of it work even better—so much better that it kicks my butt? *Go for it*! I've always tried to do my best, and if you can do better than me, great! I look forward one day to learning from you, too.

Recapping a few important lessons

A few things I've learned along the way don't reach all the way up to being full-scale Principles. They're more like observations. But they're important enough that I want to share them here anyway.

Don't Be Shy

Success in real estate is not something that comes to shrinking violets. If you want to do well in real estate, you can't hang back. You can't hide. You need to meet people and network with them. I don't just network professionally. You need to socialize with people in general and let them know—without pushing—that you're a real estate agent.

If they're people who trust you, like relatives, or people who are part of your community or tribe, people you hang out with or whom you're more comfortable with, that can work too. Just *be there*, and not in your basement playing video games. Remember what I said earlier? "Be everywhere and be the brand." Don't just be there on a billboard. Be there in person.

Being known, and being part of something that's already well-known, helps. Mr. Menary's firm was small, but it was well-known and well-respected enough to attract business on its own.

Soon after I joined, my business card was everywhere! Yes, sir: I hustled. If someone asked my name, my answer was "Faisal Susiwala—Real Estate Agent." It was automatic, like "Bond. James Bond." If an officer pulled me over to ticket me for a bad taillight, he drove away knowing that I was a Realtor.

Getting attention matters. Once a local journalist had written a story about me—'City Teen Sold on Real Estate'—people in the community suddenly all knew about me. Did it help me get business? Business exploded!

Even my youth, my appearance, made a difference—in retrospect, a positive difference. I stood out in a crowd of real estate agents even if I didn't say a word. One look, and people would wonder who that young man was, and remember me.

Sometimes a problem isn't a problem. Sometimes it's a solution in disguise. The problem is your thinking it's a problem. Maybe you think there's something about your background or appearance or heritage or age that draws attention to you in a negative way. Don't think that way. In real estate, if it draws attention to you, it's a blessing. Attention leads to calls and commissions, pure and simple.

Skin in The Game

If there's one thing I've learned about real estate investing, it's that people are much more likely to go in on a deal with you if you have money of your own in that deal. However good it looks on paper, when they ask you if you have money of your own in it, and you go, "No way!', that deal is toast. You can't ask someone to put a hundred thousand dollars into an investment when you're not willing to put a penny into it yourself. Alarm bells go off. If it's such a great buy, why isn't the person selling it putting anything in? If you're willing to risk funds of your own, they'll give it a look.

Now that doesn't mean that putting your own money into a deal is enough. It still has to look good on paper. Not just good, but better than the alternative investments they're considering. 'Monetizing your licence' carries heavy weight when you're recommending an investment. If you can give a potential partner reason to believe that you know your stuff and can analyze the deal intelligently, it matters. A licence, a track record, your brand, your reputation and your experience—they all help.

When you commit your own funds to a project, it really seals the deal. It sharpens your thinking, too. If you're wrong, it's going to hurt. Personally. Badly. When it's your own money involved, partners know that you're going to make darned sure it's well placed.

I did very well at the start of my career. Why? Because I was willing to commit. When sealing the deal meant I had to become the owner of record for a commercial building and put five per cent down, I did. My Uncle Rasheed wanted to put money into a property—provided I would partner with him. I did. Today, if I offer a townhouse complex of twenty rental units to investors, I always buy at least one of those units.

If you show that level of commitment, the people you sell to will take the journey with you. And even if the journey sours, they'll be good with it. After all, not everything works out. You took the same risks in good faith; you took a hit too. The loss will hurt, but they'll realize it's your loss as well. There'll be disappointment, but not lasting anger.

If you want to get into the real estate investing game, you can't hang back and look on from a distance as an analyst. You have to jump in. That doesn't mean you have to do it recklessly. By all means, hedge your bets. A good deal is worth taking, but not at the risk of everything you have. Keep a lifesaver near to hand—but take the plunge.

Heartset

We've all seen those motivational speakers who set themselves up as real estate gurus. They'll get up on stage and stalk around like a TV evangelist, trying to get you excited and enthusiastic and hot and bothered. "Never take no for an answer!" they holler. "Be aggressive! Fake it till you make it!"

And you *do* get all hopped up. Till the next morning when you get out of bed reluctantly because you have to make fifty phone calls and take no for an answer every single time—no, and a couple of words I don't wish to use in this book.

Well, 'heartset' is not about getting hopped up today and dropped back down tomorrow. It's not about your feelings. Your feelings come and go, and they don't come on demand just because you ask them to. Tell yourself to fall in love with that pepper shaker on your kitchen table. Feeling anything yet?

Heartset is about your values. It's about your ability to think and reason and analyze. It's about how you respond to challenges. It's about how you view what you do. Do you treat your job like a game? A burden? A steppingstone? A dead end? Heartset is about how you see yourself—your identity. My parents thought selling houses made me a 'peddler'. "Ugh! Go to college and be a professor!" My Uncle Rasheed was a professor. When he saw me making more money at age eighteen than he did, he got out his cheque book out and asked to partner with me!

Heartset isn't about mindlessly repeating affirmations. It's about noticing the words you say to yourself on the inside. "Oh no! Buyers! Now I have to stop playing my video game and go show them houses!" Good luck with becoming Number One in sales with *that* inner dialogue. Try replacing it with, "If Faisal can do it, so can I," and *really meaning* it. *You can* do it: you've got the book. You have the guidelines I didn't have.

Heartset is about your body. Your surroundings. Do you eat junk food, smoke, abuse drugs or alcohol, dress in clothes that belong in a dumpster? Friend, you need to sort yourself out. Do your friends support you? Or do they take advantage of you and tear you down when you want to make something better of yourself? Maybe you should make new friends. Do you read books about your profession, go to seminars, attend conferences? Or do you sit on the sofa playing Super Mario Brothers? Here's a game for you to play: it's called "Your Life." Turn the TV off and take a class.

Mindset isn't all in your mind. Your body and your environment support your mind. And your mind supports your actions, your family, and your future.

Heartset goes beyond just mind, though. It isn't purely about ideas. It's about what you do with ideas. It's about commitment. About decision.

Mr. Menary summed up all the business advice you'll ever need in two sentences. Do a good job. Do the right thing. That's the whole thing in a nutshell. Be competent, be ethical, be truthful with yourself and others, and see that you and they both do well.

What I didn't quite see then was that you have to *choose* to do the right thing, to *choose* to do a good job—a *great* job. To do that, you have to think analytically, to use your imagination creatively, to think in the long term, to act decisively. You have to develop yourself on the inside.

The better you can develop yourself on the inside, the better you'll do on the outside. And to develop yourself, you have to know yourself. You have to like yourself; or at least like the self you think you can become, and believe you can become one day.

No, you don't have to tie yourself into a knot about it. I don't pretend to be a genius, or a saint. Doing real estate isn't entering a monastery. I like what I do, but I'm not obsessed with it. I take time for my family and my friends. I watch TV shows and go on vacations. When I started out, I didn't analyze what it was all about or sit in yoga positions or brood about the meaning of life. I just threw myself into it, got a licence, found a broker and started marketing. I started on my journey, not entirely sure where I was going or what I would learn along the way.

But I was hungry to learn. I was willing to try. And I wanted to do right by people and not let them down. You don't need a whole lot more than that to start.

Just don't neglect getting your head straight and keeping your heart in the right place as you do it.

If you lose those, it all falls apart.

There's one more element of the system that I've saved for last. I haven't presented it as part of the Susiwala System proper because it's not really part of the system itself. It's what you can do with the system once you've put it all into operation and made yourself rich and successful.

I call it the LEXIT Strategy, and it's a way for you to take all that you've learned and built with the Susiwala System and using it to make as much money during your retirement as you did while you were working—*without* working. Even if you retire early.

Chapter 22

The LEXIT Strategy

I'm always shocked by the way the best people in real estate throw their entire business away once they decide to retire. They've built a strong brand, they've built a customer database that can stretch into the thousands, they have an impeccable reputation, networks of not just buyers and sellers but investors, contractors, suppliers, bankers, inspectors, government contacts, property managers. They've developed successful working business processes, unique and effective techniques and approaches—and then one day they throw a final office party, get on a plane to Florida, and fly away!

What happens next? Most of that agent's clients get slowly farmed out to the top dozen or half dozen other agents in the office. What's left over gets picked clean by the remaining Realtors. None of them are exactly overwhelmed to get it, either. After all, the agents don't know the people in the database. They didn't make the connection. It's just another case of picking up the phone and making a heck of a lot of cold calls, and we all know what the success rate on that is.

As for the retired agent? He may have been a rock star while he was active, and surrounded by applause at conferences and events once. Now all that's gone. He's sitting on a porch outside Miami trying to adjust to the fact that his entire income stream has dropped to zero. Yesterday he was a Diamond. Today he's dust.

Seriously. Does this make any sense whatsoever?

It never made sense to me. Since I realized I would probably retire myself one of these days, I decided that sooner or later I'd have to come up with a way better exit strategy than this.

So I did.

To tell you the truth, it isn't really an exit strategy at all. It's more of an evolution strategy that involves leveraging your exit —which is why I call it LEXIT. It's a way of taking the business you've built and lifting it to another, higher level, while minimizing your active involvement. It isn't exactly retirement. It's better than retirement. A way to keep that income stream coming in even as the amount of work you have to do for it drops down to almost nothing.

The LEXIT Strategy is an exit strategy that involves leveraging your business, leveraging your knowledge, leveraging your brand, leveraging the networks you've built up, and monetizing your licence even after you've left your office and your day-to-day routine behind.

Do it right and you'll have transformed a dead-end exit strategy into a passive multiple-streams-of-income strategy that will generate revenues for you and your family, and your children, for a long, long time. Maybe even till they retire.

How does it work?

Like this.

There are six steps.

First: when you decide to close your office, don't abandon your database to anyone who wants to cannibalize it:

Sell it. Not for a one-time cash sum (though that's an option too, if the price is right) but as a collection of leads.

Sell it as you would any other collection of leads. Do what lead generation services do: sell those leads in exchange for at least 25 per cent of any commissions made using the leads you supply.

Of course not every Realtor will agree to that arrangement, especially if the agent feels the leads are fairly cold. There are, after all, many sources of leads. Another, warmer source might yield more commissions.

So take the next few steps and heat up those leads.

Second: don't let your branding evaporate. Share it:

Think of your professional practice the way other professionals do. When a doctor retires, he doesn't drop his list of patients like a hot potato—he contacts each one, and tells them he's passing their care along to a new doctor, a qualified professional whom he's familiarized with their case, and who has his full recommendation.

Sure, they can find another doctor on their own. But why go to all the trouble of searching when someone they've worked with and trusts assures them this is the person to go to? There's no need for cold calling or extended persuasion to make this introduction and effect this transition. Just let a client know you're retiring and passing their care along to another agent. They'll agree because that's what doctors and dentists and insurance agents do.

This does involve a little work—very little. You can mention the new person or persons in your marketing material, for instance, or send a mass email. You can do more than that. You can have the new agent come along on visits several months before you retire, and introduce them personally. You can include the work this involves in your sale price. Why not? Your recommendation means the leads you've passed along and warmed up will guarantee more sales and a stronger and more frequent revenue stream.

You can also include your branding collateral and information on how to use them, and how well each works. After all, your branding involves your logo, your ad space, your phone number, email address, website, your flyers, your post cards, your YouTube, Facebook, LinkedIn, Instagram channel and accounts and your social media firm. When buyers and sellers in Cambridge see the Susiwala logo, they call. It doesn't matter if they're a formal part of my database or not. My marketing generated my leads in the first place. Why switch it off and throw it away? Why not just pass it on—for reasonable compensation?

Is it worth something to the agent receiving your leads to have the right to put that logo on their marketing material, and not to have to build up an equal level of credibility over decades from scratch?

You bet it is.

Monetize that value.

Third: sell your system. Possibly as a package involving consultation, coaching and training:

If you've built a successful real estate practice, a high revenue-generating business operation, it's because you've built effective methods—clear effective ways of listing, effective ways of presenting, effective ways of marketing. If you can give your successor (or groups of successors) a series of hands-on instruction and practice in exactly how to execute those procedures and apply them for maximum profit, it can be worth its weight in gold. You can pass along the physical materials and operations manuals of a business, and that will be a giant step forward to someone without those things. But without the skills to use them properly, what's the point? It's like passing along Eric Clapton's guitar to someone who doesn't know how to play. To someone who really wants to learn to play, lessons from Eric Clapton himself would be priceless—and monetizable.

Fourth: sell your knowledge:

What you've learned about real estate in the course of an entire career isn't valuable only to the person who's taking over your client list. Once you realize that the public regards you as a qualified professional, and your marketing has helped make you, personally, a well-known brand, there are many ways to monetize your knowledge without buying or selling a simple home—keynote speeches, master classes, consultative work, writing books, coaching, creating info-products. (I've heard it said that Robert Kiyosaki makes more money talking about real estate than he does buying or selling it. It may or may not be true, but it's certainly true of other real estate speakers and trainers).

You don't even have to wait for retirement to leverage your licence in these ways (and retirement doesn't mean throwing away your licence, any more than retiring from a university job means throwing away your Ph.D.). Call the library and offer to give a talk about buying a house. You're marketing yourself, you're building a list, and you're gaining the experience to be a business speaker. There are some people who make more money talking and writing about real estate than some people selling it. Why not do both? You don't even have to master every last thing there is to know about a subject, just enough to satisfy the curiosity of the people who come.

If you're a seasoned, experienced real estate agent, start thinking of yourself as someone with unique professional knowledge that you can share with colleagues, fellow investors, and a paying public eager to learn more—because it's true.

Fifth: leverage your networks:

If you've done a good job in the course of your real estate career, you'll have built up groups of connections that are far larger than just the database of your buyers and sellers. There's also your network of investors, for instance. Closing your office doesn't mean you'll never buy another good investment property, or partner with others to fund it. It doesn't mean you can't develop a new project, or put money into a deal someone tells you about and invites you to join.

It's much better to start developing these networks earlier instead of later. All you have to do is simply educate every client you have properly, and let them know that it makes considerable sense to take some equity out of their home and invest it in an income-generating property, and you'll quickly build a list of people interested in investing in projects projects that you yourself are investing in too. This investor list may or may not be part of the package you sell to the agent or agents who succeed you. But then those agents may be part of your after-office investment network too—showing them how to develop homeowners into wise investors may expand the network for you all.

Those aren't the only networks you've developed. A home looks like a good investment, but does it need work? You have a network of contractors too. Someone needs to manage that property? Well, you know a number of property managers, right? Contacts like those may be part of your package. Maybe you've built up a small property management firm yourself during the course of your career. Well, why shut it down? The people buying into your brand may use your lead to sell a duplex, and the client buying it may need a good property manager. Why can't you make an agreement to have leads who eventually need property management go to you?

If you've developed your real estate career properly, you aren't only an agent. You're an investor. You may well be a property manager. You probably have links to banks and legal firms and the entire business community, maybe even to the worlds of politics or education or media. Each of these networks offer wide-ranging ethical opportunities to monetize the licence you still hold.

Yes, they may take a little imagination to cultivate. But why stop playing a game you enjoy, and a profession you love, just because you're no longer doing it nine to five?

Sixth, and last: leverage your holdings:

Again, if you've developed your real estate career properly, you aren't just an agent. You're a property owner. A landlord. The owner of a plaza, or an office complex, or a storage facility. Each of these is a separate stream of income, and those streams of income don't stop flowing purely because you don't go to an office every day.

You don't have to expand those holdings. If you've found a competent firm to do it, you don't even have to manage them. You can do those things, if you want. But even if you don't, you have an ongoing source of funds that can not only cover your needs, but provide the means to fund new projects in any area you choose.

I've said from the beginning that you should monetize your licence. I can add now that monetizing your licence doesn't depend on working in an office. It doesn't even depend on doing much work at all, not if you've set things up correctly beforehand. If you have the right agreements in place, and you've set up your portfolio properly, you can keep that income stream flowing and growing all the days of your life.

But there are a couple of things you should remember about the LEXIT Strategy if you decide to make that your goal. First, I've got to underscore a very important point here. In order for the Lexit to be truly seamless, you must keep your real estate licence active. Most governing bodies require you to be licensed in order to earn commission income or trade in real estate. You will continue to do so even in retirement. Speak to your Broker of Record and ask if he or she will allow you to keep your licence registered with them for a modest fee. If this requires you to maintain a membership with the local board and you don't want to pay membership fees, there are brokerages that exist for the sole purpose of keeping licences active at a very modest annual fee. Register with them

Secondly, the strategy works best the sooner you start. It'll help build your income and help you at retirement time or at whatever point in your career you happen to be. But if you begin your career clearly targeted at building your brand, building first-rate and unique processes and services, cultivating investors, building networks and connections, building your database, giving talks, helping others, establishing not just your office but yourself as a brand—if you do what Mr. Menary taught me all those years ago, and do a good job—you'll reach the point where what you've built can continue to generate significant and steady income even without you having to be there in person to devote your time to it.

Remember too: whatever you do with your database and your business, once you've retired, you can take what you've learned and monetize just that in any number of ways, from writing to speaking to consulting to investing. You can do so at your own pace and in your own good time. It isn't just who you know or what you know that can help generate income streams throughout retirement. It's both.

As for that real estate portfolio you've built? You can use it to finance any new projects that you may decide to undertake. Or just to finance passing the time in as much luxury as possible. Any of the steps above will help you do that. All of them together make it as sure a thing as it's possible to be.

But, speaking for myself—luxury gets tiresome. Success brings money and money brings freedom and when you add that freedom to the freedom of retirement, you'll find yourself with enough space to do the things you've always wanted to do at last.

But if all you wanted to do during your real estate career was make enough money to get away from that career, you should have gone into a different business. You won't achieve success at anything if you don't like what you're doing.

Set up the LEXIT Strategy properly and you'll be able to retire very, very comfortably. You'll even be able to retire earlier than you would have otherwise.

But deep down, all of us who are good at real estate don't want to leave it behind. We don't want an exit strategy, because we don't want to leave. We like the game, and we like playing it. What we really want is to take the game to a higher level. To new horizons.

That's what the LEXIT Strategy provides—rich ongoing streams of income that free you to do the things you want, and as much or as little of them as you want, but without throwing away all you've built up over the course of a lifetime. At that point real estate stops being a job. At that point it starts being an art.

Chapter 23

The Last Word

So here we are. The last page. Wow, what a trip! From bankruptcy in childhood to Number One at the MGM Grand. From foreclosure and selling chocolate door-to-door to world travel, elegant sports cars, and multimillion-dollar homes. From circling the Qa'aba in Mecca to the smell of jet fumes at the World Trade Center on 9/11. All this, and the Susiwala System too!

Yes, it's been quite a journey. Now that it's coming to a close —for the moment—I want to sum it up in a memorable way. I know, I know—most of you aren't really interested in seeing Faisal Susiwala have a go at fancy writing. You picked up this book to learn how to do real estate. You're probably going back and underlining that chapter on Getting The Listing because you want to be out there generating commission. Hey, good for you! Get out there and knock 'em dead! And when you do make Diamond and beyond, or even come up with a tip or an idea you'd like to share, let me hear from you! Email me at faisal@therealdealbook.ca, or contact me through my social media. I value your input as much as I hope you've come to value mine.

That said, here's my last bit of input—at least for now.

I've said that being a real estate agent is the greatest job in the world. It is. But there are things even greater than that. Family. Children. Charity. God.

Life has taught me a lot about these things. What I've learned isn't hard, complicated, or mysterious. It's all been said before, in holy books, by holy men, and even by other businesspeople like me. Steve Jobs said it especially well. He made himself into one of the richest and most famous men in the world; and when he was dying, when all that he was, and all that he had, was slipping away, he wrote a letter to a friend.

This is what he said:

"I reached the pinnacle of success in the business world. In some others' eyes, my life is the epitome of success. However, aside from work, I have little joy. In the end, my wealth is only a fact of life that I am accustomed to. At this moment, lying on my bed and recalling my life, I realize that all the recognition and wealth that I took so much pride in have paled and become meaningless in the face of my death.

"You can employ someone to drive the car for you, make money for you but you cannot have someone bear your sickness for you. Material things lost can be found or replaced. But there is one thing that can never be found when it's lost - Life.

"Treasure love for your family, love for your spouse, love for your friends. Treat yourself well and cherish others. As we grow older, and hopefully wiser, we realize that a $300 or a $30 watch both tell the same time. You will realize that your true inner happiness does not come from the material things of this world.

"Therefore, I hope you realize, when you have mates, buddies and old friends, brothers and sisters, who you chat with, laugh with, talk with, have sing songs with, talk about north-south-east-west or heaven and earth, that is true happiness! Don't educate your children to be rich. Educate them to be happy. So when they grow up, they will know the value of things and not the price."

I'll leave the last word to Steve. After all, what more is there to say?

Only this: be well, my friends.

FOLLOW
FAISAL SUSIWALA
ON
SOCIAL MEDIA

Facebook:

www.facebook.com/FaisalSusiwalaHomeShack/

Instagram:

www.instagram.com/FaisalSusiwala

Twitter:

www.twitter.com/FaisalSusiwala

YouTube:

www.youtube.com/channel/UCQ0lVrC_VeyaS_FmEpgnYog

LinkedIn:

www.linkedin.com/in/faisal-susiwala-73971319

AND LEARN MORE AT:

www.therealdealbook.ca

Acknowledgements

In the name of Allah, the Beneficent, The Merciful. Praise be to the Almighty for the blessing given to me, so that, I can complete this book.

Peace and Blessings be upon the Prophet Mohammed (PBUH)

I want to acknowledge the following people. These are special people who have contributed, inspired, motivated, educated, impacted and enriched my life in so many ways.

My Parents Sikander and Hajra Susiwala

My Wife Natalie, my son Yusuf and my daughter Anisa

My Brother Zeb Susiwala, sister in-law Zulekha, nephews Aamir and Aatif

My Sister Sameera Dadabhoy, brother in-law Shoaib, nephews Azam and Raihan

My Father in-law the late Joe Buttigieg and mother inlaw Carmen Buttigieg

My late Uncle Rasheed Bond and Auntie Rabia

My Mentor the late Mr. Reid C. Menary

Abdul Kharodia

Adam Contos

Ahmed Ali and Family

Ajmal Khan

Alicia Venskaitis

Amar Singh

Amit Kohli and Family

Andrew Lesko

Angela Asadoorian

Ayoob Motala and Family

Ayub and Rehana Ahmed and family

Barney Recine

Bijabhai Family

Bilal Chapti

Bill Smith

Bill Martinek Collingwood

Blair Hibbs

Bob and Louise Stephens

Bob McMaster

Buccellatto Family

Buttigieg Family

Calvin Johnson

Cambridge Association of Realtors

Cambridge Muslim Society

Century 21 Peace and Watson

Christine Just

Christopher Alexander

Cimino Family

Cresh Marschall

Dadabhoy Family Uk

Dan Seeley Baechler

Darren Hardy

Darryl D MacPherson

Darsot Family

Dave Liniger

David Chilton

David Medeiros

David Menary

David Pascal

Dawood Chapti

Don Travers

Dr Cassim Moola

Dr Cesare Ciavarro and family

Dr Champaklal Morar and family

Dr Hakim El Ghamudi

Dr Harpreet Arora and family

Dr Jain

Dr Moona Rahemtulla and family

Dr Paul Mathew and family

Dr Shaheen Morar and Family

Dr Shekhar Pandey and Family

Dr. Hakim El Ghamudi

Fran Banks

Frank Polzer

Fred Carter

Gary Ball and Family

Gary Vaynerchuk

Gedja Family

Ghouse Mohuddin and Family

Gino Cherri

Greg Cowan

Hafiz Syed and family

Hans Madan

Haroon Patel

Homeway Real Estate

Heidi Horwat

Ian Cook

Iqbal and Julie Biswas

Jakda Family

Jalaj Arora

Jane Solonik

Janice Sutherland

Jasbir Manak

Jennifer Tavares

Jeremy Potvin

Jessie Ahier Surette

Jessie Hutchinson

Jim Dodd

Jimmy Varnasidis

Joe and Cathie Romeo

Jogiyat Family

John Dowbiggin

John E. Featherston

Johnathan Schmidt

Jose Simoes

Julian Sheppard

Katie Kertesz

Kathy Marziano

Katrina Jacomb

Kent Colquhoun

Kevin Garabetian

Khurrum Ashraf and family

Kristi Perrin

Lak Manak

Lalva Family

Late Mr Clayton Mcfadden

Late Dr Paruk and Family Jamestown

Late Mr William T Dyer

Late Mr. Gerry Stocks

Late Mr. Greg Onorato

Late Karnig Mann

Late Uncle Ibrahim Dadabhoy and family

Liz Peers

Lloyd Johnston

Lucky Sharma

Luciano Toich

Madison Turner

Mahmoudzadeh Family

Mahomedy Family South Africa

Malcolm Gladwell

Mansoor Family Cambridge

Mansour Moslehi

Marc Figuerido

Marlene Farrugia

Mary Thompson

Maurice and Rose Chelli

Mayor Doug Craig

Melanie Shantz

Mian Family Cambridge

Michael Tremblett

Michele Grieco

Micheal Polzer

Minaz and Naz Rahemtulla

Motala Family

Mr Sharma Brass world

Mufti Usman Patel

Nadir Patel

Narmeen Toorawa

Nat Mirotta

Naveed Malik

Nicole Ranton

Orlando Fantini

Palvetzian Family

Pam Alexander

Patel Families of Cambridge

Peter DeGroot

Peter Hardy

Qayum Ali

Re/Max Integra

Re/Max LLC

Renee Blair

Richard Robbins

RIS Media

Rob Turner

Robert Caldwell

Robert Cialdini

Robert Wollzeifer

Robin Sharma

Romeo Family

Rudy Matic

Rustam Fataar

Saji Family

Sajid China

Salim Memon

Salim Mian and family

Salim Sheikh

Savai Family

Scott Walker and Family

Shabbir Khan and family

Shahriar Varkiani and Mahin Derakhshanian

Shaw Poladian

Shoaib Chapti

Singh Families of Cambridge

Sister in-law Christine Lima, Brother inlaw Jaime Lima and nieces Sophia and Alesia

Stacey Chaves

Sultan Qamar

Susie Hegan

Tahani Aburaneh

Takhar Family

Taneil Currie

Teachers of Avenue Road Public School Cambridge Ontario 1975-1980

Teachers of Lincoln Avenue Public School Cambridge Ontario 1981-1984

Teachers of Galt Collegiate Institute Cambridge Ontario 1985-1989

The City of Cambridge

The Entire Chapti Family

The late Aslam Kazi

The Late Doctor Suleman Paruk, Jamestown NY

The Late Greg Onorato

The Late Howie Schmidt

The Late Mr Gerry Stocks

The Late Mr Ibrahim Mahomedy and all of the Mahomedy family South Africa

The late Oren Reid

The late Yusuf Patel and Family

The Region of Waterloo

The South Asian Community across Ontario, Canada

The Toorawa Family

Thomas Lakkas

Tim Allenson

Toby Olson

Tom Watson

Tony Figuerido

Tony Monteiro

Tony Puim

Tony Robbins

Uncle Mushu Syed and Aunty Rana

Venkatraman Kannan and Family

Victor Hussein

Victor Labreche

Walter Monteiro

Walter Schneider

My friends, colleagues and neighbours. Thank you.

Manufactured by Amazon.ca
Bolton, ON

14585662R00196